I Fell in Love with an Asexual

Navigating Needs Without Blame When You Like Sex, Your Partner Doesn't, & Asexuality Is a Possibility

DAVE WHEITNER
EVAN OCEAN

DIVERGENT

DRUMMER

Second Paperback Edition
Divergent Drummer Publications
Portland, Oregon

ISBN: 978-0-9817764-9-1

Library of Congress Control Number: 2018901966
Library of Congress subject headings:
Family & Relationships—Sexuality
Self-Help—Sexual Instruction

Inquiries: Please see the contact page at asexualbook.com.

Divergent Drummer Publications
Portland, Oregon
Version 2.0

Praise for This Book

. . .

"Outstanding! Elegantly weaves personal exploration with concrete education and scientific data on asexuality. I wish I had this book as a resource to offer several former sexual-asexual couples I have seen in my practice. While written with the sexual partner in mind, it is a valuable book for asexuals who desire romantic attraction as well, as they are most likely to find themselves in partnerships with sexual individuals. This book has provided some concrete recommendations for future clients."

**Lori A. Brotto, PhD, R Psych, Professor,
Division Head, Gynaecologic Specialties,
Department of Obstetrics & Gynaecology,
University of British Columbia,
Director, UBC Sexual Health Laboratory**

"It's time to put the A (asexual) into LGBTQ, and *I Fell in Love with an Asexual* is a heartfelt, informative foray into an extremely important topic that's woefully misunderstood and under-represented in academic and popular literature. A trail-blazing, comprehensive book that will speak to anyone who wants credible insight into asexuality in all its facets."

**Ian Kerner, PhD, LMFT, sex therapist and
NY Times best-selling author of *She Comes First***

"This authoritative exploration of mismatched sexuality . . . is a unique addition to the literature on sexuality, addressing a range of human variation usually ignored or misunderstood. Its broad overview offers creative self-help guides for anyone engaged in mixed-orientation intimacy. Above all, it assures readers that they are not alone in their hidden journey."

Carol Grever, author,
When Your Spouse Comes Out,
and *My Husband Is Gay*

"The first book to explore the dilemmas of sexually motivated partners who have asexual partners . . . skillfully offers the reader opportunities for self-reflection by asking hard questions in a remarkably supportive manner . . . thoroughly details the myriad options involved in staying in or leaving the relationship . . . offers heartfelt support in the process of reintegrating one's sexuality . . . and gives others lots of permission to be human!"

Karla Baur, MSW, sex therapist and co-author of
***Our Sexuality*, the best-selling college textbook**

"Through candid personal exploration, well-researched data, and practical advice . . . offer[s] credible and thoughtful insight to anyone in a relationship with an asexual partner."

PsychCentral

"Inherently fascinating, impressively informative, and ultimately inspiring . . . An extraordinary and unreservedly recommended addition to both community and academic library Human Sexuality reference collections and supplemental studies reading lists."

Midwest Book Review, Small Press Bookwatch

For our next generation:
May our courage today
create a tomorrow
where you can live and love
fully, joyfully, and authentically.

Contents

• • •

Disclaimer, Limitations, & an Important Request

• • •

This book is intended to be an informational and educational resource, for your consideration only. It is not a substitute for the services of qualified mental and medical health professionals. Human sexuality is complex, and this work is not a diagnostic or prescriptive tool. Other resources, including a few sites that list professionals, are included later in the book. Whether and how you use the material contained herein is up to you.

Asexuality is still highly misunderstood, despite continued awareness-building efforts of many asexual individuals. Many of the viewpoints here are based upon personal observation and theory rather than empirical scientific study. Because each situation is unique, some but not all dynamics may apply to your situation.

Generally speaking, an asexual person is simply someone who does not experience sexual attraction.[1] A large majority do not feel favorably about personally having sex.[2] However, some asexuals are exceptions to these general rules. I am assuming that you love someone who has little or no desire for sex, and who may or may not also be asexual. You may not yet know whether they fit into both categories, and they may not yet know either. For simplicity, I often use the term *asexual* or *asexual partner,* but I sometimes use *potentially asexual partner* or *low-interest partner* interchangeably. Later, I'll describe asexuality in more depth, and draw distinctions between lack of attraction and lack of desire.[3]

Some individuals within the asexual community advocate for use of the words *non-asexual* or *allosexual*, rather than *sexual*, to denote all individuals who are not asexual. One argument for this is that asexual individuals do not lack all traits associated with the traditional meaning of *sexual*, such as genitals or a desire to masturbate.[4] This stands in contrast to the original definition of *asexual*: the opposite of *sexual*. This concern about confusion is understandable, and I have attempted to address it through detailed explanations of what asexuality is and is not. However, because the language is still evolving, and disagreement remains, this book uses *sexuals* to refer to individuals who are not asexual, and *asexual-sexual couples* to refer to mixed-orientation couples. Please keep the limitations of this imperfect language in mind, and know that the two categories are not mutually exclusive opposites. Over time, clearer terms will evolve.

I have endeavored to provide a fair representation of asexuality, to encourage consideration of both partners' points of view, to point out that no one orientation is superior, and to emphasize that neither partner may be "at fault" for anything. I've also attempted to minimize a bias toward relationship preservation or separation, simply providing options and considerations. However, my perspective undoubtedly reflects some biases of a predominantly heterosexual cisgender male.[5] In addition, because this book is geared toward sexual partners, it has a sexual bias. To gain a broader perspective, I also recommend reading a few books written from an asexual viewpoint. I have listed several under "Additional Resources."

An important request: Most of this book was written by one author (Dave). However, I have drawn many of the personal relationship details from the experience of Evan Ocean, with his full permission. Because he wishes to remain anonymous, Evan Ocean is a pen name. I have sometimes blended in details from my own life, as there are many commonalities between my experience and Evan's. I have altered many potentially identifying details, including names and locations. To maintain continuity, and to reflect the commonalities between our experiences, I've written most of the book in first-person singular.

This arrangement has made it possible for me to blend first-hand experience with academic knowledge and professional training, and to share the insight that comes with this pairing, while still maintaining a degree of privacy and anonymity for others.

You could determine Evan's identity, as well as the identities of others in the text, with a bit of detective work. However, out of respect for them, I kindly request that you not publicly speculate about real identities, online or elsewhere. I am deeply grateful that others support this book being published under this arrangement. It is their gift to you and others whom we hope the book will help. I look forward to the day we can all share our sexual information more freely, with less concern about judgment.

PART ONE:
Lay the Foundation

Part One Overview

• • •

SEXUALITY IN GENERAL is a sensitive topic, and having a partner who seems sexually uninterested in you can be deeply frustrating and painful. It's a tough and confusing time for both people. Like you, I've been there. With this book, I aim to provide you with enough insight, perspective, options, and hope to recover the intimacy and joy you deserve, whether that means remaining with your current partner or ultimately moving on. By the time you have finished this book, I want you to feel like a more evolved person.

This is no small goal, and resources are sorely lacking for sexual partners of asexual and potentially asexual people. I have pulled together a wide range of topics to support you. It is important to build an initial foundation before moving on to some of them.

Part One outlines the book's purpose, structure, intended audience, and overall content. It includes my story, illustrating that you are not alone in your struggles and sharing the source of some of my perspective and expertise. Elements of my experience may resonate strongly with yours, while others may feel very different. It may inform your sense of which later suggestions and insights you wish to consider, and which ones you wish to modify or ignore.

Part One also provides a detailed explanation of what asexuality is, and what it is not. As there is still a great deal of misunderstanding on this topic, it can help to have a handle on the basic concepts before further discussing the topic with your partner. You want to avoid jumping to premature conclusions or making assumptions that could further frustrate you and your partner. Many counselors, therapists, and coaches are still gaining an understanding of this topic, so this knowledge can increase your odds of enlisting and receiving helpful support if you so choose. It may even provide you with additional insight into your sexuality.

For clarity, I'll repeat the definition of *asexuality* and outline a few key facts here. A deeper discussion of related concepts follows the memoir chapter.

An asexual person, per the Asexual Visibility and Education Network, is simply "a person who does not experience sexual attraction." However, some aces (individuals on the asexual spectrum) experience sexual attraction on rare occasions, or under specific circumstances.

A majority of the time, but not always, the lack of sexual attraction is accompanied by a lack of favorable feelings about having sex. From the 2015 Asexual Census, with more than 8,000 ace and nearly 500 non-ace respondents:

> "Approximately a third of ace respondents feel repulsed about personal engagement in sex (36.6%), while nearly half of the respondents felt either indifferent (28.5%) or uncertain (21.3%). Only 7.5% of the ace respondents had a favorable feeling about personal engagement in sex, in contrast to the 67.4% of non-ace respondents with favorable feelings about personal engagement in sex."[6]

It is important to remember that some asexuals view sex as enjoyable, even though the percentage is small. Also, 41% of aces on the same survey said they'd be willing to consider sex with a relationship partner who wants it. Being asexual doesn't automatically make someone sexually incompatible with you if you like sex.

At the same time, because lack of sexual attraction is so frequently linked to lack of favorable feelings about having sex, many asexual-sexual relationships may pose challenges. This is especially likely if one or both people are initially unaware of their differences.

Also note that some sexuals don't care for sex either, meaning that a lack of interest in sex does not necessarily mean someone is asexual.

1. About This Book: Addressing Pain & Providing Hope

• • •

If you are reading this book, you have probably been struggling with some exceptionally challenging emotions and questions. Having been with a low-interest asexual partner for more than a decade, where neither of us initially understood our differences, I know how difficult the territory can be. That is why I've written you the book I wish had been available to me.

I know what it is like to desire something very different from what the person closest to you desires. To feel the pain and disconnection of not being able to express your love fully. To feel largely alone and misunderstood by family, friends, and even well-credentialed therapists. Even with an amazing partner who was exceptionally loving and giving in many ways, I often felt unwanted and undesirable.

For the majority of people, sex is a vital part of life. Mutually expressed, loving contact nourishes us, connects us, and fills us up in ways that enable us to live more fully. For many people, sexuality plays a key role in creativity and spirituality. But for a small portion of people, estimated to be around one percent of the population, sexual attraction—and quite often, interest in sex—does not appear to be part of the intimacy equation.[7] That can be very tricky to grasp, especially when it seems true for someone you deeply love and desire.

Even after obtaining six years of formal training in psychology and counseling, participating in a number of sexuality and relationship workshops, and poring through many books, the process of healing and reclaiming my sexuality has been challenging. Few resources are custom-tailored to sexual people who have fallen in love with asexual people. Many mental health therapists remain skeptical that asexuality even exists. In many ways, I have had to cobble together my decision-making and recovery process. I hope that the many hours and dollars I've spent building my knowledge, alongside the many firsthand challenges I've experienced, can now benefit you.

An asexual-sexual relationship may pose an incredible challenge for two partners who otherwise love each other very much. What is supposed to be a very pleasurable and intimate bonding experience can stir up a range of negative emotions—rejection, guilt, anxiety, anger, loneliness, inadequacy, and resentment are the tip of the iceberg. Unable to meet each other's basic needs, you and your partner may need to question long-held assumptions about sex, romantic love, and institutions such as marriage. These are not easy questions.

Creating this book has been one of the most emotionally dynamic and challenging experiences of my life. Another was returning to my previous city to attend Charlie's fifth birthday party. My ex-partner, Katie, and I had co-parented Charlie for a few years. She was now raising him on her own.

As I mingled in a room with dozens of familiar faces, I occasionally fought to hold back tears. I had agreed with Katie that it was supposed to be a happy day. I had promised that I would step out if I became visibly sad or upset.

Part of what I felt was genuine joy. I was very happy for the two people I dearly loved, posing for photos in front of the birthday cake. The other part of what I felt was deep loneliness, shame, and guilt. My heart intermittently pounded with anguish, and my mind spiraled downward.

I had already noticed that Charlie was acting much differently toward me—much more hesitantly than he once did. He seemed to recognize me, but clearly not in the same way as when he had seen me every day. I knew that because he was so young, he would eventually have little or no conscious memory left of me. Perhaps only a felt sense. I wondered if right now, he felt abandoned or hurt in some way. That would continue to haunt me for years.

I also lamented that I had abandoned my life partner, best friend, and teammate. I felt like I had checked out of the game after we had supported each other through so much. Katie had been so wonderful to me in many ways. I was now merely standing on the sidelines. Largely for shallow, primitive reasons.

Shallow, primitive reasons like sex.

But I knew it wasn't quite that simple. Several months earlier, profound differences in sexual needs had been driving both Katie and me crazy, affecting other areas of our lives.

I anxiously wondered what others in the room were thinking. Dozens of mutual friends, colleagues, and former neighbors had come to show their support and celebrate. This was the first time most of them had seen me in nearly a year. After living in that city for a number of years, I had slipped away quietly, with little explanation to others. Katie felt that matters involving sexuality were private, and I hesitantly obliged.

How had I ended up in such an unusual situation, with someone so amazing, and at the same time incompatible in such an important way? Why couldn't we live in a culture where people talked more openly about sexuality?

I feared that others wouldn't understand my departure without knowing that key piece of the story, and I had been ashamed to show my face to many of them. "How could he just move across the country and abandon such a kind, loving, gentle woman and such a beautiful child?" I imagined the thoughts around me.

What our friends would understand even less were the things that I had seen and experienced since leaving. I had immersed myself in a community with a surprising abundance of physical intimacy—both erotic and platonic—and the options of this very different world nearly overwhelmed me at times.

At a conference focused on the links between sexuality and ecology, I had met a woman who enjoyed sex a great deal, and who shared a passion for studying sexuality and intimacy. This provided a fertile ground of learning opportunities: I had to relearn how to relate to someone who was not only sexual but also more sexually empowered than the average person. She had several lovers when we met, including a female sex blogger and a wealthy spouse of a sex coach. This situation offered even more self-growth opportunities, beyond the ways you might initially imagine. More on that later.

Over the following year, I explored a range of events that often stretched my comfort zones. I discovered resources and communities that I did not previously realize existed. I not only reclaimed much of my sexual energy and desire, but I learned a great deal about nourishing platonic touch as well.

Later I will share much of what I learned along this roller coaster segment of life. This learning includes resources for reclaiming sexuality and authenticity, and for increasing physical affection in general. While suddenly being in a world of abundant sexual and sensual possibilities was exciting in many ways, it wasn't a cakewalk either. I exercised a lot of discernment, but my energy and decisions were not always coming from the healthiest places. At the same time, I needed to have some healing and growth experiences.

There are probably also parts of your story that few people would understand. You may also be trying to figure out what experiences you need to have so you can move forward. I hope that this book will help you to start dissolving loneliness and misunderstanding.

I have designed this book to help you if you are a sexual person but have or had a partner whose lack of interest in sex has impacted your relationship and happiness. They may already self-identify as asexual, or one or both of you may suspect that they are asexual. I aim to give you more than just a Band-Aid solution to your current crisis. I aim to give you a foundation for a better sex life, regardless of what your partner determines their identity or preferences to be, and regardless of who your future partner(s) may be.

Perhaps you have not yet enlisted the support of a professional coach or therapist. Perhaps you've already tried at least one coach or therapist and are frustrated that they haven't yet been helpful.

I assume that you are in one of the following situations:

➤ You are in a relationship where you want sex much more than your partner does. You're struggling to figure out whether and how you can make the relationship work.

➤ You have already left a sexually mismatched relationship and are now single. You're trying to get past the pain and confusion of what has happened so you can move on.

➤ You previously left a sexually mismatched relationship and have already begun another relationship. You sense that you have "personal baggage" that is hindering your ability to relate.

I also assume that when you initially fell in love with your partner, your differences were not clear to you. Maybe they didn't give you a clue because they didn't know either. Maybe they tried to let you know, but you didn't believe or accept it. Maybe they sent mixed messages because they were uncertain about their identity or their desires. Maybe you sensed it but were hesitant to talk about it.

In the case that your differences *have* been clear from the beginning, some of the material on trust and feeling deceived may be irrelevant. However, much of the other information should still apply.

If your partner once had a sex drive but has lost sexual desire completely and irreversibly due to physical or medical conditions, you may still find much useful information here. If your partner came out as gay or lesbian when you thought they were heterosexual, you may still find much useful information. If your partner has rarely or never experienced sexual attraction to anyone, the conversation is geared toward you in particular.

Maybe you are considering romantic involvement with an asexual person who has little or no interest in sex, and you want additional perspective before making a decision. If that is the case, I hope this book is helpful. Keep in mind that each situation is different.

I have organized this book into several parts for you:

➤ **Part One: Lay the Foundation** outlines the book's purpose, structure, and overall content. It includes my story and provides a detailed explanation of what asexuality is and is not.

> **Part Two: Look Within** guides you to clarify what you want out of your relationship, courageously explore some of your sex-related attitudes, and approach your situation with refreshed perspective. Topics include the Madonna-whore complex and the Devil's Pact.[8]

> **Part Three: Broaden Your Possibilities** recognizes that traditional relationship boxes don't always fit uncommon relationship situations. It presents new ways of approaching your dilemma and options for thinking outside the box.

> **Part Four: Improve Your Sexual Abilities** covers topics ranging from communication to masturbation and porn, tailored specifically to partners of potential asexuals. It is intended to help you to make the best of your current situation, or to show up even more powerfully with a future lover, recognizing what you have the ability to change.

> **Part Five: Connect, Integrate & Look Ahead** provides guidance on talking more with your partner, enlisting additional support, and amicably ending the relationship if that seems necessary. It also addresses potential baggage to avoid carrying into future relationships, and ideas for meaningfully placing your struggles into a larger context.

> The **End Matter** includes a range of information and resources for extending your exploration beyond this book.

As each situation is unique, I do not attempt to answer the most difficult questions for you. However, I do attempt to provide you with a framework for assessing your situation and moving forward, supported by empathy and compassion. Very little research on asexual-sexual couples currently exists, so much of the information is my best interpretation based on personal experiences and education. I hope that additional information on such relationships continues to become available.

Above all, I want you to know that you are not crazy and that you are not alone. Perhaps, like me, you have experienced some of the following:

➤ You have sometimes lain awake in bed, next to a person you fell in love with, feeling alone, unfulfilled, and misunderstood.

➤ You have a great deal of love to give, but your partner has seemed unable to accept it in the ways you've needed.

➤ You have tried many things in an attempt to get your partner more interested in sex, but nothing seems to work. You have often wondered if you were doing something wrong.

➤ Eye contact and interaction between other couples seems to have a certain energy that your relationship lacks.

➤ You have often sought ways to make yourself more attractive, but it hasn't seemed to impress your partner.

➤ You have often felt forced to "turn off" a key part of your authentic self-expression, sometimes right when you seem to be getting the most playful or excited.

➤ You often feel guilty, shallow, selfish, or dirty for wanting sex from your partner, and for not being able to see other aspects of the relationship as enough.

➤ When you try to bring sexiness into different aspects of your interactions, whether it's dancing, music, flirting, talking, or otherwise, your partner seems uninterested or perhaps even frustrated.

➤ There is a sexual part of you that desperately wants to come to life but has been painfully squelched and ignored.

➤ You have tried a sex or relationship counselor, but they seem to be missing something.

➤ You love many things about your partner, and it seems crazy to give up what you have just for the sex—but you really want more passionate sex!

In the pages ahead, I will share with you how I have experienced many of these challenges. I will share ways I have discovered for reclaiming my sexuality and related parts of myself. Whatever decisions you ultimately make, I hope this book helps to make your journey easier and more fulfilling.

In closing this introduction, I'll share two important questions that have driven the creation of this book. Because they have also supported my healing, I hope that they can serve you.

The first question: **How can I take the love I've experienced, including the painful and challenging parts, and transform it into more love?** I didn't want to label my years in relationship with a wonderful, loving person as a failure, because there was a lot of love there. I also didn't want to keep to myself what I had learned through our struggles—struggles we had endured largely because others had been silent about sexuality. I decided to delve into some of the challenging places, and to create a resource that could make life easier for other mixed-orientation or sexless couples. Sharing intimate details of my life has felt very scary at times, but I believe that courageous risk and vulnerability create love and change in the world.

The second question: **How can I redefine key elements of my life purpose that I previously defined through my relationship?** Transitioning from "Dad" to "a loving non-parent adult" has been incredibly difficult. I felt like I had lost much of my purpose. I realized, however, that providing a day-to-day safe and nurturing home environment for a child is only part of the picture. Another important task is creating a world in which they and future generations can thrive. No gardener would put hours of loving care into nurturing seedlings indoors, only to plant them in a bed of arid, depleted soil. Creating this book has been a way to help water and enrich the garden bed, playing a "parent" in a more indirect and broader way.

These have been difficult questions for me to consider, and the answers didn't surface overnight. However, you may find them helpful to ponder for yourself. How can you transform your experiences into more love? Regardless of how you transform your relationship, how can you live your purpose in new ways?

2. My Story: Best Friends

• • •

Growing apart

The impact of sex and gender issues has been apparent to me from an early age. In elementary school, I spoke with an unusually soft and high-pitched voice for a male. Classmates sometimes taunted me, calling me "fag" and "queer." Although I am attracted almost exclusively to women, I've long had strong empathy for anyone whose sexual orientation or gender expression falls outside the norm. I once even organized a relatively large event for same-sex couples' rights. But little did I know just how close to home sexuality-related issues would hit.

Or how hard.

The shit started to strike the blades one December, a month when it's usually too cold in Cleveland to even run a fan. Katie and I were lying side by side in bed, both exhausted from heated discussion. I couldn't believe we had gotten to this point. We had survived long-distance dating and living together in a tiny apartment. We were best friends. We had supported each other through many challenges and had experienced wonderful intimacy together. I once felt certain that we would happily grow old together.

However, we now faced some exceptionally difficult relationship challenges. The most obvious and openly discussed issue was that Katie really wanted a child—and eventually, probably a second one. I still felt uncertain about having one child and was almost certain I didn't want two. I had insecurities about my career and the costs of raising children.

29

There was also an elephant in the room. I had developed many concerns about sexual intimacy over the last few years. I was almost always the one to initiate sex. I felt fortunate that Katie was often willing to go along, especially given that some long-term couples rarely or never have sex. However, I had gotten an increasing sense that it was primarily for my benefit. It often felt loving, but not enthusiastic. This was even though Katie could be very romantic and generously showed deep affection in many other wonderful ways. She often wrote loving, expressive messages in the cards she gave me for birthdays, anniversaries, and other events. She often got me little "treats" of my favorite snacks or desserts when she did the grocery shopping. She enjoyed snuggling with me while reading in bed. But none of these things ever seemed to have sexual energy attached to them.

I had previously written off our sexual differences as a normal female-male dynamic, accepting the stereotype that most women have lower—often much lower—sex drives than men. I had a partner and friend who was already loving on so many levels, and I tried to be grateful for that. However, I began to question things upon overhearing female friends complaining about their male partners' low sexual interest levels. Also, female friends sometimes flirted with me with a certain energy I had never really felt from Katie—even when we had first met. My additional reading and online research confirmed that there are many women who have high levels of interest in sex. This fact remains largely hidden for a variety of reasons, including the way our culture shames women for expressing their sexuality.

I was already anxious that something was off with our sex life. Furthermore, having a child would make it even more challenging to find time for intimacy. I feared that in our case, intimate time would become virtually nonexistent—at least for the first few years of parenting. I wondered whether having a child would feel less threatening if I had a more sexual partner, but that was difficult to imagine.

Additionally, we had just survived a several-year stretch where we had devoted significant emotional energy and time to assisting Josh, an extended family member, with some major challenges. It felt like we were jumping from one marathon right into another, with little chance to recover.

While lying next to Katie, feeling worn out from our head butting about kids and sex, I finally uttered words that neither of us had ever spoken: "Maybe—maybe we should consider splitting up."

Upon hearing those heavy, previously off-limits words, she was silent for several moments.

"Maybe you are right."

The big revelation & difficult questions

A day or two later, Katie explained that she felt a sense of relief—like a weight had been lifted from her shoulders—after I mentioned the option of separating. Feeling fear and concern, I clarified a bit.

"I meant it as just one option for further discussion. I mean, it might end up being the best one, but I'm not saying I definitely want to end our relationship. I'm just not coming up with any other options."

Then she prepared me for the additional revelation she was about to share.

"I know that we love each other very much. I also know we're on different pages about kids. We've always been very honest with each other about that. But there is something else other than the kids issue."

"What's that?"

"The stuff around sex. I mean, it has been an issue for us for a while. And I'm also getting pretty worn out by it."

"Yeah, I am hoping it improves soon. Are you saying that you don't see that getting any better?"

"It's not just sex that doesn't feel right. Even kissing you feels kind of like making out with a sibling."

"Huh?"

I stopped cold. That revelation surprised me. I knew that neither of us was trying to be mean or attack the other—she said it very matter-of-factly, and with an air of sadness. But it still hurt to hear, and I struggled to get clarity.

"Like a sibling? I'm not sure I understand. Is it how I kiss? Is it that some people say we look a little bit alike, with our similar smiles?"

"No, it's none of those things. For me, it's just—it just feels inauthentic. It's hard to explain."

"So you're not physically attracted to me anymore?"

"I—I don't know."

"Could it be stress from me not making money from my business yet? Or from all the attention you were giving to Josh's situation?"

"No, those things aren't it. It's been this way for a long time. And I'd be fine if you were bringing in just a bit of money part-time alongside getting your business running."

"Hmm. So have you *ever* been physically attracted to me?"

"The best way I can explain it is that I chose my best friend, thinking I'd eventually feel attracted to you—but it just never happened as I had hoped."

"So you're saying it's been like this all along?"

"Yeah."

"What about with other people, when you were a teenager, or in college?"

"Nope. I don't remember being attracted to anyone."

"But didn't you date a few guys, and kiss them, and do some sexual things with at least one of them?'

"Yeah, but looking back, I wasn't really attracted to them. Parts of it felt nice, but part of me was just kind of going along with things."

"What about famous people that a lot of people believe are hot? Brad Pitt? Rob Lowe? Harrison Ford? Are you attracted to any of them?"

"Nope."

"What about women? Angelina Jolie? Marilyn Monroe? Madonna?"

"Nope. I'm not attracted to women, either."

"So you've never been attracted to anyone, ever?"

"No, I guess not."

I was dumbfounded. Also, I knew that the questions I was asking weren't easy for either of us.

"I know I'm almost always the one to initiate sex. But you often go along, and there have been many times when you've seemed to enjoy it at least some. You often have orgasms with oral sex. What about that?"

"Parts of it do feel really good. I know you try hard to make it good for me, and I appreciate all the reading you've done, different things you've tried, and so on. It's just that it doesn't feel like me. It doesn't feel authentic."

My curiosity and confusion started to mix with anger and frustration.

"I'm trying to figure out how you didn't know this earlier. I mean, we both have educations involving coursework in sexuality. We've both volunteered with people with different sexual orientations. We're pretty open about this stuff. And we've been together for quite a while."

"I'm sorry. I don't know. Again, I thought I'd become more attracted to you over time."

"None of this makes any sense, though. I know it sounds horrible to bring this up, but is it possible you were abused when you were younger and are repressing it? Not by your parents, because I know they would never do anything like that, but maybe an extended relative? A babysitter?"

"No, no, no. I wasn't abused when I was a kid."

"But we've only been to therapists for a handful of sessions. That wouldn't be enough to uncover something like that."

"I'm tired of talking to therapists."

"And what about possible physical causes? Weren't you going to get an additional medical test?"

"I've already had my doctor check several things that can affect sex drive, but I'll think about it."

I was in such emotional shock at the time that it's difficult to remember all the things that were said. However, the above covers the highlights of the initial "coming out" conversation, and the discussions over the next few intense days.

Loneliness, hope, & parenthood

Less than two weeks after our separation discussion, I slipped on ice while jogging and fractured my leg. My primary form of exercise and stress relief was out of the picture for a while. And, of course, not much sex.

The stress was already intense enough. I was struggling with the realization that my relationship might soon end. I had many concerns about career and money. I felt ashamed that I wasn't more willing to provide my partner, my life teammate, with something she wanted so badly—a dad to help her raise children. Even though I had always been honest that I might never want kids. Was I avoiding the grown-up, mature thing to do?

And now, on top of all that, I had a broken leg and a partner who had apparently never been sexually attracted to me. Furthermore, I had to depend on Katie physically in a way that I never had before, after having suggested that we consider separating. I was embarrassed and ashamed.

The anxiety often felt unbearable. I would hobble downstairs in the middle of the night and pace back and forth on my crutches. From kitchen to living room and back, from living room to kitchen and back, I'd burn off some of my nervous energy. The rubber tips of the crutches thudded on the wooden floor as my heart raced. Our cat, sometimes observing from atop his cat tree, probably thought I was crazy. At that time, he would have been correct. I soon developed shingles, which can be triggered by extreme stress that compromises the immune system. Fortunately, it was a mild case with minimal discomfort, and I recovered within a few weeks.

Over the next few months, my leg healed. I gradually returned to regular exercise routines and regained my physical independence. I reduced my anxiety levels. Springtime approached and brought with it new hope.

Following a few deep conversations, Katie and I agreed to take in an extended family member—a small child—who would need a temporary home. This would give both of us a chance to experience parenting firsthand while Katie explored her sexuality. It seemed like a sensible way to try things out, as the child would likely be with us for only a short time anyway. So if we ended up not being able to work things out with each other, it wouldn't be the end of the world.

Over the next few months, as we prepared our home for a child, I remained hopeful about Katie's sexuality. I held out for some discovery, shift, or test result that might change things. I fantasized about possibilities: Perhaps parenting together would create such a profound emotional shift for Katie that she would feel attracted to me. Perhaps she would agree to do a bit more therapy, and uncover something from her childhood. Perhaps we would discover that something about our interpersonal dynamics had created a lack of desire. Or maybe there was some medical test that hadn't been done yet.

Then, one winter evening, baby Charlie arrived. That was simultaneously one of the most exciting and scariest moments of my life. There before us was a cute, crying, tiny human who couldn't even sit up on his own yet. I had no idea what I was doing. That morning, I stayed up until 4 a.m. Googling the health implications of green poop and the potential dangers of allowing an infant to sleep on his stomach.

The next several months were quite an adventure, and there were many fun moments amid the craziness. Although I approached parenting hesitantly, I felt a greater sense of identity and purpose. At the same time, not surprisingly, our relationship issues took the back burner. Katie didn't continue therapy, alone or with me. But she did ask her doctor about other possible physical causes for lack of interest in sex. Tests revealed nothing new or helpful.

At the same time I bonded with Katie over the parenting challenges we faced together, I became even more sexually lonely and frustrated. I signed up for free accounts on several online hookup and dating websites. While I never attempted to contact anyone, I sometimes sat alone in silence, scrolling through one profile after another, wondering why my partner never wanted sex like many of the online women seemed to. I occasionally reminded myself that many of the profiles were probably fake or exaggerated, set up just to attract more men to the sites. However, spending time on these sites reinforced my perception that everyone in the world except me seemed to be getting it on—and that every woman in the world except my partner desperately wanted to.

Katie soon expressed an increasingly urgent desire to move into a new home that was more child-friendly. We had talked about it previously, but now that we had a child it seemed more urgent. By the end of the year we found one just a few miles away. It needed some interior renovations but could be ready to occupy in a few months. We agreed the new house should be solely in her name, as our chances of making things work still weren't looking much better.

In the meantime, parenting consumed even more time than we had anticipated, with frequent caseworker visits, birth family visits, and all the standard needs of an infant. Katie was more enthusiastic about the hands-on aspects of parenting than I was, so I focused more on supportive roles such as renovating her new home and cooking. As I worked inside the empty house getting it ready to move into, often alone until late at night over several months, part of me still hoped that Katie and I could eventually work things out.

I continued to become more attached to Charlie than I had anticipated. As I sanded and refinished the wooden floors, I thought about how the new surfaces would be safer and more comfortable for Charlie and other kids to crawl around on while playing. I carefully made them as smooth as possible to avoid any splinters. As I built a new wooden railing, I made sure it was strong enough for those times Charlie would be leaning over it to call downstairs for Katie. As I mounted and painted cabinets and shelves in the bedrooms, I imagined the fun toys he might keep in them, and I envisioned him enjoying the bright colors. I hoped that even if Katie and I didn't work things out, I would be leaving enough tangible things behind to be remembered by, enough things to make it clear how much I cared.

But I wasn't yet prepared to focus on the possibility of leaving.

Finally, a name for it?

Katie and I continued to have our occasional frustrating encounters. One day as we passed in the upstairs hallway, I felt the urge to embrace her and kiss her as I previously had on many occasions. I recalled what she had said about kissing feeling inauthentic or gross, but I was feeling increasingly frustrated with my inability to express my affection. We wrapped our arms around each other for a hug. However, when I attempted to venture beyond a peck on the cheek and into a passionate kiss, she became upset and pulled away. In retrospect, I understand how uncomfortable it must have felt for her. She felt betrayed, given what she had previously told me about being uncomfortable with kissing. At the same time, it was traumatic for me. I felt rejected, unattractive, lonely, and confused. Both of us were on the verge of tears.

Such encounters motivated me to do more research. Soon, I discovered the term *asexuality*, on the Asexual Visibility and Education Network (AVEN) site. I had a hard time believing it at first, but it sounded like Katie. I didn't mention it immediately, as I wanted to learn more, and I didn't want to risk slapping on a label prematurely. As I continued to read, it matched much of what she had described to me.

A week or two after discovering AVEN, I mentioned it to Katie and suggested that she look at it. The information surprised her, too. She agreed that it did sound a lot like her; perhaps she was asexual. In the following few months, she seemed to become more convinced of this.

We gradually let a few of our closest neighbors know about our differences, our possible separation, and the reasons we would be moving soon. While Katie wanted to keep the sexual orientation element private, I worried that our closer friends might judge me if they thought our differences were solely about kids. Hesitantly, she agreed that I could tell a few people.

Amy, a close neighbor and therapist, initially reacted strongly to my disclosure about our orientation difference. She explained that men always seem to blame women for sexual issues, when often the problem has more to do with how the man is managing the relationship. I agreed this was often the case, and explained that I certainly wasn't perfect in my relationship with Katie. However, our situation was different. I told her about the asexuality website.

Amy later apologized to me, explaining that my revelation had triggered some things for her. I responded that while I had been a bit shaken up by her reaction, I understood that sexuality is a taboo topic. My hope was that people could start talking about it more openly so that they didn't have to suffer alone. She seemed to agree.

By the following spring, we had moved into the new house and sold our old house for a profit. It had been a lot of work. It was incredibly emotionally challenging, as I had grown close to many of our neighbors. I had volunteered a great deal of time working on neighborhood issues. It was tough to leave all those relationships, all that social support, behind.

More than a year after his arrival, Charlie was still with us. This followed a few cycles of returning to his birth parents briefly and then coming to live with us again. These cycles were especially stressful because Katie was becoming more hopeful about the possibility of adopting Charlie. She had become very attached to him. I was becoming more attached to him, too.

After we moved into the new house, Katie had more time to read again and ordered *Asexuality: A Brief Introduction*. She read it eagerly, completing it in only an evening or two. It seemed to give her new energy and a sense of relief. She then offered it to me to read. Much of the author's life experience, she explained, resonated strongly with her. The things the author had experienced as a teenager, the awkwardness and loneliness they often felt, the numerous questions they had about their differences, were all very familiar to her.

As I read the book and talked with Katie about it, I felt a range of emotions. On one hand, I was happy that we seemed to have discovered some answers. I was glad that a person I loved deeply had found some relief. On the other hand, I feared that this was one more step toward our relationship finally ending.

An open relationship

Despite the profound incompatibilities Katie and I seemed to have, I was not yet ready to give up completely. While the lack of a mutual attraction was frustrating and often drove me nuts, I still loved Katie in many ways. Could there be a different way to arrange our relationship?

The term *open relationship* generally refers to any relationship that is not sexually monogamous. There are some variations on this. Later we'll cover several of them, alongside special considerations for asexual-sexual couples.

By early summer, I started poring through books on polyamory. I learned everything I could. Poly people often remain closeted, due to strong societal judgments about lifestyles that people aren't as familiar with. However, the love I felt was clearly going to be difficult to maintain within the boundaries of a traditional monogamous arrangement. And in a culture where half of marriages lead to divorce, I knew that others' judgments had limited merit anyway. There was no guarantee with any type of relationship.

I knew of a few couples who had experimented with polyamory, both successfully and unsuccessfully. Some individuals on the AVEN site had tried it with their relationships. Perhaps if I could find another outlet for my sexual energy, someone with whom I could share that part of myself, I would feel more complete and could relate to Katie even better. While Katie was skeptical that it could make our relationship work, she said she would probably be happier if I could meet some or all of my sexual needs elsewhere.

Googling for various groups and events where I could learn more about polyamory, I soon discovered an event that fascinated me, given my combined interests in sexuality and environmental issues. It offered a range of workshops and experiential exercises focused on the linkages between human relationships and sustainability (social, environmental, and economic). This included discussion of polyamory.

During an evening walk-and-talk, as Charlie slept in his stroller, I talked with Katie about the idea of going to the event. I also asked her thoughts on any boundaries regarding potential romantic connections. The conference would have many people who were enthusiastic about polyamory. If I met someone and there seemed to be mutual sexual interest, was it okay to have a fling with them?

This felt very awkward and scary to ask Katie about, as we had always been monogamous. At the same time, the possibility of being involved with someone who shared a mutual attraction, even if for just an evening, was exciting.

Katie said she saw no issues with it, provided I was physically safe. I asked her a few times if she was entirely sure. She responded that while it did feel a bit odd, I had her blessing. I was deeply grateful. At the same time, I felt sad that Katie and I were unable to experience more sexual intimacy together.

A few weeks later, I was across the continent in Seattle. One of the very first things I noticed was that many women attending the conference were not only sexual, but were very confident with their sexuality. As I entered one of the preconference volunteer events and noticed a few women staring at me with interest—a difference from the usual "just being friendly" look—I experienced a new energy. Women occasionally flirted with me in other settings, but I hadn't allowed myself to notice in recent years. After all, I was in a committed relationship, and even allowing myself to flirt had been off-limits.

During that weekend, what I encountered drew me out of my head and into my body much more. I experienced several sensual but non-sexual workshops where participants exchanged nourishing physical touch, in safe spaces created by skilled facilitators. I had never had the opportunity to request touch from three other people and then feel them all massaging me at once. It was wonderful. I had never danced just in my underwear in the middle of a hotel ballroom, where many other people were doing the same—and some were completely naked.

These experiences were quite exciting, and they marked a few critical turning points for me. For one, this was the first time in years that I had substantially exchanged affectionate physical touch beyond brief hugs or handshakes with anyone other than my partner. Doing so had felt taboo, a major no-no, akin to cheating. Secondly, they marked the beginning of my exposure to many fascinating outside-the-box people, versed in many connective body, mind, and spirit integration practices. These included Tantra, Ecstatic Dance, various forms of mindfulness meditation and rituals, and snuggling.

Alongside that, I met someone with whom there was a mutual spark. We kept bumping into each other throughout the weekend, experienced a few workshops together, and had a wonderful time dancing. Before the weekend ended, we spent the night together. While we refrained from some activities because we didn't know each other that well yet, we had a pretty sexy time.

Long-distance polyamory & fire hosing

As I left Seattle, my head spun with a broad range of emotions. Sophia, the woman with whom I had connected, seemed very sweet and thoughtful. She phoned and texted to see how I was doing and to let me know that she had had a wonderful time. So had I.

I felt a strong connection with Sophia while also realizing she lived a very, very long way from where I had spent my entire life. I broke down crying in the airport a few times, seemingly out of overwhelm. I had experienced a great deal over the last few days, and it would take some time to integrate. Before I returned home, a previously planned stopover to visit a dear old friend helped me to regroup.

A few days later, it felt scary and awkward to tell Katie about my adventures, but she didn't seem that bothered.

"Do you think you will keep in touch with Sophia?"

"I'm not sure. It would be nice to talk to her again. What are your thoughts on that?"

"I'm okay with that. In fact, it might be nice for you to have someone to provide another outlet for your energy."

On one hand, Katie's being okay with things felt liberating and even loving. On the other hand, I was concerned that she didn't seem jealous. It reminded me that she didn't desire me in that way.

I decided that I did want to keep in touch with Sophia, and at least get to know her better. Given how far away she lived, I had no idea where things might go, but I looked forward to more great conversations. In addition to sharing an interest in sexuality and environmental issues—not a surprise, given the topic of the conference at which we had met—we seemed to share other interests and values.

Sophia and I started out by sending each other emails, alongside talking via phone as we had time. After a month or so, we decided to try talking by phone roughly once a week, video chatting when possible. We connected on a number of levels, and I began to feel increasingly attached to her. I also enjoyed her flirtatiousness during our conversations. While Katie had always expressed much love and affection, the attention from Sophia had a different, more sexually charged quality.

My connection with Sophia initially created some additional discomfort for both Katie and me. My conversations with Sophia often left me feeling more aroused. But I wasn't comfortable with phone or Skype sex, so Sophia didn't provide the "outlet" for me that Katie had envisioned. Because I was still also attracted to Katie, I was now even more interested in having sex with her.

At the same time that I was still having sex much less frequently than I desired, Sophia was actively having sex with several different people—people who sounded exciting to have sex with. One was a woman who wrote for a well-known sexuality site, starred in an explicit sex education video, and occasionally organized masturbation parties. Another was a wealthy executive who had studied Tantric sex extensively, and whose partner was a sex coach.

"Toto, I've a feeling we're not in Kansas anymore."

Sophia and I mutually agreed to be very honest with each other about our sex lives, and I felt like I had no right to have any say in her sex life. Not only were we at a distance from each other, but we were just getting to know each other. I had no idea whether we would eventually end up being a couple. While it was a perfectly fair arrangement, it wasn't always emotionally easy. I sometimes felt knots of jealousy in my stomach when Sophia told me she had been on a date with someone else, or when I saw comments or photos from her other lovers on Facebook. I knew that *date* sometimes but not always meant sex, and I was often afraid to ask.

I recalled that outside of the few people whose discussions I had read on AVEN, most people with open relationships shared a mutual attraction with their primary partner *in addition to* sharing intimacy with others. Their additional bonds complemented the physical intimacy with their primary partner, rather than just taking the place of it. Furthermore, their additional partner(s) were not at a distance. The arrangement I was experimenting with was probably uncommon. There was also a certain irony: I was now spending time on two relationships that provided very little physical intimacy—one due to lack of interest, and one due to being at a distance. I still often felt frustrated, unable to experience intimacy and connection fully.

I wanted emotional support from others, so I joined a Meetup group focused on alternative relationships. I asked others in open relationships how things were working for them, and asked if they had ever heard of asexual-sexual couples having open relationships. Nobody had heard of asexuality. But at least they had some empathy around open relationships, and around having a sex drive.

As I got to know Sophia better, I expressed more and more of the sexual energy I had suppressed. Since I couldn't be with her physically, I channeled it into my emails to her, my conversations with her, some of my music, and even some poetry. I was essentially directing a fire hose of pent up sexual energy right at her. She didn't complain and seemed to enjoy it. However, I eventually realized that it was more sexual energy and attention than I could realistically sustain over time, without neglecting myself. Later under "Be grateful & giving but not codependent," I'll share how I refocused some energy on myself and other priorities.

Katie's courageous experiment

Because I had found the Seattle event so transformational, I wondered if an interactive weekend event with sensual and possibly sexual elements could also change Katie's perspective of her sexuality. She still didn't seem entirely certain about her identity, and I felt that anything that could help to clarify matters was worth a shot.

Would Katie be willing to try an event that would stretch her boundaries? Even if she needed to try having sex with one or more other people, to see if that might create a spark that she couldn't experience with me, I'd be okay with it.

The idea of attending a highly sensual, potentially sexual interactive workshop did not excite Katie a great deal. She said she'd be willing to consider it, though. I found a weekend intimacy event with exercises for getting more in touch with one's sensuality and sexuality. It also offered the potential for interacting with other people at one's discretion, although explicit sex was not an official part of the program. It was just a few weeks and a short flight away.

Katie contacted the facilitator to describe our situation and to ask a few questions. While the facilitator didn't seem to believe in the concept of asexuality, she ensured Katie that she'd always be at choice regarding the activities. After much consideration, Katie reserved a slot and booked her flight.

Due to confidentiality agreements, Katie was able to share only limited information about her experience after she returned. However, it was clear that it had been more intense than the Seattle event. While Katie had some fun, some of the activities made her very uncomfortable. She sometimes felt frustrated, alone, and very different from the other attendees, as she was unable to enjoy some of the things that they were. However, she had made a few friends, including Peter. She felt an emotional bond with him and planned to follow up to talk about their experiences.

From a selfish perspective, I was disappointed that attending the event hadn't yielded any "sexual awakenings" for Katie. At the same time, I was saddened that some of the activities had made her so uncomfortable. She had stretched well beyond her comfort zone, and I admired her courage. I was deeply grateful that she had given it a try. This was far more than most partners would have been willing to do.

Over the next month, I continued to enjoy my conversations with Sophia at least once a week. We did seem to have a lot to talk about, and at least she had empathy for my sexual frustration. Her having a few sexual partners still made me uncomfortable, but I decided it was an opportunity to practice managing some of my emotions and insecurities. We started to talk more about how we'd like to relate over the longer term, and if or when we'd see each other again.

At the same time, Katie was spending an increasing amount of time communicating with Peter. She sometimes spent extended periods emailing or talking to him on the phone late at night. He lived a few states away and wondered whether he should visit. Intrigued, I asked Katie whether she felt any sparks with him. She felt warmth and found him attractive, but not in what seemed to be a sexual way.

While I loved Katie a great deal, I was also becoming more attached to Sophia. I realized that I couldn't sustain devoting so much time and energy to two relationships, especially when neither was providing me with the physical intimacy I wanted. I greatly valued friendship and meaningful conversation, but I was also seeking a lover. Not to mention that I was doing this while co-parenting, adjusting to a recent move, and trying to determine whether Katie was actually asexual.

Exploring with other lovers

I planned a return to Seattle in late September for a weeklong visit with Sophia, so we could get to know each other in person better. The thought of moving to Seattle was a bit scary for me, as I had never lived outside the Northeast and Midwest. At the same time, my future in Cleveland with Katie was uncertain. Sophia was clear that she was very attached to Seattle. I would be the one moving if we decided to continue dating in person. That made sense to me, especially as she had previously moved to accommodate a partner and had spent a lot of time developing her local connections.

In the meantime, Katie also planned another experiment to help her to gain clarity. While I was in Seattle, Peter would drive to visit Katie and spend a few days at our home. He was fully aware of her likely asexuality, and they had talked about the possibility of sexual exploration if it felt right. Even though I was going to sleep with another person myself, I felt some jealousy and concern about another man possibly sleeping with my partner while I was gone. At the same time, I supported anything that might help Katie get clarity. Might Peter spark something within her that I had been unable to?

I was very excited to be back in Seattle, getting to spend a full week in person with Sophia after being limited to phone and Skype for so long. In addition to talking, we could also enjoy other activities together, and share physical intimacy including sex. During my time there, we did have plenty of sex, and I had so much energy that I felt like I had shaved 10 or 15 years off my age.

While camping in a tent on a warm September night, Sophia and I stayed up half the night making up silly sex jokes. Allowing long-dormant parts of myself to play was wonderful. Being able to love two people in such different ways surprised me. I realized that I had known Katie much longer and had been through a lot more with her. Sophia and I were still in an infatuation and honeymoon phase, boosted by hormones that would dissipate over time. But I wondered: Was either type of love more "noble" than the other, or were they simply equally important parts of human existence?

My trip was not all lighthearted fun, though. There was also some learning accompanied by discomfort. It became clear that during my years with Katie, I had taken for granted that I rarely felt insecurity or jealousy over other men. This was likely because Katie wasn't sexually attracted to anyone. Sophia and I, on the other hand, had already had some challenging discussions around the other people with whom she was actively involved. Visiting her in person made it even more tangible.

Having been monogamous for a number of years, I also wasn't used to having detailed discussions around topics such as safer sex. For example, what precautions should be taken around oral sex with another partner? How current should STI testing be? How much should I trust Sophia's other partners? She assured me that they all seemed careful in this area, but I didn't personally know them or their other partners. I honestly expressed my preferences, even though the conversation became charged at times. It was a lot to process at once, and it was emotionally messy, but Sophia and I managed it. Alongside that, we did have some wonderful times together.

Sophia and I agreed that we would probably continue to have a lot of fun dating, and could learn a great deal from each other. At the same time, we both realized several other things. Katie and I were still trying to figure things out; and even if we split up, hopping from one relationship right into another might not be wise. Also, what if I moved all the way to Seattle, and Sophia and I didn't get along that well? And on top of that, what if I didn't like Seattle? It seemed like a big risk from my end. Furthermore, Sophia was enjoying the permission she had given herself to be a bit "wild" for a time, dating several people at once. It was a lot to consider.

When I returned home from Seattle, Katie and I had a lot to talk about. Even though we had been very honest with each other about our intentions, which included having sex with other people, it felt awkward and scary at first.

"So did you have a good time in Seattle with Sophia?"

"Yeah, it was really good to have a chance to get to know her better."

"And there seems to be a mutual attraction there?"

"Yeah, that's definitely there. However, it still feels uncomfortable to talk about—like I'm comparing the two of you or something. There are things about you I love that nobody else could ever replace, and there are things about her that I appreciate, too. How did things go with you and Peter? Did he visit?"

"Yeah, it was a great visit. He wasn't able to stay for quite as long as he had hoped, but he spent a night here."

"So did you guys try connecting? Physically, like through sex?"

"Yeah, we did."

"How was it? Did you feel anything new or different?"

"It was pleasant and different. But it's not something I feel the need to do again anytime soon."

"Hmm. So no new revelations about sex?"

"No, I don't think I can imagine myself ever wanting to have sex more than once a month or so, if that."[9]

The message seemed clear: Katie didn't believe she'd ever have more interest in sex. It was time for me to accept Katie as she was, and to take additional steps so that both of us could move on. We had given it our best shot.

A parenting milestone

As the end of the year approached, we experienced a major milestone with Charlie. After many months of Charlie being in our home, his birth parents decided that permanent adoption would be best for him. Katie and I would have first dibs.

After being a part of the journey for so long, and being supportive the best I could despite our differences, I felt a mix of emotions. On one hand, I was happy and somewhat relieved. Katie was now almost guaranteed to have her dream, and Charlie would continue to have a wonderful home. Because of that, I felt a little more comfortable with the possibility of leaving. I had done my best to accompany Katie to the next step in her journey toward one of her biggest dreams. On the other hand, I was deeply saddened by the prospect of leaving. I still loved Katie a great deal, and I had become more attached to Charlie than I had anticipated. Even little things, like the fact that Charlie would often eat kale the way I liked to prepare it, warmed my heart.

Therapy, snuggling, & sensual feasting

Now that Katie and I were not being sexually intimate at all—and I was no longer comfortable attempting to initiate—I felt additional motivation to leave. Even though Katie's generosity around cuddling and massage trading helped to take the edge off, I often felt frustrated. It now felt like I had to turn part of myself off completely.

I began seeing a therapist more regularly, sometimes twice a week. Fortunately, she had extensive knowledge of polyamory and other sexuality issues, and she seemed understanding about the asexuality. I expressed to her my various fears and uncertainties. What if I settled into another house or apartment locally, and soon thereafter decided I wanted to move to Seattle? What if I moved to Seattle and didn't like it or didn't get along with Sophia—or both? What if I realized that I needed more space and time to myself between relationships?

I also reconnected with Jordan, whom I had met the same weekend as Sophia. She was forming a snuggle party and massage trade group. I was eager to learn how I might create such events in Cleveland or get involved with the Seattle group.

My Seattle experience and talks with Jordan inspired me to attend a very different event for New Year's and my birthday. Network for a New Culture, a group devoted to exploring alternative, sustainable ways of living, was hosting a retreat in the snowy mountains of beautiful West Virginia. It was within a day's drive of Cleveland. It would be my first birthday apart from Katie since we had met, but she was supportive of my going.

At that retreat, I experienced my first snuggle party, with a small group of people I had known for only a day or two. I initially felt awkward, but as I relaxed into it, I experienced a blend of connection and happiness that is difficult to describe. I also experienced the power of other simple but profound connective techniques: eye gazing, synchronized breathing, and a "sensual feast" in which we slowly and deliberately fed one another desserts and other delicious foods. I left that long weekend with the same broadened sense of connection and possibility that I had felt after my trip to Seattle.

After returning home a few days later, I was very happy to see Katie. I had missed being with her for my birthday. But as I excitedly shared various elements of the event that were fun for me, I noticed how the smile on her face seemed slightly forced and non-enthusiastic. She was doing her best to listen, but what was fun for me did not sound like fun to her. I recalled our fundamental differences.

With my therapist's support, I soon came up with a plan to move to Seattle, in a way that would allow me to "check things out" for an initial three-month trial period. I'd move there with a minimum of belongings so that I could move back easily and cheaply if needed. This removed much of my fear and indecision. Katie was willing to let me keep many of my things in the basement, and Sophia was supportive of the idea. I would plan to live separately from her when I got there, and we'd continue to experiment with polyamory after I arrived.

Along with being deeply sad about leaving my partner and a wonderful child we had co-parented, I was incredibly scared. I would soon be separated from the person I had long relied on for the vast majority of my physical intimacy needs. However, my recent connective experiences had given me a ray of hope. There were additional ways to connect with others, to feel supported.

Katie did her best to accommodate our situation; she was even fine with sleeping together as long as I didn't try to persuade her to have sex. Nonetheless, I chose to sleep alone during our last month together for a few reasons. First, it would help me to transition to sleeping alone in my apartment. It felt better to be starting this phase out of choice, knowing that I still had a "backup" if needed. Secondly, sleeping with Katie and trying to avoid initiating sex altogether seemed too challenging for me.

Moving to a strange land

Early on a bitterly cold morning in late January, my best friend and partner drove me to the airport. I'm still unable to write about that morning without crying. Charlie slept peacefully in the back seat, unaware that he would no longer regularly see the man he had learned to call "Daddy."

Katie and I had decided that whenever I called, I would be an "uncle," or we would just go by my first name. Shifting from "Daddy" to "Uncle" was very emotionally challenging for me. But I knew it was the right thing to do. We figured that after all that Charlie had already been through, his little heart didn't need any more confusion about who loved him, who did and didn't want him, and so on.

Long after that, I would continue to worry whether my leaving would create another scar that Charlie would have to heal later in life. I knew that it would take *me* a while to heal. For several years, few days passed when I did not think of Charlie. Whenever I came across a photo of him, I would begin to cry. Often when I passed a playground or saw a parent walking with a small child, I'd get tears in my eyes.

There is a reason babies are so cute, and attachment to them is wired deeply into us. I hadn't anticipated how attached I could become to a child who wasn't biologically mine. My heart goes out to all asexual-sexual families where a child is involved, and where separation seems like the best option.

Just a few hours after a painful goodbye to Katie and Charlie, I was several time zones away from the region where I had spent my entire life. Amid a mix of emotions, it was a massive shift. I had given up many of the material belongings and human connections with which I had previously identified myself.

Each night during my first week in Seattle, I struggled to fall asleep on a camping pad in my basement room. As I watched the cold winter drizzle through the window, I feared going crazy. Fortunately, I already knew one of my housemates—Jordan had posted a want ad for a housemate shortly after I made the decision to move, and we decided it could be great fun to live together. Coincidentally, I had already seen the room via Skype, during a snuggle group planning meeting they had held there.

From asexuality to polyamory in person

When I first learned more about polyamory, it seemed like the greatest thing since sliced bread. After having an asexual partner, I feared having another partner who might lose interest in me. So being open to multiple partners seemed like a great insurance policy. Additionally, because I was so grateful for Sophia's enthusiasm for sex, I was probably more open to possibilities than I might otherwise have been.

So even though polyamory couldn't save my previous relationship, I was still willing to experiment with poly when I arrived in Seattle—or so I initially thought. I had read several books on it and had technically already been practicing polyamory while dating Sophia at a distance.

However, things felt much different in person. I had not yet experienced in-person dating with someone who also had other lovers. Just the shift from an asexual to a sexual partner alone presented some unanticipated challenges, which I will share more about later.

Polyamory on top of those challenges, alongside getting to know Sophia and an entirely new place, was a massive shift.

Even though I now had housemates, living apart from a romantic partner was an adjustment. I struggled when Sophia and I didn't see each other for a few days in a row. She seemed to have a busy schedule that varied a lot, and she was still dating a few other people at that time. I'm rarely bored during "alone" time, and personal space was necessary for my healing and transition process. Nonetheless, I had to find other ways to meet some of my social needs in this new place. Being under exceptional stress, in a place where I knew very few people, seemed to magnify challenging emotions like loneliness.

I often got jealous and frustrated about our time scheduling and the need to "share" Sophia with other lovers. We hadn't clearly hashed out our expectations as to how we'd prioritize each other over other lovers, especially near important events such as holidays and birthdays. What would our "couple boundaries" be, when she had other lovers also wanting her time and energy?

Because I was moving across the country largely for her, I expected her to prioritize me in more ways than I had explicitly communicated. Understandably, this felt like a lot of pressure to her, as we were still getting to know each other. She didn't want to give up her other romantic relationships when we weren't yet sure whether she and I were even going to work out. That made sense, even though it was hard for me to accept.

At the same time, I remained uncertain about whether I wanted to remain in Seattle or return to the Midwest, which understandably increased Sophia's fears of committing too much too quickly. Her fears, in turn, further triggered my uncertainty, in a continuous loop. While we had talked a lot over the phone and Skype, we had left out some important details.

Partially because of this, we ended up having conflict near Valentine's Day, when another lover was co-hosting an event that triggered some of my insecurities. We had conflict again near Sophia's birthday, when events involving members of her poly community made it challenging for us to schedule a time just for the two of us to celebrate. This included the birthday of another lover.

An otherwise relaxing group camping weekend got off to a tense start after a former lover—one who would also be present at the event —texted her about "unfinished business" as we were on our way there. An annual social event that I had co-hosted for years with Katie took on a different feel the first time I co-hosted it with Sophia: Another romantic interest showed up without my realizing he was attending, and I felt blindsided and jealous while they spent time together. Then there was the former lover whom I didn't feel had respected my boundaries, and who became angry with me when I expressed this. I became jealous when Sophia remained relatively neutral rather than siding with me. I appreciated the efforts Sophia was making to balance different people's needs, but for me it felt overwhelming.

Additionally, I found myself triggered by different aspects of Sophia's other current and recent love interests. Two people were significantly younger than I was, so I sometimes found myself worrying that I was losing attractiveness with age. One was relatively wealthy and had taken her on some fancy dates, so I found myself worrying about not having as much money. Another blogged for a famous women's sexuality site, so I fretted about whether I had enough sex appeal. And so forth and so on.

I was already feeling insecure, having partially internalized Katie's lack of sexual interest in me. The presence of other lovers encouraged comparison, which merely magnified my insecurities about being undesirable. To make matters worse, because Sophia was openly bisexual, I initially feared that she might eventually not want or need men at all—or that alongside being with a male partner, she would inevitably need occasional "recharges" with female partners in order to feel sexually fulfilled. (This is a common and unfortunate misconception about bisexual people, as it leads to the belief that they are incapable of fidelity.)

The above are just a few examples, and the finer details of the situations don't matter. In most cases, everyone involved was simply doing their best during a confusing time, but things got messy. I merely want to illustrate that polyamory is not necessarily a simple solution to one's lack-of-sex woes. It may bring up any insecurities you haven't yet dealt with. On top of that, you may also experience the effects of several other people's insecurities and emotional triggers.

Amid all this, I felt like I had too much on my plate for more than one romantic relationship at the same time. So beyond going on a few dinner dates and attending a few somewhat risqué dance events, I didn't attempt to date anyone else myself. After a confusing period of mutual ambiguity about polyamory, Sophia wisely suggested that we try monogamy. I eventually agreed.

My current opinion of polyamory is that the practice itself is neither good nor bad. It is simply different and has both pros and cons. Because it is one strategy for managing asexual-sexual relationships, we'll talk about it more later. This includes questions to ask yourself and your partner to determine whether it is worth exploring.

There was a certain irony to my "poly flip-flop." Several months earlier, I had wondered how on earth Katie didn't realize her orientation sooner. Along the same lines, Sophia wondered how I didn't anticipate my negative reaction to polyamory before moving to Seattle.

I regretted that my sexual confusion had caused Sophia and her other lovers additional pain. At the same time, my flip-flop gave me more compassion for Katie and her confusion. Sometimes you just don't know until you fully dive into a relationship. Over time, the more I was able to forgive Katie, the more I was finally able to forgive myself for my sexual bumblings.

More touch-positive events to the rescue

At the Network for a New Culture event, I had learned that there is an additional way to be polyamorous, with some of the same benefits but fewer complications. It is possible to enjoy many types of nurturing touch with other people, without being romantically or sexually involved. In other words, you can be polysensual without being polyromantic or polysexual.

Sometimes, especially after I hadn't seen Sophia for a few days, I simply wanted to exchange a 5- or 10-minute neck and back massage with someone, or just wanted to cuddle for a few minutes after dinner. I had taken for granted how even brief exchanges of physical touch helped tremendously: a short neck rub in the car while I was driving, or an extended "good to see you" hug after a busy day. Now, I sometimes simply sat alone and cried. I also worried that my neediness would overwhelm Sophia.

Fortunately, because my new housemate and her partner were snuggle enthusiasts, things soon began to improve. Within a month or so, I was attending, co-facilitating, and sometimes creating snuggle events held in our home. As Jordan and I got to know each other better, we started doing occasional massage and snuggle trades. Another friend began to invite me to smaller private snuggle parties. Also, Jordan and her partner Jamie had been polyamorous for some time. It was helpful to have someone to talk with about my experiences. Both were empathic listeners.

All of this was incredibly helpful as I adjusted to various big changes in my life. It even benefited my new romantic relationship in a few ways. I was no longer as desperate for physical touch across the board, especially when I didn't see Sophia for a few days, or when we were having normal relationship growing pains. I was able to ease into things a bit more, as I knew I had a few other supports. The physical touch helped me to feel emotionally closer to my new friends, further increasing my sense that I wasn't overly dependent upon just one other person. While it didn't erase the grief I felt from my separation, it helped me to cope with it.

Also, exchanging massage often helped me to relax and get in a romantic mood more quickly, but giving lengthy massages had been a part of Sophia's day job for many years. She was understandably often too tired to exchange that type of touch with me. My getting some of these needs met elsewhere helped both of us.

Through the touch-positive events, I met many other people at the forefront or "cuddling edge" of the snuggle movement. This included individuals who had created a book and several cutting-edge workshops on healthy touch, another who writes about human relationship issues, and several members of a visionary group called LoveTribe that facilitates heart-centered, touch-positive events.

I learned a great deal by speaking with many of these deeply insightful and creative people, alongside attending and co-facilitating touch-positive events. The combination of snuggling, massage, and conversation left me feeling wonderfully energized and relaxed at the same time. Witnessing creations such as the new Tribal Love Network (a website for organizing snuggle parties and other touch-positive events) and participating in a brief video about snuggling got me excited about the possibilities. Attending touch-positive events with Sophia gave me firsthand insight into how event dynamics can affect couples.

Furthermore, I immersed myself in Seattle's ecstatic dance community, which is also very cuddly in nature. Walking into the dance events, I had never seen so many people greeting each other with lengthy hugs and dancing with various partners in touch-positive ways. At other outings where many of these people were present, even musical performances and birthday parties, it wasn't unusual to see small groups of people happily snuggling. It was quite a shift from what I was accustomed to. These experiences influenced me so profoundly that I spoke in depth with several experts in the touch-positive community and created a guide for hosting some of these events. See "Additional Resources" for touch-related books and websites.

Platonic touch-positive events can benefit single people—especially newly single people—and also those in relationships. For asexual-sexual couples, such events can help both partners practice more ways to get touch needs met. They can also help you feel less "needy" around touch, which in turn can help you come across as more comfortable and confident while dating. If you are in a relationship, and you and your partner have very different touch needs, such events can provide an additional outlet for the higher-need person.

I also attended many other events that stretched my boundaries around intimacy and connection—not just physical touch, but verbal and emotional connection. Pujas, for example, include interactive sensual but non-sexual exercises designed to foster connection and heightened awareness. These might include eye gazing while focusing on a particular theme, exchanging massage in groups, synchronized breathing in pairs, or talking about intimate topics in small breakout groups. I even tried a clothing-optional dance and had a lot of fun. Through a group called Authentic World, I participated in a range of games and exercises designed to tear down facades and encourage connection.

At the same time, the breakup, separation, and divorce support group I regularly attended offered a stark contrast. There I often heard stories about how touch-deprived people felt. When I described some of the local touch-positive resources, several faces often lit up. Someone would eagerly ask, "Where I can sign up?"

I came to realize that whether I was in a romantic relationship where many of my touch needs were being met, or between relationships, there were advantages to having a greater degree of physical touch with others. There were also advantages to cultivating other types of intimacy.

Homecoming & big healing steps

After a few months of monogamy with Sophia, I still couldn't tell whether I'd ever be able to put certain events from our polyamory experiment behind us. While we loved and respected each other, we frequently second-guessed each other while communicating, and both of us seemed to have difficulty with trust. We often disagreed over issues such as how to manage relationships with her recent ex-lovers. I missed certain things about the Midwest, and I was still healing from my previous relationship.

I finally decided I needed a break from Seattle and my current relationship. I was pushing myself too hard, and I needed some space and time to absorb everything that had happened. I wanted to see my family and to visit Katie and Charlie. I planned to return to my hometown in Ohio for at least a few months. From there, I could decide if I wanted to come back out to Seattle. Leaving Sophia and my other new friends in Seattle was incredibly difficult. Sophia and I agreed to stay in touch, to see where each of us stood in a few months. I didn't know if I would return.

Outside, it was a temperate and sunny day when I said goodbye to Sophia at the airport. Inside, my emotional weather was mixed. I was somewhat relieved that I had made a decision, and I was excited about seeing family and other familiar faces again soon. At the same time, I knew I would miss Sophia a great deal, and I was very saddened to say goodbye to her. A dark pit of uncertainty churned in my stomach: Had I made the right decision? Would I ever see Sophia again? Would I feel at home back in the Midwest? How much would Katie and Charlie even want to see me, and would I still even feel comfortable around them? Where could I rebuild a sense of family and home?

Just a few hours later, I was back on the other side of the continent, in my small Ohio hometown. Being back home with my family was a treat, as I hadn't visited for more than a long weekend since I was 17. I enjoyed spending time with my parents, sister, and other close family members. We had a better chance to process some of the changes together, and to mourn some of the losses. They also deeply loved Katie and Charlie, and our separation hadn't been easy for them, either. They were also excited and curious to learn more about Sophia and my life in Seattle.

I did feel somewhat out of my element due to the lack of other social settings in my small hometown. However, this also meant fewer distractions, leaving more time for important introspective work.

Several steps during that time aided my healing process. I'll share those that may be helpful or inspiring for you. First, I spoke more openly about my life transitions with a few old friends and family members. This included the reasons Katie and I had separated. While sharing in a support group had helped, sharing with people already familiar to me provided additional healing.

Second, I sought actions to convert some of my negative energy into positive energy. This didn't mean ignoring those emotions, but just doing things that would get me into a more empowered mode. For example, when I felt lonely and disconnected during winter in my hometown, I volunteered to spearhead a "Happiness Sprinkling." This involved holding up inspirational signs at a busy intersection, to cheer up otherwise anxious holiday shoppers. It was a connective experience that boosted others' moods alongside my own.[10] I also spent many hours in a coffee shop working on two self-help books including this one—projects using the learning from my struggles to create resources for others.

Third, I returned to Cleveland to visit Katie and Charlie and to get my remaining items out of Katie's basement. Although Katie had kindly allowed me to store many of my items for as long as necessary, I knew that retrieving them would release an emotional tie for me.

That visit also helped me to heal more around my "sex is a shallow need" belief and the accompanying guilt. While going through old holiday ornaments, I broke down crying. I expressed my recurring concern that I had abandoned Katie and Charlie, and that I had done so for shallow reasons. Katie gently reassured me that we had both done our very best, and that she didn't believe I had abandoned them. She reminded me of other ways our differences had affected us. That was helpful to hear again.

Fourth, I attended Charlie's birthday party. As described earlier, this was one of the most emotionally challenging days of my life. This visit also helped me to integrate and appreciate some of the positive highlights of my last few years with Katie.

Finally, I spent time reflecting upon my insecurities that had been triggered by Sophia's other lovers while I was in Seattle. I wrote and emailed each of them a detailed message outlining some of my insecurities and apologizing for any friction or coldness that I had conveyed. Their responses were generally positive, but the important thing was that I was speaking my truth where I had not before.

The healing & adventure continue

Following two months in Ohio, I decided that I didn't need to have the next decade of my life figured out. It was okay to feel uncertain about some things, and it was okay if I still had healing to do. So I returned to Seattle to reconnect with new friends and to continue exploring life with Sophia. And to continue healing and growing.

Since returning, I've been in a more introspective space than I was in when I first arrived. At that time, exploring, rediscovering my sexuality, and connecting with new people seemed of paramount importance. I've still continued some of that. Lately, however, it has been more about channeling my journey into resources that can help others. That includes this book.

I continue to enjoy many aspects of life in the Pacific Northwest, including getting to know Sophia and myself better through our new relationship. I'm experiencing different aspects of intimacy than I had before. Sophia is a wonderful lover and friend on many levels, and we have shared a great deal of passion. She has also motivated me to grow and develop myself in new ways, extending well beyond what I share in this book. I've even enjoyed the company and friendship of some of her former lovers who once made me intensely jealous—this is due not only to my self-growth work, but also to Sophia's commitment to open and honest communication.

Sophia and I have also wrestled with some differences. More than two years after returning to Seattle, several moving boxes remain packed in my closet and the garage. This is partially due to mutual concerns about compatibility. We aren't sure whether certain personal priorities and aspects of our styles are compatible over the longer term. Each of us wants the other to thrive, regardless of what form our relationship takes in the future.

Those few remaining boxes also remain packed due to other internal dynamics still boxed up inside me. Following Katie's surprising revelation, I formed a "wait and see" mindset. No therapist confirmed her asexuality, and many professionals still doubt the existence of asexuality today. It has taken time for me to accept and love her for who she really is, not who I want her to be. I've carried my habit of remaining uncertain into other relationships, and I've cautiously held others at an emotional distance in certain ways. While I've made some wonderful new connections, I'm still learning to open up and trust others and myself again. I didn't initially realize how much growing and healing I had to do.

At the same time that I love Sophia, Seattle, and other friends in Seattle a great deal, I still love and miss Katie and Charlie. I miss my family and Katie's. I cry when Katie tells me that Charlie still sometimes refers to me as "Daddy" when he sees my picture. Given all of this, it's taking a while to redefine what I ultimately want my family to look like, and whether the Pacific Northwest will ever fully feel like home.

Unexpected glimpses of ecstasy

Several times over the last few years, during other activities, I've experienced a blend of emotional openness, vulnerability, connection, and excitement that I once believed was possible only with sex. It hasn't been at the same depth or level of intensity, but there's a similar sense of seeing and being seen, of loving and being loved. I initially glimpsed this during touch-positive events like snuggle parties and pujas. I have experienced it during ecstatic dance and sometimes even during deep conversations. It's the feeling of looking into another person's eyes and forgetting about everything outside of that moment. It's knowing that you're on the same page as your bodies flow to the same music, or as you exchange ideas, energy, smiles, laughter, or touch. Beyond that, it's difficult to put into words.

I'd like to become better at experiencing this more frequently. I'd love for you and others to experience such things frequently, too. I hope that some of the learning I share with you will enable that.

What kept me from having such experiences previously? I believed that such emotions could occur only with sex, so I wasn't looking for them or allowing them in other settings. Once I got past that assumption, I still believed that fully allowing myself to experience and express such feelings was the equivalent of feeling and expressing romantic and sexual interest. Sometimes following these experiences, I have allowed myself to imagine what it might be like to make love to the person I was with. So opening myself up felt not only like risking rejection, but also like cheating on my partner emotionally. Because of this fear and shame, I'd often do one of two things. Even if someone seemed very receptive to my energy, I'd turn down my energy and close myself somewhat. Or, if I allowed myself to fully open up around someone, I'd be more controlled and possibly avoidant around them in the future.

I still wrestle with how to handle these experiences. Am I limiting my love and blocking the affection of others? Should I talk about my experiences with those around whom I've felt this way? For now, I'm simply happy that I can allow myself to experience more openness without feeling like it *has* to be attached to sex. Then, when the two are attached, it's like icing on the cake. I have practiced sharing deep appreciations and verbal expressions of love with a few close friends. It has felt very connective, and it's really fun to see their faces light up.

Perhaps you've also faced challenges navigating different types of affection and connection alongside fear and shame. We'll talk more about this later.

Finding completion & fulfillment

I had hoped that shortly after Katie and I separated, I would experience feelings of completion and relief. But those feelings have taken a while to develop.

There's still an occasional sense of incompletion.

Some of the incompletion is due to the natural grieving process, which can take many years after ending any long-term relationship. Pangs of grief crop up unexpectedly. I miss catching up with Katie while eating dinner together, or while pushing Charlie in his stroller. I miss hanging out with them around a backyard fire. I miss the warmth and connection of events that we hosted, and the sense of teamwork and accomplishment we shared afterward. I miss the creative holiday cards we sent to family and friends.

While I still have difficulty imagining myself as a full-time parent, I sometimes mourn the loss of certain aspects of parenting. I miss the opportunity to share with a little person the same holiday magic that my parents shared with me, and to watch their eyes light up with the same joy and wonder that mine once did—while decorating jack-o'-

lanterns, making holiday costumes, sharing delicious food, stringing up Christmas lights, and discovering toys under the tree. I missed being there for Charlie's first bicycle ride.

I've missed the opportunity to be there for some of the tough times, too. When Katie let me know over the phone that Charlie was in the hospital with pneumonia, I worried a lot. When Katie shared that she was having difficulty getting Charlie to sleep, I wanted to be there to help.

Some of the incompletion is due to unfinished emotional business. In many ways, moving to a new setting gave me more space to process an otherwise overwhelming amount of personal "stuff." The change in perspective enabled me to grow, and it provided a lot of experience and insight for this book.

But the move also enabled me to postpone some emotional work that I continue today. I said goodbye to two people I love a great deal. That has been more painful than I had anticipated. The knowledge that I've faded from Charlie's memory as his dad continues to haunt me. Whenever I look forward to seeing him again, I also fear the emotional difficulty of returning to my former home. Where I once played a significant role, things have moved on in my absence. It felt like part of my identity died when I left Katie and Charlie, and I've had to reinvent it. Accepting my new and different role in their lives has been challenging.

Some of the incompletion is due to lack of understanding about asexuality. There's still not that much formal research on the topic. Partially because of this, I'm also still working toward 100% acceptance of, and belief in, Katie's asexuality. I'm probably around 99% there, but there's still that lingering 1% of me that wonders, "Is she *really* asexual? Could it be something else?" You, too, could find yourself with such doubts. But as I'll talk about later, you'll ultimately need to accept what your partner believes if you wish to move forward, regardless of whether you fully believe or understand it yourself.

Some of the incompletion stems from the same energy that motivated this book—a realization that we are far from alone in this journey. Many of the same challenges that Katie and I have faced also affect countless other people, including you.

I've accepted that things will never be truly complete, as life is an ongoing series of challenges. However, several things will bring me fulfillment.

I'll feel fulfilled when people who deeply love each other, but who have profound sexual incompatibilities, can openly consider a range of relationship options and family structures without worrying about others' judgment.

I'll feel fulfilled when such couples can more easily "come out" to family and friends.

I'll feel fulfilled when anyone who feels that they're sexually or romantically different in some way can talk about it openly and safely with others from the very beginning.

I'll close this chapter with some of the biggest lessons I've learned. One source of love never replaces another; they simply complement one another. We need many types of love and connection, just as we are each capable of giving many types of love. It is possible to love multiple people deeply and equally at the same time, in different ways.

Also, our love for someone can shift and even expand when we "end" one type of relationship and transition into a new season. I still love, admire, and trust Katie deeply. In many ways, I appreciate her even more than I did before we separated.

I haven't discounted the possibility that in some form, Katie and I will still grow old together. It just won't be in the way that I originally envisioned. Perhaps there will be occasional visits where we sit side by side on the beach, lounging in Adironack chairs, facing a sunset. Maybe even snuggling, or walking hand-in-hand alongside the waves while reminiscing about old times. Talking about Charlie and the rest of our families. Simply enjoying each other's presence and company.

But there will be no sex on the beach. Unless I have a sexual partner who also happens to be there.

Later I will share with you insights from the experiences already described, and from experiences since returning to Seattle. This includes recognizing and working through some of the "personal baggage" from being in an asexual-sexual relationship. I hope that this information helps you to heal, to clarify what you want, and to increase the love and happiness in your life.

3. How to Understand Asexuality

• • •

Keep an open mind, at least initially

Your partner might have already done a lot of exploration and self-reflection and feel secure in their asexuality. But if you have begun to use the term *asexual* without much prior research, some words of caution are in order.

Differences in levels of sexual interest are a common issue in relationships, even in the absence of asexuality. Research suggests that at least a third of women experience low sexual desire.[11] Sexuality expert David Schnarch explains that there is usually a higher-desire and a lower-desire partner. Few couples share exactly the same natural level of interest in sex.[12] Such differences can be masked in the early or honeymoon phase of a relationship, when most lovers' bodies secrete a flood of natural chemicals that enhance the sexual charge and promote bonding. Later, as this initial charge wears off, and each person returns to their "baseline" level of interest, significant differences may become apparent—even if both partners are sexual.[13]

While the lack of sex may be the most obvious problem, other issues may lie just beneath the surface. Other relationship dynamics or stressors can cause or exacerbate sexual tensions: the addition of children to the family, concerns about power and money, and natural aging processes, for example. Some people desire sex more when they experience stress, and others desire it less. If you and your partner respond very differently to stress, you'll sometimes feel out of sync, even if you both experience attraction and enjoy sex.[14]

A decrease in sexual interest can result from one or both partners feeling emotionally distant. Conversely, it can result from one or both partners being too emotionally enmeshed and not independent enough. Interdependence, the balance between intimacy and autonomy, can be tricky to achieve and maintain.[15] Also, ironically, attraction and sex may seem less intense in a stable and safe relationship than in a dysfunctional or abusive relationship, where insecurities may drive a desire for more sexual connection. Fortunately, approaches are available for addressing the above.[16] A relationship professional may be helpful if you suspect that such dynamics are at play.

While less likely, it is even possible that your partner is another orientation or gender identity—for example, perhaps they are lesbian, gay, bisexual, or transgender—and they are not yet ready to come out. Also, as you will see, asexuality is not the same thing as a lack of libido or sex drive. Therefore, it is wise to remain open to a range of possibilities, at least initially.

The temptation to apply a label quickly can be great because it provides a neat and tidy package to explain a complex range of issues. However, a label can lead to a self-fulfilling prophecy, where a person lives up to the expectations attached to a label, even if the label didn't totally fit them in the first place. This may hinder open-minded exploration of who they are.

David Jay, often credited with being the founder of the asexuality movement, emphasizes that orientation labels are best utilized as tools used to describe what you want, not to govern your behavior. As quoted by sex columnist Dan Savage:

> "There's no such thing as a 'true' asexual. If the word seems useful, use it. At the end of the day, what matters is how well we understand ourselves, not how well we match some Platonic ideal of our sexual orientation, and words like *asexual* are just tools to help us understand ourselves."[17]

Jay makes an important point here. In many cases, such flexible thinking can help people continue to feel free to explore who they are, rather than feel the need to fit into a specific box and stay there.

However, things become more complicated if someone is already in a serious relationship with a sexual person. In some cases, simply using a label if it seems useful might actually encourage the behavior Jay wisely warns against—trying to match some Platonic ideal of an orientation label. This is because many people have difficulty relating to labels in a relatively loose way.[18]

Once a person begins to use such a label, it may influence their decisions and other behaviors, as well as those of people close to them. When other people are already deeply involved, including a sexual partner, I believe it is important for a person to consider whether they are a "true" asexual. You probably want to know, for example, whether your partner's lack of interest is temporary or relatively permanent, and whether there is a way to increase their interest.

Ironically, a few days before Katie and I informed a few relatives of our incompatibility, one of them forwarded this joke via email. It's about a couple who have been married for many years.[19]

> Four guys have been going on the same fishing trip for many years. Two days before the group is to leave, Ron's wife puts her foot down and tells him he isn't going. Ron's mates are very upset that he can't go, but what can they do?

> Two days later the three get to the camping site only to find Ron sitting there with a tent set up, firewood gathered, and dinner cooking on the fire. "Ron, how long you been here, and how did you talk your missus into letting you go?"

> "Well, I've been here since yesterday. Yesterday evening, I was sitting in my chair, and my wife came up behind me and put her hands over my eyes and said, 'Guess who?'"

> "I pulled her hands off, and she was wearing a brand new nightie. She took my hand and pulled me to our bedroom. The room had candles and rose petals all over. On the bed, she had handcuffs, and ropes! She told me to tie and cuff her to the bed, and I did."

> "And then she said, 'Do whatever you want.'"

> "So, Here I am."

Ron obviously does not have the same sex drive as his wife. What makes this joke humorous is that it holds elements of truth for many couples. Because most couples have a lower- and a higher-interest partner, most will face sexual challenges at some point.[20] This is particularly true if they've been together for a while. In other words, a large difference in sexual interest between two partners doesn't necessarily mean that one of them is asexual. But it might.

Avoid label overwhelm

In the following sections, I cover many different terms and definitions. Don't feel the need to memorize all of them, and don't try to determine with certainty which labels fit your partner. As David Jay noted, words are merely tools to assist with understanding. Whatever the case, you will still need to talk with your partner to clarify preferences around physical intimacy, given that any label is open to different interpretations by different people.

If all you seek is a very basic understanding of asexuality, don't spend too much time on finer details like the different types of attraction or the subtle differences between attraction and desire. If you seek a deeper understanding that will help you to understand yourself and partner regardless of their orientation, then you may find the finer details in the following sections valuable.

Asexuality: The official definition

Before speaking with your partner in more depth, it is important to learn the basic facts about asexuality. Your partner may or may not actually be asexual, and even if they are, they may not understand it yet.

According to the Asexual Visibility and Education Network (AVEN):

"An asexual is someone who does not experience sexual attraction. Unlike celibacy, which people choose, asexuality is an intrinsic part of who we are. Asexuality does not make our lives any worse or any better, we just face a different set of challenges than most sexual people. There is considerable diversity among the asexual community; each asexual person experiences things like relationships, attraction, and arousal somewhat differently."

Because the prefix *a-* generally means "the opposite of" or "the absence of" the word that follows it, many people initially believe that *asexual* simply means "the opposite of sexual." This confusion is understandable, especially given that language in this area is rapidly evolving. In fact, asexuals often refer to themselves as *aces*, a word that excludes *sexual* altogether. However, these words generally denote the absence (or near absence) of one specific element of sexuality: sexual attraction. Asexuality doesn't necessarily mean that a person lacks other characteristics or desires falling beneath the sexual umbrella.

Asexuality is not caused by a traumatic or abusive past, a shame or guilt reaction, or a medical disorder. If at one point your partner regularly experienced sexual attraction to you or others, then they may not actually be asexual. Something else might have occurred in their life that triggered a loss or suppression of their sex drive. If, on the other hand, they have rarely or never experienced sexual attraction at any point in their life, they could be asexual. But, as we'll talk about, this may not be easy to determine.

Attraction, desire, libido, & arousal

"You know that look that women get when they want to have sex? Me neither."

Steve Martin

Understanding the subtle distinctions between *sexual attraction*, *desire*, *libido*, and *arousal* can help you to understand asexuality. There is still debate over the extent to which attraction and desire are separate from one another. While many people experience them as nearly the same thing, for some people they are more distinct. The following synthesize some of the best descriptions currently available.[21]

Levels and patterns of sexual attraction, desire, libido, and arousal can change significantly for a given person over time, whether they are sexual or asexual. Physical age, the age of a relationship, physical and mental health, stress levels, the physical and emotional environment, and many other factors can have an impact.

sexual attraction

This is an involuntary, internal, relatively unconscious impulse to initiate sexual contact with a specific person or people. It could be anyone, and may be due to appearance, personality, perceptions of power and status, scent (including pheromones) and hormones. Because it is essentially sexual energy triggered by another person(s), it can also be defined as directed libido. It is a feeling, not an intention.

Sexual attraction may be accompanied by physiological components, such as shifts in breathing and heart rate, sweaty palms, and pupil dilation. While attraction is closely connected to desire for many people, it does not necessarily lead to desire. Also, attraction is not necessarily required for desire. We'll soon discuss a few examples to clarify this.

sexual desire

This is a more conscious wish or intention to initiate sexual activity, usually with a specific person who meets certain criteria. The motives behind this desire may vary, and can include one or more of the following: finding someone attractive, wanting to experience physical or emotional pleasure, wanting to experience connection, and wanting a significant other to feel pleasure.

libido

Also frequently called sex drive, this is the physical craving for sex. It is usually connected to attraction in sexuals, and for this reason, some define sexual attraction as "directed libido." However, libido is not necessarily connected to attraction in asexuals. It is possible for an asexual person to have a physical desire for sex, but not crave it with a partner. An asexual person may be just as happy satisfying their libido on their own.[22]

sexual arousal

Arousal is more about the body's subsequent physiological responses, usually once desire has been established. This may include additional shifts in breathing and heart rate, increased blood flow to the genitals, and heightened physical sensitivity. Arousal is largely about the body saying, "Okay, I'm getting ready for action!"

To help you understand how attraction, desire, and arousal may be separate for an asexual person, here are some examples of how they can be either linked or separate for a sexual person:

attraction and desire linked

You find the person sitting across from you on the bus from you, who says hello to you every morning, incredibly attractive. While you know very little about them, you occasionally fantasize about them and consider asking them for their number. In this case, sexual attraction and desire are closely intertwined.

attraction but no desire

You also find a neighbor who lives across the street from you very sexually attractive. The first time you spoke to them, you got that excited butterfly feeling in your chest and stomach. However, when they started talking to you about their favorite hobbies, it bored the snot out of you and turned off any desire you had to try to sleep with them. You still find them fun to look at and occasionally fantasize about, but when you think about it on a conscious level, you don't actually want to sleep with them.

desire but no attraction

You have been together with a partner for several decades, and you both look very different than you did when you first met. While neither of you finds the other unattractive, your appearance alone doesn't generally trigger either of you to have that "Must jump in the sack with you!" feeling that you did many years ago. However, you still want to have sex with each other regularly, even if it is now much more driven by factors outside of sexual attraction.

Here's another possibility that may or may not resonate with you: You're camping with a good friend. You don't find yourself attracted to them or ever having sexual fantasies about them, but you are very comfortable around them and don't find them unattractive, either. As you are sitting at the campfire, they reveal to you that they haven't had any physical intimacy—sex or otherwise—for some time. You share that you are in the same boat, and you appreciate how your friend listens intently. Later, as you try to fall asleep next to your friend, you wonder what it might be like to pleasure them sexually, and to allow them to pleasure you.

arousal without attraction or desire

It is also possible to experience sexual arousal in the absence of attraction or desire. Some rape and sexual abuse victims, both female and male, report physical arousal to the point of experiencing orgasms, even though they had no desire or intent to have sex with their perpetrator.[23]

Some asexuals may become aroused by witnessing others engaging in sexual acts, such as by watching pornography, even if they don't find the individuals sexually attractive.[24] If this doesn't make sense, find a porn scene where you don't find the actors very sexually attractive—not repulsive in any way, just not a turn on for you. Avoid fantasizing about someone else. If you eventually become aroused, physical attractiveness probably wasn't a factor in your arousal.

Master the attraction types

Another distinction is important to grasp so that you understand asexuality: the difference between *primary sexual attraction* versus *secondary sexual attraction*.

Primary sexual attraction is the physical attraction you feel right off the bat with someone, either just after meeting them or perhaps simply after seeing them. Secondary sexual attraction is something that develops more over time, as you get to know someone and learn more about their personality, interests, and so on.

While some asexuals experience neither primary nor secondary attraction, others may experience only secondary sexual attraction. In other words, they rarely find someone "hot" right off the bat, but may come to find someone sexually attractive after getting to know them. Of course, this experience is not limited to asexuals; it can also happen with sexuals. You might recall experiences in your life where you didn't feel much of a spark with a person initially, but once you got to know them, found yourself more sexually attracted to them.

Some writers propose that asexuals can experience different types of attraction outside of sexual attraction. These include the following:

> **aesthetic attraction**: an attraction to another person's physical appearance, without a sexual component

> **romantic attraction**: an attraction that leads one to desire a romantic (but not necessarily sexual) relationship with another person

> **sensual attraction**: an attraction to engage in sensual, touch-related, but non-sexual activities with another person

It is difficult to know whether some people experience these attractions in the same relatively automatic and unconscious way that many of us experience sexual attraction, that is, with the same intensity and associated physiological responses. For some people, there may be a less automatic, more conscious wish to engage with someone, more closely following our earlier definition of *desire*. It likely varies from person to person. Sexual people may also experience these other types of attraction.

The important thing to note here is that people experience attraction, desire, and arousal in different ways. Even if your partner doesn't experience sexual attraction, there may (or may not) be other ways in which you turn each other on.

Attraction can be complex for sexuals, too

When I first started learning about asexuality, I thought, "Wow, asexuals seem so complicated compared to the rest of us." You may have similar sentiments. However, that is not necessarily the case. Even for sexual people, attraction and desire can be complex, and many of the above distinctions apply. Most of us just don't think about it as much. When we are in the majority and most other people are relatively similar to us, we don't *have* to think about it as much. Unlike asexual people, who often feel very out of place, sexual people can still often maintain a basic state of happiness and connection, even in blissful ignorance. Only once a crisis hits do we become motivated to gain greater awareness about ourselves and others. This can be uncomfortable at first, but it can increase our potential for happiness and connection.

Here is an example of my own complexity in the realm of sexual attraction and desire: I often encounter women who immediately trigger a "Wow, she's hot!" thought, followed by a brief visualization of what it would be like to have sex with them. In my mind, this sex is wild and animalistic. These fantasies usually don't last more than a few seconds before my mind moves on to other things.

At the same time, I know a few women who didn't trigger such a strong immediate response, but whom I've found increasingly attractive as I've gotten to know them better. There might be things that they do, things they believe in, or ways that they have of showing up and connecting that I appreciate, admire, and respect deeply. When I allow myself to feel my love for them fully, I sometimes imagine getting naked with them, making them feel as much pleasure throughout their body as I possibly can, wrapping myself around them and feeling them wrapped around me, devouring them while they devour me, basking in each other's warm glow.

However, I've gotten in touch with this latter part of myself only recently. Because I currently prefer monogamous relationships, I previously didn't even allow my mind to go in this direction while having a partner. Having only very brief fantasies about women I didn't know that well felt less threatening. I've become more comfortable allowing myself to think about such things occasionally, recognizing that it doesn't mean that I need to act on them, whether I'm currently in a monogamous relationship or otherwise.[25] Such fantasies may, however, tell me something about how I prefer to interact sexually, and I sometimes incorporate elements of them into lovemaking with my current partner.

Likewise, even if your sexual attraction style seems simple on the surface, you may discover complexity if you allow yourself to explore it more deeply. Alongside helping you to appreciate the complexity of others, it may help you to enjoy better sex.

Asexuals & sexuals: Diverse & overlapping groups

While this book often uses the words *asexual* and *sexual* as though they are two distinct categories, it is important to understand that they simply represent different ranges along the same sexual attraction continuum. Each group is very diverse. A "pure" asexual falls at the lowest end of the continuum, representing no sexual attraction at all. A "gray asexual," someone who experiences occasional attraction, falls a small distance up the continuum.

People describing themselves as sexual would fall along the remainder of this broad range, with those experiencing very high attraction (hypersexual) falling at the upper end.

**Potential Range of Asexuals and Sexuals for
Level of Sexual Attraction Experienced**

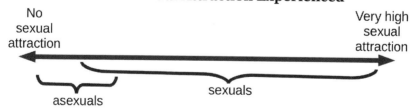

There is some overlap between the upper end of the asexual spectrum and the lower end of the sexual spectrum. For example, one person who experiences sexual attraction roughly once a year may still consider themselves sexual. At the same time, another person who experiences attraction roughly four or five times a year may consider themselves a gray asexual. In other words, some sexuals may experience less attraction than some gray asexuals. The labels may sometimes be misleading, as they are determined largely by how people prefer to identify themselves.

Where a person falls on the attraction spectrum may or may not correspond to how strongly or frequently they are interested in having sex. For example, one person who frequently experiences sexual attraction may be happy having sex once per week. Another person who never experiences sexual attraction may prefer to have sex three or four times per week. The same differences may occur between two people who rarely or never experience sexual attraction.

Potential Range of Asexuals and Sexuals for Level of Interest in Sex

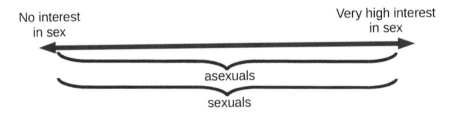

Keep in mind that for asexual individuals, desire for sex isn't necessarily linked to sexual attraction as it is for most sexual individuals. Survey data suggest that it is far less common for asexuals to have frequent and strong sexual desire, but it is still possible.[26] An asexual person may desire to have sex in order to feel close, to establish or deepen a bond, to help the other person feel pleasure, or to enjoy the different physical sensations of sex. Such desire may or may not happen automatically from time to time, as can be the case for sexual people. Like sexuals, some prefer sex within the context of a sexual relationship, and some prefer it casually.[27] An asexual person may sometimes initiate sex. The first time Katie and I ever had sex, she played a significant role in initiating. She also did on a handful of occasions after that.

The diversity among asexuals and sexuals is important to keep in mind to avoid comparing yourself or your partner to others. This, in turn, can help you to avoid setting standards that are inaccurate and unfair.

In a public online forum, one asexual expressed sadness that their sexual partner had dumped them specifically because they had refused to have sex. Others responded with examples of sexual partners who had been fine with not having sex. Why, they wondered, could this person's sexual partner not have done the same?

There are a few possible answers. While many unique factors affect any given relationship, some sexual partners who remain with asexual partners may have lower sexual interest levels than those who choose to separate. Also, some high-interest sexuals who remain with asexuals may have different sexual outlets—masturbating with or without pornography, having sex with someone else, and so on. They may or may not be honest with their partners about these outlets.

In other words, don't beat yourself up just because you know of someone else out there who seems to be handling a low- or no-sex relationship better than you seem to be. You may not have all the details.

At the same time, it's not fair or helpful to say to your partner, "I've heard about other asexual partners who were willing to have sex just to keep the relationship together. Why can't you do the same?" Even if your partner is asexual, they may fall at different points on the libido and attraction spectra than the other people do. Everyone is different.

What asexuality is not: Addressing several myths

"Don't have to make love, 'cause love made me, and I'll be happy just by myself," sings Greg Brown in "Just by Myself." While this might initially sound like a potential anthem for asexuality, things aren't so simple. An asexual person might not want to eliminate lovemaking altogether, and they might still desire a committed relationship—possibly one with romance.

The previous examples and distinctions involving sexual individuals can help us to dismantle some common myths about asexuality.

First, just as sexual preferences among people who identify as sexual can vary, attraction levels among people who identify as asexual can vary. *Gray asexuals,* already mentioned, experience sexual attraction only once in a great while. *Demisexuals,* a type of gray asexual, experience sexual attraction only after forming an emotional bond with someone—in other words, they experience only secondary sexual attraction, as discussed earlier. This bond may or may not be romantic.[28]

How strongly asexuals identify with their specific labels also varies. Many of the labels evolved through conversations in online communities. Some self-identified gray asexuals and demisexuals believe that their preferences are subject to change.[29]

Second, as noted, asexuality does not always mean lack of desire for sex. I repeat this because it's probably one of the biggest points of misunderstanding. Asexuality also does not always mean a complete lack of interest in fantasizing about, reading about, talking about, or viewing sexual activities. While research remains limited in this area, some people who identify as asexual are aroused by others having sex, and some experience strong sexual urges. Some even write erotica. These interests and urges may or may not be connected to anyone in particular, and the person may or may not have an interest in participating in real-life partnered sex themselves.[30] As 27-year-old Mike puts it, "I want to have lots of crazy, kinky sex, just not *with* anyone. If someone tried to initiate something, I'd throw my hands in the air and run out of the room screaming."[31]

You may feel confused and even misled if your partner, like mine, occasionally initiated sex early in the relationship, but then completely stopped later. However, know that this dynamic often happens even with sexual partners.[32] Intimate relationships can bring a lot of powerful emotions and needs to the surface, especially early on; and not all are dependent upon sexual attraction.

Third, asexuality does not mean an inability to become aroused. An asexual person may become aroused by another person's touch or by their own touch, even if they don't experience sexual attraction or desire. Related to this, asexuality does not mean "broken equipment." An asexual person may still enjoy masturbation, and they may still respond to your physical stimulation with arousal and orgasm. This is irrespective of whether they desire or need to experience such sensations with another person, or whether they ever fantasize about another person while masturbating.

This can be confusing because masturbating and having orgasms obviously involve the sex organs and are thus generally considered *sexual* experiences, regardless of how many people are involved. However, the term *asexuality* refers specifically to sexual attraction, not to arousal.

Fourth, asexuality does not necessarily mean a lack of interest in romantic relationships and activities. Sexual attraction and desire for romance are two distinct things. For many people, romantic activities like giving or receiving flowers, going out to a romantic dinner, or watching the sunset together can set the mood for bedroom activities. For other people, such activities do not increase the desire for sex. This romance-desire connection is not necessarily dependent upon whether the couple experiences mutual attraction. Watching a sunset together may increase Lisa's desire for sex while making Bobby wish he were in bed sleeping. One asexual person may find that romance stimulates openness to have sex with their significant other, while another asexual person may never connect romance with sex.

In *The New York Times*, one asexual writer put it this way:

"For many . . . sex and romance are indissoluble, like two-in-one shampoo and conditioner. But for anyone who identifies as either asexual or aromantic, they're more like separate bottles of shampoo and conditioner. They may work well together, and sometimes do, but having one doesn't necessarily mean you have the other."[33]

Katie, for example, sometimes wrote me wonderfully romantic cards and letters, filled with warm, passionate, loving statements. She enjoyed settings with candlelight and soft music. She sometimes bought—or even made—me clothing that she knew would make me feel sexy and loved. She often surprised me with food treats she knew I enjoyed, and sometimes left me little love notes. Katie taught me many things about how to be more romantic. This was despite her experiencing no sexual attraction and little interest in sex.

An asexual person, like a sexual person, can have romantic preferences falling within any of the following categories. For some people, these preferences can vary over time:

➤ **aromantic**: don't enjoy romance with anyone

➤ **heteroromantic**: enjoy romance with people of the other sex

➤ **homoromantic**: enjoy romance with members of the same sex

➤ **biromantic**: enjoy romance with either women or men

➤ **panromantic:** enjoy romance with people of any sex or gender identity, including people who don't identify as male or female

Fifth, just as asexuality does not necessarily mean a complete lack of interest in sexual activity, it also does not mean a lack of interest in other types of sensual, intimate touch. An asexual person may very much enjoy snuggling, massage, and other types of touch, perhaps even naked. Katie, for example, enjoyed snuggling and generously sharing massage with me. However, such touch may rarely or never lead to sexual desire and arousal for them. In some cases, it might. Each person is unique.

Furthermore, asexuality does not mean that a person is "sad" or "missing out." It is easy for a sexual person to think, "Wow, if only that asexual person knew what they were missing out on, they would enjoy things." However, many asexuals are perfectly happy with how they are, and some grow tired of others asking them how they could possibly be happy.[34]

Just as it is important to honor that sex may be very important and valuable to you, it is important to honor that it is not currently important to your partner, and may never be. Your partner is probably interested in certain things that you are not, and you probably wouldn't want them pushing you to do those things too often, either.

Tragically, some individuals who have come out as asexual have even been victims of "corrective rape." A perpetrator forces them to have sex, partially out of a belief that they will find the experience enjoyable and realize that they actually do like sex.[35] This is disturbing and unfortunate enough as it is. Even worse, if the victim does happen to have repressed sexual energies, the added trauma will likely make it even more difficult for them to access that part of themselves.

Related to a few points above, there is not necessarily a correlation between asexuality and how much sex a person has or hasn't had in their life. Asexuality is about the absence of sexual attraction, not sexual behavior.[36] Just like a heterosexual male doesn't actually need to have sex with a male to know that he's not sexually attracted to them, an asexual person doesn't need to have sex with anyone to know that they are not sexually attracted to them. At the same time, an asexual person may have tried sex many times, but still never have experienced sexual attraction toward anyone. They may or may not have enjoyed the sex.

As a sexual person, you may find much of this difficult to comprehend fully. I admit that while I understand much of asexuality on a cerebral level, I cannot fully imagine life without sexual attraction. However, it is still possible to imagine parts of it, and it is still possible to respect it. Likewise, asexual people may find it equally difficult to imagine the experience of sexual attraction, even though it seems like such a fundamental thing to the rest of us.

Asexuality isn't yet broadly understood

In 2012, Barack Obama declared, "I think same-sex couples should be able to get married." It was one of the boldest statements an American President had ever made in support of non-traditional families. In 2015, LGBTQIA (lesbian, gay, bisexual, transgender, questioning, intersex, asexual) community members and allies celebrated a major victory. The U.S. Supreme Court ruled that states cannot ban same-sex marriages. While such events catalyzed a range of reactions, they accompanied a gradually increasing public acceptance of at least some individuals outside the heterosexual and cisgender norms.

Such acceptance in the U.S. has been very slow in the making. In many other parts of the world, it has been even slower. In the meantime, countless families have experienced the turbulence and aftermath of mismatched relationships, due to misunderstood or closeted sexuality. Amity Pierce Buxton, author of *The Other Side of the Closet*, estimates that at least 2 million heterosexual Americans are or have been in a marriage with someone who is lesbian, gay, bisexual, or transgender.[37]

As the LGBTQIA community gained more public acceptance, and being vocal about one's sexuality became less dangerous, a "coming out crisis" occurred in the '80s and '90s. Many gay men and lesbians, having married heterosexual partners while still closeted, announced their true orientations. It has been estimated that only a small proportion of families with a heterosexual and homosexual partner—between 11% and 15%—stay together.[38]

Today, with increased understanding and acceptance, the number of closeted gay and lesbian individuals married to heterosexual partners has likely decreased. However, we are still far from a full understanding and acceptance of individuals who identify anywhere on the LGBTQIA spectrum. Among these categories, asexual people remain among the least understood and accepted. That, in turn, translates into limited support and understanding for sexual partners of asexuals.

While some believe the overall LGBTQIA population to be as high as 10%, a 2011 Williams Institute Report puts the U.S. LGBT population around only 3.5%.[39] Asexuals are presently thought to make up an even smaller percentage: perhaps only around 1% of the population.[40] However, if this estimate is correct, that's still more than 3 million asexual people in the U.S. alone, and more than 70 million worldwide.[41] That is not a small group of people.

Are we on the verge of another large-scale coming out crisis, this time among asexuals?

Many questions about asexual-sexual couples and families remain unanswered: How many asexuals are currently in relationships with sexual partners, without both partners even knowing or understanding this? How many asexuals continue to enter long-term relationships with sexual partners today? In a culture where 50% of marriages fail, and where sexual challenges remain one of the most frequently cited reasons for incompatibility, could many long-term relationships simply be suffering from asexual-sexual mismatch? What proportion of asexual-sexual couples ultimately remain together? Do the sexes, orientations, and gender identities of the partners influence how they handle differences after one person comes out as asexual?[42]

I still love Katie very much, and I am deeply appreciative for all the wonderful years we had together. I'm very grateful to have her as a friend today, and I hope to remain friends for the rest of our lives. We have already learned a great deal from each other. However, had we known about asexuality years earlier, we probably would not have committed to a long-term relationship that included sex. We could have adjusted our expectations early on, and could have avoided much pain and frustration. But we did not have that understanding then, and it is just beginning to permeate our culture now.

As mentioned earlier, I regularly attended a breakup, separation and divorce support group for many months. A few women in the group shared stories about their male partners coming out as gay. Nobody seemed to question the women's situations or decisions—it made sense that a gay-heterosexual relationship would be difficult to maintain. However, when I mentioned that my ex-partner was asexual, I sometimes observed puzzled looks and received questions. I didn't mind answering the questions—I appreciated that they wanted to understand my situation—but it reinforced how little collective understanding we still have about such relationships.

In mid-2015, I met a woman who had recently moved from San Francisco, where she had earned a graduate degree in marital and family therapy. She also claimed to have much knowledge about the LGBTQIA, polyamory, and kink communities. However, despite having spent a decade in a city known for its exceptional sexual openness, and having attended a graduate program focused on human relationships, she had not heard of asexuality until moving away. As her knowledge of asexuality was still very limited, I enthusiastically answered her questions.

A few years ago, I participated in a two-day training with the American Association of Sex Educators, Counselors, and Therapists (AASECT), to learn more about the field. I discovered that I had already become quite a sex geek, winning a competition for knowing the most sexual slang terms. Although we spent time passing around multicolored sex toys, talking about our genitals and sexual preferences in small groups, discussing various sexual orientations, and so on, the term *asexual* was not mentioned a single time.

Many therapists don't yet believe that asexuality exists. They maintain that everyone must be sexually attracted to someone, at least to some extent. This is often simply because they have not yet learned about the concept. If a person does not experience sexual attraction toward anyone, therapists often assume that there must be repressed trauma, psychological issues, or medical issues blocking a person's sexual energy. While this is sometimes true, it is not always the case. It can be helpful to understand some of the distinctions between a few common disorders and asexuality.

Sexual disorders versus asexuality

The *DSM-5* is the most recent version of the *Diagnostic and Statistical Manual of Mental Disorders*. It is the guide used by many therapists and psychologists to diagnose patients, especially when reporting to insurance companies for medical coverage. The *DSM* includes a condition called male hypoactive sexual desire disorder, or HSDD. Male HSDD is defined as "persistently or recurrently deficient (or absent) sexual/erotic thoughts or fantasies and desire for sexual activity," taking into account the patient's age and cultural context.

The *DSM* also includes female sexual interest/arousal disorder, defined as "lack of, or significantly reduced, sexual interest/arousal," with at least three of the following symptoms present:

> little or no interest in sexual activity

> no or few sexual thoughts

> no or few attempts to initiate sexual activity or respond to partner's initiation

> no or little sexual pleasure/excitement in 75%-100% of sexual experiences

> no or little sexual interest in internal or external erotic stimuli

> no or few genital/nongenital sensations in 75%-100% of sexual experiences

In both cases, symptoms must exist for at least six months and cause significant distress. A diagnosis can not be made if the symptoms can be better explained by another condition. Also, simply having less desire than one's partner is not reason enough for a diagnosis. One addition to the *DSM-5* is of particular importance: If a person's lifelong lack of desire is explained by self-identification as an asexual, then a diagnosis is not made.[43]

Over time, the broader psychological community has come to acknowledge that other non-heterosexual orientations can exist without being clinical disorders. They have just begun to do the same with asexuality. However, several criticisms of the initial *DSM* descriptions exist.[44]

One criticism is the requirement that the person be experiencing significant distress to be diagnosed with a disorder. Some argue that a person may not see their lack of attraction or desire as an issue simply because they have no way of knowing what they're missing—especially if they've never experienced sexual attraction or desire. However, the most recent *DSM* essentially states that this is the individual's call, not the clinician's.

On the other hand, if the person is experiencing significant distress, it could be because they are in a relationship with a sexual person, and have not yet recognized or accepted their asexuality. They might be much happier if they were simply in a relationship with few or no sexual expectations. Also, if they truly are asexual, they may be distressed largely because they feel like a misunderstood minority in a mostly sexual world.

A second criticism is that in some cases, lack of desire may actually be an understandable and even adaptive response to other things going on in a person's life. This could include, for example, relationship stress or financial distress. While this may fall under "accounted for by another condition," one could argue that the potential role of a partner deserves a little more emphasis.

Third, of all the people who self-identify as asexual, how can one know how many are actually of this orientation, versus how many actually have a disorder? It's probably a mixed bag. Someone who identifies as asexual may fit into any of the following categories:

People who identify as asexual and truly are asexual, with no evidence of psychological or physiological "issues" that might be causing their lack of sexual attraction.

People who identify as asexual and truly are asexual, even though they have histories or physical conditions commonly linked to low interest in sex. Even if a person who identifies as asexual discovers that they have a history of abuse, trauma, or physical conditions commonly linked with sexual desire disorder, it doesn't necessarily mean that these factors are the "cause" of anything. In other words, it doesn't necessarily mean they are actually sexual, hidden beneath layers of repression. They could have been asexual in the first place, independent of the abuse, trauma, or physical conditions. Asexual individuals are no more likely to have suffered a history of abuse than sexual individuals.[45]

People who identify as asexual and have sexual attraction or desire that has been repressed. This repression may have occurred in response to life events, undetected medical conditions, or relationship issues that involve their partner. These people may identify with asexuality for any number of reasons, and may or may not realize that they can experience sexual attraction and enjoy sex. It's hard to say whether they would ultimately be happier continuing life as an asexual or uncovering their sexuality. While it might be possible for them to change, it could take significant effort to do so.

Moreover, it is ultimately up to them, not you, whether they do any such exploration.

Even if a person is initially willing to explore possibilities like past trauma or abuse, medical conditions, sexual shame, or relationship issues, they may start to uncover things but hit a point where they don't want to go any further. What they discover might be too scary. Or, they may discover things and make significant progress in understanding them, but still experience little or no change in their sexual attraction or desire for you. For example, what if your partner is actually attracted to people of a different sex than you, and they are so ashamed of this that they have repressed their sexual attraction altogether? The discovery and healing process could take many months.

If a person chooses to end their exploration without discovering a long-repressed sexual attraction, it may be impossible to know whether just a bit more work could have generated a shift, or whether there was no attraction in the first place.

In late 2014, researchers announced a 12-question survey that accurately identifies people who experience no sexual attraction versus those who do, regardless of whether they identify with the label *asexual*.[46] This is great progress, but it doesn't appear to distinguish between people who were never wired to experience sexual attraction in the first place, and people whose sexual energies are repressed for whatever reason.[47]

These realities leave some uncertainty regarding the percentage of self-identified asexuals who are actually sexual. In other words, if your partner seems to be asexual, it's difficult to know whether or how much they may ever be interested in sex, even if they wish to explore their identity. Perhaps one of the few estimations you can make is that someone with a lifelong lack of attraction or interest is less likely to shift—but even that is impossible to know for sure. It is up to each person whether they wish to explore their identity.

Consult other resources

Because this book is aimed at sexual partners of asexuals, it covers only a portion of what books devoted solely to describing asexuality cover. If you believe that your partner is asexual, I would recommend checking out at least one or two books written firsthand by asexuals. A few are listed in the "Additional Resources" section. For example, reading *Asexuality: A Brief Introduction* was reaffirming for Katie and me, as it finally gave us an explanation as to what had been going on. As a reminder, just be cautious about applying an identity label too quickly, and explore other possible reasons for your partner's lack of attraction to you.

PART TWO:
Look Within

Part Two Overview

• • •

YOU HAVE NOW HEARD my story, and you have a grasp of some basic concepts surrounding asexuality and lack of attraction. At this point, you are likely experiencing a range of thoughts and emotions. You probably recognize that you are not alone. You may have a stronger sense that your partner is asexual, or a weaker sense. You may feel a sense of relief that there are a few possibilities. You may feel a sense of frustration that figuring things out may take more effort.

Whatever you are experiencing, know that your feelings are valid and understandable. You are not on an easy journey. Living with uncertainty can be challenging, especially when it involves a person and relationship very dear to you and some of the most primal (for most of us) human needs.

Like me, you have likely spent a great deal of time focused on your partner, and what seems to be your partner's "issue"—lack of sexual interest in you. How can you convince them that your needs are important? Why don't they seem to understand?

Paradoxically, during this time of trying in vain to get your needs met, you may have lost sight of yourself. Focused on what your partner is and is not doing, you may have forgotten that you are half of the relationship equation. Focused on getting any sex at all, you may not have allowed yourself to dream about what you want sexually in detail.

Furthermore, like many people, you might have grown up with sex-negative and guilt-based messages that sabotage the happiness you deserve, in both the bedroom and elsewhere. You might have given little thought to the actual sources of your loneliness. You may now have difficulty accepting not only your partner but also yourself.

You owe yourself some loving attention and courageous self-exploration. In Part Two, it is time to look within. If your conversations with your partner lead to endlessly frustrating loops, stopping to build and maintain your foundation can be especially helpful. Many of the upcoming topics are important whether you remain in your current relationship or eventually move on to another.

4. Assess What You Want

• • •

Manage painful emotions

It is normal to experience a range of challenging emotions. Around the time when Katie revealed that she was likely asexual, I was feeling a great deal of anger, loneliness, betrayal, confusion, and pain. I was also experiencing a lot of anxiety, and some elements of depression. Such thoughts and emotions require recognition, time, and space. As we'll talk about more in "Begin to Accept Past, Present, & Self," the healing process can take a while.

In the meantime, it can help to focus at least some of your energy on what you would like the future to look like, rather than to focus all of your energy on what has upset you in the past. Things are much more likely to change that way. This can also better equip you to utilize a therapist or other helping professional, as you will have a clearer idea of the changes you would like them to support you in creating.

However, you might be so emotionally shaken up, especially if you and your partner were initially unaware of your differences, that it is difficult to focus on the future just yet. Maybe you are having difficulty even concentrating on this book. If that is the case, consider enlisting a therapist or joining a support group as soon as possible. This is especially important if you are losing significant sleep, are having difficulty completing day-to-day tasks, are having difficulty interacting with your partner amicably, or are thinking about harming yourself or others.

While I never felt any urge to harm Katie or myself physically, I did sometimes shout and express anger verbally. I wish I could take back some of the things I said to her, as I know they were hurtful. Once I sought out emotional support from others, things became a bit easier to manage. This was especially important while we had a small child in the home, as I wanted her to be in a peaceful environment. You likely want the same for those closest to you.

I have included some thoughts on seeking support in Part Five under "Come Out & Seek Support." While the suggestions there are intended to accompany additional conversation with your partner, you might wish to get support just for yourself much sooner, and consider ways to involve your partner later.

Reframe entitlement

You may have invested a great deal of time, energy, and other resources into your relationship. You may have promised many things to your partner, perhaps including monogamy. In return for your commitment, you have probably developed many expectations of your partner.

You may have what seem to be good and legitimate reasons to expect sex. You might have explicitly communicated your preferences and expectations early in the relationship. Or, you might not have, believing that your expectations were implied in other ways. If you had sex early on, it probably seemed safe to assume the sex would continue. If you are married, regular sex may seem reasonable to expect, given that having sex with anyone else without your partner's consent could be considered grounds for divorce.

However, when it comes to creating a more sexually fulfilled life, it doesn't matter how entitled you feel, or how valid your reasons are. You can't *make* someone want to have sex with you. The only person you have control over is yourself. The best you can do is to focus on your self-development, become the most attractive partner you can, get to know your needs better, and learn to communicate them as well as you can.

If that's not enough to make your partner want to have sex with you, or at least willing to have it in a way that meets your minimum needs, it's your choice whether to remain, leave, or attempt to negotiate new relationship terms that work for both of you. Nobody, including your partner, is making you stay. If they insist that they are unwilling or unable to have sex with you, even at risk of losing the relationship, that's something you ultimately need to honor. Sure, you might be able to persuade someone to have sex with you through nagging, guilt-tripping, or letting them know why you feel entitled, but is that the type of connection you really desire? If you truly care about your partner, is that what you want for them?

Upon reading these words, you may be thinking, "But it's not a choice—the costs of ending the relationship would be devastating!" True, there may be massive costs involved with separating from your partner, especially if you have been together a very long time, are married, have one or more kids, or share a lot of property. The emotional, financial, time, and energy costs of separating may indeed be quite large. There may be religious and spiritual considerations. We'll talk more about some of these later. Whatever the case, staying or leaving is ultimately your choice. This may sound blunt, but blaming your partner for "boxing you in" is not likely to help.

Should you find yourself seriously thinking about forcing yourself upon your partner, or if you have already attempted to do this, please seek additional professional support as soon as possible. That's a clear sign that the relationship needs to change in a major way for you very soon, or you need to transition out of the relationship. Even if you feel that your partner misled you, and this feels intensely unfair, anger or force won't help anyone. You don't want to hurt someone you care about and create further pain and complications for both of you.

After realizing that Katie was asexual, I sometimes found myself very sexually frustrated. While I never physically attempted to force her to have sex, I did sometimes use emotional manipulation. If she showed disappointment when I requested sex, I might emotionally withdraw, or tell her that a task or errand I had previously been happy to do now felt like an inconvenience. I feel terrible that I acted that way toward her, as I know it didn't help either of us. At the same time, I have done my best to forgive myself, knowing that it was a challenging situation I could not have anticipated.

Always remember, there are billions of people on the planet, the majority of whom are sexual, and many of whom are seeking companionship. This may be very difficult to see right now, and may sound like a platitude. I know because I have been there myself. However, it is true.

Questions to keep in mind

As you continue to read this book, having the following questions in the back of your mind may be helpful. Some of them will give you a framework for integrating later topics.

A first question worth asking yourself is one of my favorites from life coach training. You can consider it alongside each of the other questions below: **Are you currently thinking and acting out of love, or out of fear?**

Love includes consideration for your partner's higher well-being, as well as yours. When you feel consistently deprived of a basic human need, it is easy to veer away from love and toward *fear*. Yes, most people can easily survive extended periods without sex, so it's not an absolute survival need; but many people do need it to feel fulfilled and connected. People often act out of a combination of love and fear, but sometimes the motivations are weighted toward one end.

Which types of sexual activities do you need to be happy, and with what frequency, at a minimum? How does this mesh with what your partner is willing to do? Later in this chapter, we'll talk about getting more specific about what you want, and cover one exercise for comparing your wants to those of your partner.

How much do you need to feel needed by your partner in these activities? Another way to ask this: In addition to receiving pleasure from your partner, how much do you need to feel like they are receiving pleasure, too? How much do you need them to express excitement? Keep in mind that your partner may never want or need you sexually in the same way that you need them. In a later chapter, we'll talk more about loneliness and "wanting to be wanted."

Related to the above: **How much do you need your partner to have an experience of sex that seems similar to yours?** The truth is that even for two partners with similar levels of sexual interest, their perceptions of any given sexual experience may be very different. However, for mixed orientation couples, things may always seem *very* different.

If you can't get your "giving and feeling needed" needs met through sexual activities, how much can these needs be satisfied with non-sexual activities? Later we'll cover different types of intimacy and different ways of giving and expressing love. If you already seem to have strong bonds in other areas, that may be another "plus" for striving to preserve the relationship. If your relationship is weak in many of these other areas as well, then you may have much more to consider than sexual compatibility.

If your partner has a permanent lack of attraction or interest in sex, how well can you continue in the relationship without holding this against them? If you feel that you are going out of your way to tolerate your partner's lack of sexual interest, and you expect special treatment from them in return for your sacrifice, that may cause problems. This includes expecting them to put up with sub-par treatment or effort from you. For example, when our sexual differences were at the forefront, I sometimes resented when Katie asked me for things like watching Charlie for a few additional hours. Even though watching him was sometimes enjoyable, I resented that Katie expected me to show up as a parenting teammate when she couldn't show up as a romantic partner in the way that I needed.

Are you totally okay with always initiating and never expecting your partner to initiate or have sex on their mind? Can you do this without feeling as if you are putting your partner out for asking them to put out? Can you do this without playing games? Can you agree to an arrangement that doesn't rely upon your partner to initiate? For example, a realistic agreement might regularly reserve times x, y, and z of each week for sex if you would like it then. Some sex books state that the low-interest partner needs to initiate sometimes for a relationship to work; but where asexuality is a factor, sex may rarely be on a person's mind. Later we'll talk about asking for what you want, which may also be helpful for this—and for other areas of life.

How do you manage behaviors or situations that often lead you to desire sex, but that do not arouse your partner? For example, your partner may want to enjoy an evening of dinner and dancing in a way that gets you turned on for lovemaking. But they would prefer that the evening end with going to bed early—and going to sleep. Maybe you and your partner enjoy gazing into each other's eyes for extended periods—but your partner prefers to do it without any expectation of making out. Perhaps your partner likes to cuddle naked with you in bed, but rarely or never wants sex. Maybe they like to exchange naked oil massages, as long as it doesn't lead to sex. Your expectations need to be clarified and expressed so that these situations don't always leave one or both of you dissatisfied.

What other things do you need to meet your sexual needs? Is your partner okay with them? This might include pornography and sex toys. You don't need to discuss every detail or instance with your partner, and you might even have a "don't ask, don't tell" agreement that works for both of you. But if you find yourself regularly engaging in many sexual behaviors that you have never talked with your partner about at all, you might want to explore what that means. Is it a secrecy that affects your connection? Later we'll cover several ideas for managing pornography and masturbation in relationships.

How authentically playful can you be with your partner in the realm of sex? Consider yourself in your most fulfilling years of having sex, whether this was with your current partner or previously. How playful and energetic were you? Can you act this way with your current partner, or do you feel you have to behave unnaturally? For example, if foreplay is important to you, how much is your partner willing and able to provide this without a "let's just hurry up and get it over with" vibe?

What other areas of your life are closely linked to sex for you, and how much can you enjoy them with your current

partner? For example, artistic expression and spirituality are intertwined with sexual energy for many people. If you enjoy dancing in a sexy way, can you do this with your partner? Or can you enjoy it with someone else in a way that's acceptable for all of you?

How much will you feel the urge to change your partner if you remain together? For example, perhaps you have always wanted to see how your partner looks in black pumps and a plaid miniskirt, or tight jeans and a form-fitting V-neck, but this just feels very inauthentic to them. Can you let such things go? Later we'll talk more about acceptance and forgiveness, which apply regardless of whether you remain together.

How content can you be socializing with sexual-sexual couples, without envying what they have? Later we'll revisit the concept of envy, and how to use this energy.

Is exploring an open relationship an acceptable option for both of you? If you and your partner cannot achieve a mutually acceptable monogamous compromise, this is another possibility. We'll discuss this in depth later, as there are some special considerations for asexual-sexual couples. It's not something to jump into without prior planning and very honest dialogue.

Determine your desire to improve yourself

You might discover that the primary cause of tension between you and your partner is that they do not experience sexual attraction. On the other hand, you might discover that your thinking and behaviors are a big part of the equation. Or both.

For example, there may be reasons you *chose* a partner who doesn't experience attraction as you do, or who doesn't have as much interest in sex as you do. Under "Neither partner may be to blame," we'll discuss challenging things I had to admit to myself. Your ongoing sexual differences could be a distraction from other personal growth opportunities. If so, those challenges will remain, and will require courage and personal effort to address, even once you have an abundance of sex.[48]

If you are asking your partner to consider changes, and you want things to work, you will probably need to make changes as well. This is the case if they are already certain about their asexuality, and you are asking them to be more sexually accommodating of you. It is also the case if they are not certain that they are asexual, and you are asking them to seek professional support to explore this. How are you willing to accommodate them?

In addition to any exploration your partner is willing to do on their own, are you also willing to seek support, including seeing a couples counselor or coach if needed? If it turns out that your partner has repressed sexual energy due to issues in how the two of you relate, you will both have personal development work to do. If your partner confirms that they are asexual, will you need support in accepting this? If your partner finds that their lack of desire is linked to a traumatic early life experience, will you be prepared to get any support you need as they work through that?

The bottom line here is that it's not going to be just your partner doing the work—if they are willing to make efforts, you will likely have homework as well. Keep in mind that whatever work you do on yourself is likely to benefit you for the rest of your life. Whether you stay in your current relationship or eventually move on to another one, you will be a wiser person.

Determine what you need to be happy

At this point, you have a pretty good idea of what you *don't* want: a relationship with little or no sex. You know that, among other things, you would like to have more sex and more romantic spice in your life. But it's not enough just to run away from what you *don't* want; you will likely find it easier to remain motivated if you can envision the life that you *do* want.

Obviously, in real life, nobody gets what they want all the time from their partner. There will always be compromise. But it can't be *too* much of a stretch for either person. If you are inwardly resenting your partner, it won't help anyone in the end. To determine whether you can meet in the middle, you first need to get clear on your needs.

Clarifying what you want will be helpful regardless of whether you remain with your current partner or eventually enter another relationship. You'll have difficulty feeling satisfied with anyone if you're not willing and able to communicate what you want.

Here I'm not talking about what you need just to make the relationship tolerable, but something enjoyable, without resenting your partner. Without worrying that 10 years from now, you are going to regret having remained in the relationship.

Get specific. For example, do you want to be having sex at least once a week? Twice a week? Vague statements like "I like to have sex a few times per week" can mean different things to different people. Turning that into "I like to have intercourse at least three times per week, including at least once during the weekend" is specific.

Do you need them to initiate sometimes, or is it enough that they are sometimes willing when you initiate? Do you need to have a better sense that they are enjoying it? Do you just want to be having sex with someone period, even if it is someone else?

If you want to get even more specific, consider body parts, locations, and types of motions. This could be more than you and your partner are capable of communicating with each other right now, but it may be helpful later. For example, "I like being licked down there" can be expanded to, "I like it when my partner slowly licks my labia from bottom to top for several seconds, and then quickly and lightly moves their tongue back and forth over my clitoris, occasionally stopping to suck on it." When both people are open and present, it's possible to get this specific. And it can be quite fun and pleasurable to do so. In addition, feel free to imagine and jot down things you've never even experienced, but are curious to try.

Also, consider whether your sex-related wants are just about the sex itself. Are there other related things that you would also like to see shifting? Jot those things down, too.

Don't try to judge what's right or wrong, or politically correct, or noble. Just write what comes to mind. Try to rule out things that feel like "shoulds"—things that you have been taught are right or wrong, but that you inwardly resent having to do. An example: "I *should* be okay going a month without sex because when you truly love someone, you are willing to put sexual needs aside." Another: "Expressing a desire for sex before my partner initiates is a sign of impatience and disrespect."

If you have difficulty getting specific about what you want, take a few moments to list how improvements in your sex life will affect other areas of your life. This may include your relationship with your partner beyond sex, your relationships with other friends and family members, your career, your physical health, and your emotional well-being.

Keep the above questions in mind as you continue to read. As you gain additional perspective, some of your desires may shift.

Dig deeper with your wants & needs

After you have allowed yourself to brainstorm, ask *why* you need the above at a minimum in order to be happy. What makes it important? Sometimes, but not always, digging deeper leads to other ways to meet the same needs. Moreover, it may lead you to realize that certain things are either less or more important than you previously thought.

For example, you may realize that a deeper need is feeling wanted and appreciated by your partner, but that it doesn't necessarily need to be sexual that often. Or, you may decide that you want to experience the feeling of mutual physical attraction. Digging deeper, you realize that mutual attraction helps you to feel understood. That, in turn, helps you to feel more connected. Perhaps you realize that mutual attraction also gives you a greater feeling of power balance in the relationship—you are no longer the only one who needs sex. These are just examples of what you might discover by digging into your wants and needs.

Clarifying your needs will not only benefit your well-being, but it will also help you show up more powerfully for your partner. Because sexuality is intertwined with other areas of your being, you may have difficulty being emotionally and physically present in other ways if you're shutting off that important part of yourself. For example, you may find it hard to relax and enjoy a romantic film while snuggling with your partner if you're worried that the slightest sign of sexual arousal might make them uncomfortable. To apply a humorous analogy to a challenging situation, living with an asexual partner for me was sometimes like trying to urinate at half velocity without totally cutting off the stream. I often had to keep myself from getting too excited, but I didn't want to shut off my vital energy altogether. Not an easy thing to do, and not comfortable or sustainable.

Special considerations: Kids

As mentioned earlier, one of the most difficult aspects of separating for me was leaving the little boy Katie and I had parented together. I often cry as I recall simple activities like rolling a ball around a field and watching him chase it. Simply jogging by a playground, or seeing a small child on a bicycle, sometimes triggers me. It still pulls my heartstrings when I hear that Charlie sometimes sees my picture around the house and refers to me as "Daddy."

I have sometimes wondered whether I would enjoy parenting with a partner who prioritized sexual and romantic intimacy. The quality of closeness I feel with a person can influence how I frame other things; for example, I'm even more enthusiastic about mowing the lawn shortly after having sex. It's hard to say—the commitment required to raise a child is obviously much greater than that required to mow a lawn. I do know that I feel grief from missing that specific little person, a person whom no other child could ever replace in my heart. These are not easy issues to work through. Even after many hours of therapy and support group discussion, I still wrestle to clarify what role I ultimately hope to play in my former family members' lives.

My heart goes out to you if you are a parent. Even though each of us has a unique experience, I know a bit about the depths of sadness that are possible.

If you happen to have kids with your partner, this will undoubtedly weigh heavily into your decision-making. Numerous factors such as the age of the child, availability of nearby relatives and friends to assist with childrearing, and economic stability of each partner may play into the decision-making.

An asexual-sexual partnership can bring up questions and concerns that not every stressed family with kids must contend with. For example, one thing that made it especially difficult to leave Katie was worrying that she had a lower likelihood of finding another partner. Would she always be alone? Would she always be a single parent? Or was that even that big a deal for her? Perhaps I was incorrectly assuming she feared loneliness in the same way that I did.

Also, who wants to risk being perceived as abandoning their kids so that they can have more sex? I took on this risk when I agreed to try parenting with Katie while having uncertainties about our sexual compatibility. Society has difficulty acknowledging parents as sexual beings. Also, there's a commonly held notion that sexual love and romantic love are inferior to certain other types of love, such as parental love. We'll talk more about this later.

It's possible that your partner came out to you very shortly after you had kids. This may make things even more challenging. Recall that Katie came out to me when we were having major disagreements about children. I'm grateful that she came out while we were having the conversation, and not after we had already had kids. Not everyone is so fortunate. Similarly, when gay or lesbian partners come out to a heterosexual partner, the revelation is often catalyzed by some sort of stress or crisis, such as having children, a serious illness, or a death in the family.[49]

Long after separating from Katie and Charlie, my guilt and shame around leaving them for "shallow" reasons still crop up sometimes. I occasionally find myself questioning whether I deserve the pleasure of sex. Individuals in a few settings—both a relative and a member of a support group—have expressed surprise that I would leave both a partner and a child for something like sex. I do my best to explain that I still love and miss them very much, but that the love didn't enable us to meet some of each other's basic needs.

You'll also want to consider whether you and your partner can model a relationship that will be healthy for your kids. This includes being reasonably happy and expressing a reasonable level of affection for each other regularly.[50] It also includes maintaining a bond with your partner that isn't significantly weaker than your bond with your kids. Without a reasonably strong partner bond, it will be harder to maintain a unified parenting approach when your kids need your teamwork and consistency the most. Additionally, you run the risk of having an overly child-centered relationship, which can create other issues.

Whatever the case, your kids may benefit from professional or peer support. If they have witnessed conflict or lack of affection between you and your partner over an extended period, they may doubt their own ability to form intimate relationships. They may have many questions they've been afraid to ask and emotions they've been afraid to express. The resource pages of the Straight Spouse Network's website list several resources for families of mixed-orientation couples. While they currently appear to be geared toward families with someone who has come out as lesbian, gay, bisexual, or transgender, some of the dynamics will still apply to asexual-sexual families. As more individuals speak out, children and families of asexuals will receive more attention.

Special considerations: Religion & spirituality

You and your partner may have religious beliefs surrounding your wedding vows. You may have promised, "until death do us part," "in sickness and in health," and so on. Such vows can be very difficult to break. At the same time, these vows likely included an agreement to be sexually monogamous. Each of you is the other's one and only option for sex. Does this imply that each of you is willing to meet the other one's sexual needs, at least a reasonable amount of the time? And what if one person is unwilling and unable to do this, and it's not even because of an illness or accident, but because of their fundamental nature? How does that affect the rest of the agreement?

This is tricky ground. Perhaps your partner is willing to continue having sex, not because they inherently enjoy connecting in that way, but because they fear that not doing so will violate their religious duties. How will this affect your ability to experience connection? Or perhaps your partner is rarely or never willing to have sex, and you decide that you'll do your best to go without sex. Can you continue to love your partner in the other ways you agreed, alongside that?

The intersection of religion and sexuality, or more broadly, spirituality and sexuality, can create additional frustration for people who don't experience sexual attraction or who lack desire for sex. For many people, sexual attraction and union are spiritual experiences— experiences that can create a deep sense of connection and incredible energy, perhaps even an increased closeness to God or a higher power. Just meeting a person you find very attractive can be exhilarating. Because of this, society teaches us that blissful sexual union, so intense that it is spiritual, is an ideal to which we should all aspire. This is bolstered by the widely held religious notion that sex is the icing on the cake of a God-sanctioned union between two people.

Regardless of how much you agree with such notions, they are widespread, part of our standard social programming. Such high ideals and the pressure to live up to them can present challenges even when a person is sexual. This includes not only how sex should be for you, but also how it should be for your partner. Given that, imagine the pressure that someone who experiences little or no sexual attraction or interest in sex might feel. Much of the world seems to rave about an element of spirituality that just doesn't fit into their spiritual experience.

If sexuality is an important part of your spirituality, can you find other ways to feel connected to a partner for whom this is not the case? Any two people—even two highly sexed people—are going to have different experiences of sex. It's a matter of how much of a perceived difference you are willing to experience. The section "A source of loneliness: Not being understood" provides more thoughts on this.

While religion and spirituality can provide a grounding and guiding force, they play a different role for each person and situation— especially when it comes to sexuality and relationships. Only you can ultimately determine what options will honor your values.

5. Soften Your Dragons: Sexual Guilt & Shame

• • •

Defining guilt versus shame

Sexuality is so rife with guilt and shame that many books could be written just on this topic. Like Reverend Arthur Dimmesdale in *The Scarlet Letter*, many of us psychologically flagellate ourselves for our sexuality. If you've been in a relationship with a low-interest partner, these dynamics may affect you even more.

The words *guilt* and *shame* are often used interchangeably, but they are somewhat different. *Guilt* involves an awareness of having done something that you believe has wronged another person. It is a bad feeling you experience about your actions, driven by empathy. *Shame* involves self-judgment, concern about the type of person you are, and how you appear to yourself and others. Shame may or may not be a result of your actions.[51]

In moderation, both emotions can keep you from doing things that are harmful to others. But when shame, in particular, becomes extreme or long-term, it can cloud your ability to feel other emotions including joy. It can also lead to isolation and self-sabotaging behaviors. When you feel bad about yourself, you may become defensive and hypervigilant for judgment from others. This doesn't help anyone. Sources of shame can be difficult to pinpoint, given that the associated self-judgment can provide a strong motivation to avoid looking beneath it.

For example, earlier I mentioned how I felt guilty for leaving Katie and Charlie. After a while, this guilt turned to self-judgment or shame. How could I be the type of person who would leave a loving partner and child for something as shallow as sex? I struggled with this later, even after Katie reassured me that we had done our best and that I hadn't abandoned them. For a long time following our separation, my shame triggered difficulties in allowing myself to experience pleasure —not just sexual pleasure, but even things like attending parties or allowing myself to relax while not writing or doing other work.

If you have separated from your partner or are considering doing so, it's possible that you are wrestling with similar guilt and shame. One of the first steps in dealing with it is simply being aware of it, and understanding some of the dynamics that play into sex-related shame, especially as they can impact asexual-sexual couples. You deserve to be happy and fulfilled.

Being different from your partner is okay

With sex, as with most things, different people may want or need different things to make them happy. For your partner, sex may or may not be connected to emotional intimacy or commitment in the same way that it is for you. Because of this, your partner may never fully understand your viewpoint, and you may never fully get theirs.

Related to this, you may believe that the situation is much rougher for you than for your partner because you need sex while they don't seem to need it at all. The truth is that it may not be easier for either of you—the challenges and frustrations you each face are simply different. Trying to determine which of you is in more pain may only keep you in a cycle of trying to one-up each other with complaints of how you've been hurt.

Some asexuals on the AVEN boards lament not being able to comprehend why their partners have such a need for sex. They feel that if their partners truly loved them, they'd be willing to go along with much less sex. On the other hand, many sexual partners lament how they feel not only horny, but also lonely, unloved, and unable to connect with their partners. Neither partner is right or wrong. Alongside accepting that it is okay for your partner to lack interest if that is simply who they are, it is important to accept your attraction and pursuit of sexual fulfillment as okay—and important, joyful, and connective.

As one asexual blogger puts it, "You're not automatically a bad person if a sexless romantic relationship isn't for you. If you have needs that it's impossible for your partner to meet without being made unhappy, you are incompatible, and it's no one's fault."[52]

If you & I are shallow, so are many others

If you and I are shallow for wanting sex in our relationships, then a whole lot of other people are shallow, too. In fact, having good sex is highly important to more people than is having adequate money or shared interests with their partner.

A 2007 survey asked more than 1,600 people about the most important factors determining marital satisfaction. "Faithfulness" and "happy sexual relationship" were at the top of the list, with 93% and 70% of respondents respectively reporting each as very important for a successful marriage. Faithfulness, of course, has a direct tie to sexual relationships—the common assumption is that if your partner isn't having sex with other people, they'll be more available for sex with you. Sex was more frequently ranked as highly important than "sharing household chores" (62%), "adequate income" (53%), and "shared tastes and interests" (46%).[53]

Heal your virgin-whore split

Sex therapists like to talk about the "Madonna-whore complex," referring to the Biblical figure thought to be a virgin, not the pop singer. It's sometimes called the "virgin-whore split." One of the most prevalent causes of sex-related shame, this term refers to a tendency to place women into one of two categories:

➢ saintly, wholesome, committed, virgin-like, maternal women whom you can admire and proudly bring home to your parents, and who are suitable for long-term relationships and marriage

➢ sexual women who are wonderful to have sex with, but not the kind you would bring home to your parents—women devalued as sluts and whores, not capable of loving commitment and not suitable for long-term relationships

This view of women stems partially from social expectations that mothers are not supposed to be sexual. If men and women cannot accept that their own mothers are sexual human beings, then they may have difficulty imagining the female(s) in their own relationship as sexual beings. This is especially true if the couple plans to have kids or already does. This view also stems from sex being viewed as a lower-level and base aspect of relationships, compared to other types of intimacy and commitment.

It is a dichotomy, an expectation that any given woman is unable to embody characteristics from both categories. Our culture also holds either/or attitudes about men that may not be quite as deeply rooted, but that have some similarities: the "nice guy-bad boy complex." These ways of thinking can also negatively affect same-sex couples.[54]

Because such dichotomies take the components that make up a whole human being and split them into parts, they make it difficult to honor and express all parts of a person and their needs. People are expected to turn parts of themselves off and on in unrealistic ways. This leads to people giving each other very mixed messages, because what they truly want on the deepest level conflicts with what society has taught them that they should and shouldn't want.

These attitudes can also lead to contradictory and unrealistic expectations. Some men still expect women to be good at sex from the beginning, while at the same time expecting them to have had little or no previous sexual experience with others. Apparently, they are supposed to develop their sexual skills by magic. Additionally, phrases like "retaining virginity" and "losing virginity" perpetuate the attitude that simply having sex somehow makes a person less valuable or pure.

Some sex therapists report that it is relatively common for couples —even those who have been happy sexually active for some time previously—to develop physical intimacy issues shortly after marriage or commitment ceremonies. This sometimes occurs because the partner now bears the label of *life partner, wife,* or *husband.* With such labels, they may no longer fit the sexual category in their partner's mind—and possibly in their own mind. They are respectable and lovable, but not as sexually exciting. This also helps to explain the dynamics of some sexual affairs. One or both partners seek excitement with other people who aren't associated with any of these labels in their minds.

So how does this all tie into asexual-sexual relationships? First, it may help to explain why you chose someone who is less sexual than you. Because they didn't give off as much of a sexy vibe as other people, they might have seemed safer, more wholesome, and more capable of being a committed long-term partner. Perhaps you didn't believe that the same partner could provide both excitement and safety, both passion and commitment, both adventure and groundedness, both hot sex and wholesomeness. So on some level, perhaps not fully consciously, you felt like you had to give up one for the other. This is, of course, just one possibility among many; you were likely attracted to them for a range of reasons.

Second, the Madonna-whore complex may tempt you to place the asexual partner on morally higher ground and yourself on lower ground as a whore or a bad boy. You may be tempted to beat yourself up for not being able to put other aspects of your relationship above sex. It might feel like you are viewing your partner largely as a sex object, even if you obviously value other aspects of the relationship.

Third, the Madonna-whore complex is powerful enough to cause sexual difficulties for people who experience sexual attraction. Therefore, it could be powerful enough to eliminate sexual interest for someone who doesn't experience sexual attraction, but who may otherwise be open to sex. In other words, even if your partner is asexual, an inability to enjoy sexual interaction with you *might* be partially or largely attributable to sexual shame. I emphasize the *might*; it's up to your partner whether they explore this possibility.

Additionally, sexual shame can keep us in relationships that are less than what we deserve. One woman I know grew up receiving strong messages that good men want to marry only virgins. After much pressuring from a boyfriend, she decided to have sex for the first time. After they broke up, she no longer believed she could attract a decent partner, due to having lost her virginity. Largely because of that, she then tolerated two relationships with partners who treated her poorly. Fortunately, after those learning experiences, she met a more compatible partner and is now happily married.

If you and your partner were each other's "first," that's a special bond that you share. However, if you are staying together partially out of obligation due to that, or out of fear that you will be seen as "used goods" by other potential partners if you move on, take a closer look at how this will serve you, your partner, and others close to you. If religious values and beliefs are intertwined, this may be very challenging to examine—especially in a culture where some sex education programs compare non-virgins to chewed gum, used toothbrushes, and even worn-out sneakers.[55] Only you can determine which personal values are most important for you to honor.

The bottom line here is that people are complex creatures. It is possible to be caring, warm, loving, and sensitive while also being highly sexual. This might include a sexual history with multiple partners. The quality of sexuality can range from soft and sensitive to rough, animalistic, and primal, all within the same person, depending on the setting and mood. In addition, most of us are going to treat each other as sources of pleasure sometimes, using our bodies and minds to connect powerfully and share energy—not just sexually, but in other ways as well. When done consensually, this doesn't have to equate to disrespecting or devaluing one another.

If you have fallen prey to the Madonna-whore complex, be gentle with yourself. It's human nature to categorize and stereotype to simplify our understanding of the world. This is particularly the case with topics where knowledge is limited. Sexuality is one such topic, given the lack of education and honest discussion surrounding it. The most important thing is to exercise self-awareness from this point forward.

You might also explore some of the attitudes about sex that you learned growing up. Here are a few questions to ask yourself that might provide insight into your Madonna-whore thinking:

➤ How did your parents interact in your presence? Did they show affection, or did they tend to hide it?

➤ Were you ever caught by an adult or someone else behaving sexually, such as masturbating? If so, how did they react? (This might have occurred at such an early age that you can't remember it.)

➤ What messages about sex did you receive as part of your religious and spiritual upbringing?

➤ What are some of the earliest opinions you recall others expressing about sexually active members of your sex and of the opposite sex? About non-sexually active members?

Also know that the virgin-whore split is about much more than virginity versus sexual experience. It's about safety versus risk, familiarity versus novelty, home versus adventure, and calmness versus excitement. Life is a constant dance of balancing these polarities. It's acceptable and normal to crave characteristics at both ends of the spectrum and anywhere along the middle, even if our culture tells us we should feel guilt or shame for some of our desires. Furthermore, we don't apply these dichotomies just to people—we may also apply them to other important factors in our lives, such as different geographic locations or career options. These are some of the forces that drive many midlife crises.

My virgin-whore split spanned more than 3,000 miles. In some ways, Katie and Cleveland represented safety, familiarity, home, and calmness. Sophia and Seattle represented risk, novelty, adventure, and excitement. Initially, the differences between these people and places seemed very pronounced, and I excitedly anticipated having everything I felt I had been missing. Over time, as I recognized how much my attitudes influenced my perceptions, many of the differences became more nuanced. I realized that a different person or place could only do so much—I also had to look within myself. I had to begin healing my own virgin-whore split.

Question the hierarchy of love

Closely related to the Madonna-whore complex is a widespread tendency to judge certain types and expressions of love as superior to others.

While Katie and I parented Charlie, some who knew he wasn't our biological child treated us like saints: "Oh, my gosh, what you're doing is so wonderful! That must be so incredibly challenging!" It was indeed challenging for both of us, even with Katie taking on a greater share of the direct care responsibilities. Additionally, the parental love I developed for Charlie was quite powerful. As mentioned earlier, I still miss Charlie deeply, and I often feel a profound sense of loss. Few days go by where I don't think about how he's doing.

Indeed, parental love is a noble, admirable, and incredibly powerful thing. But did anything make the parental love we gave a child any *better* than the myriad other ways in which people share affection? Did anything make it better or more noble than the romantic and sexual affection I wanted to share with Katie? Or was it merely *different*?

I've found it helpful to keep a few things in mind. Hopefully they'll help you as you sort out any shame or guilt around your sexuality, especially if you and your partner have children.

First, while sex is sometimes separated from love, it can also be a profound way of expressing and receiving love. As with other types of sharing and giving, if done honestly and with integrity, it's a way of spreading energy that can have an exponentially positive effect—just like more socially praised forms of love and sharing.

If you doubt this, think about the last time you received or gave deeply gratifying sensual touch. It could have been a passionate kiss, a massage, sex, or a long embrace. If it has been a while, consider a passionate artist's work that resonated with you. It might have been a live music performance, a song on the radio or in a dance club, a play, or a painting. These are just a few products of love, passion, and energy directed in different ways. How have such things affected you? How did that, in turn, influence your interactions with other people, your work, and so on?

Chances are such pleasurable experiences have often helped you to show up more powerfully and energetically in the world—in your various relationships, work, hobbies, and so on. When your cup is overflowing, you have more to give and share with others. I have experienced this. For example, when Katie was willing to be physically intimate with me, I found it easier to be playful and relaxed around Charlie. On the other hand, when I felt deprived of the types of affection I wanted from Katie, I found it harder to tolerate stressors such as a toddler's crying.

Additionally, most types of love, even those that seem the most selfless, have at least some selfish element. Just from parenting for a few years, I learned that parenting takes a lot of selflessness. However, as Katie and I discussed various motivations for having kids, I realized that such motivations aren't always selfless. For example, many individuals value the companionship and care that they envision their children providing as they grow older. Or they want to relive fun elements of their childhoods vicariously through their children. There is nothing inherently wrong with these reasons. They simply have some elements of self-interest, just like romantic and sexual love do—sometimes to a lesser extent, but sometimes not.

Stop depriving yourself & others of pleasure

We are often taught from a very young age that experiencing pleasure is wrong. We deal with this enough as it is in our culture, let alone in a sexual/asexual relationship. Women, in particular, have long dealt with messages that it's not okay to enjoy sex. Even worse, we learn that the pleasurable aspects of relationships—including sex—are used to manipulate others and get what we want. These messages, delivered in many subtle and not-so-subtle ways, influence our attitudes about love and sex.[56]

For example, you might have observed a parent or other adult withholding affection as a form of punishment to get what they want. This might have included one person giving the other the silent treatment, or even one partner being "in the doghouse" and having to sleep alone. Interestingly, some research suggests that children under three years old are already capable of practicing *relational aggression* —the intentional withdrawal of attention or affection to punish or get what they want.[57]

This learned connection, carried into adulthood, may affect asexual-sexual couples in a few specific ways. First, suppose you learned that whenever Daddy wasn't getting affection from Mommy or vice versa, it meant that the deprived partner had misbehaved. You may later assume that whenever your partner isn't willing to provide physical affection, you must also be undeserving or "bad" in some way. If you develop shame around this, you could become more defensive with your partner. The truth, of course, is that your partner could be unwilling simply because they are not that interested.

Second, suppose that you don't get the affection you are seeking from your partner even when you are trying to "be good." You could resort to the punitive patterns of withholding affection that you learned as a child. Such patterns aren't likely to strengthen your bond with your partner. When your partner does give in, it may be more out of desperation than out of love, and they may resent it. Over time, you might develop a habit of withholding affection or withdrawing from a partner as soon as you feel desire. You'll then miss opportunities where they would have given you what you wanted if you had simply asked kindly. This is a self-defeating pattern.

If you catch yourself withholding love, ask yourself how often that behavior has gotten you what you want. Then ask yourself how you can be more loving, even if it's difficult in that moment.

You also might have learned other false beliefs about pleasure that can affect sexuality:

➤ You must in some way earn every bit of pleasure you experience. While this may be true for some pleasure, it is certainly not always true.

➢ Even wanting sex, or openly asking for what you want in an honest way, is being overly assertive or aggressive. While this belief clearly affects women, it also impacts men.[58]

➢ Suffering and self-deprivation are noble. Martyring yourself is more respectable than enjoying yourself is.

➢ Everyone else needs to feel great, or you need to take care of them, before you are allowed to request, receive, or experience pleasure.

➢ It is not appropriate to request, receive, or experience pleasure alongside "negative" emotions like sadness or frustration.

Perhaps one or more of these false beliefs boosted your attraction to someone who is not very enthusiastic about sex, even when you are. Perhaps your relationship has further reinforced one or more of these stories. Shame about pleasure and sexuality is embedded so deeply in our culture that it is no specific person's fault. However, once you are aware of it, you have the power to transform it.

Amity Pierce Buxton observed that many heterosexual partners of individuals who came out as gay or lesbian had engaged in self-depriving behaviors. Some took on a "superhero" partner role, over-performing in other areas of the relationship. This might have been a strategy to cover up or distract themselves and others from their partner's profound differences. Or it might have been a vain attempt to earn their partner's affection. Others played an overly nurturing, almost parent-like role while suppressing their own needs. Buxton likened it to the behavior of a partner of an alcoholic, placating and overachieving to help hide their partner's secret identity.[59]

It is difficult to know how many of the dynamics observed in heterosexual-homosexual couples also apply to asexual-sexual couples. Either partner could take on some of the same roles described above, either as a distraction or as an attempt to compensate for differences. Have you developed similar strategies for coping with a sexually uninterested partner? If so, you have probably already realized that such behavior is neither pleasant nor sustainable.

Beyond pleasure rationing & self-sabotage

Another common belief about pleasure often gets in the way: For any pleasure you experience, you must experience an equal amount of work or pain. Even in the absence of sexual differences with their partner, many people have a tendency to self-sabotage by creating or focusing on problems whenever the going gets good. This happens with both individuals and couples. As Gay and Kathlyn Hendricks note in *Conscious Loving*, it's as though humans are socially programmed to place an upper limit on how much fun or pleasure we allow ourselves to experience. Once we reach that point, we feel obligated to experience work or pain.

In a mixed orientation relationship, you may have learned to place even more limits on pleasure. Ideally, intimate partners engage in frequent and natural give-and-take, without too much "keeping score" once the relationship is established. In a mixed orientation relationship, however, this sort of keeping score may become common with sex, because both people have such different needs. The couple might attempt to create harmony by developing a spoken or unspoken understanding that sex happens only once every several days, not more than once in a given weekend, and so on.

When I attempted to initiate foreplay with Katie within a day or two of having had sex, I would often be greeted with a response of, "What? We already did it once recently." I would often feel rejected, and this would sometimes turn to anger, silence toward one another, and redirection of our energies into other activities. We would usually apologize to each other later, but this never resolved the underlying issue.

Due to this pleasure rationing, I experienced numerous instances of what I call an "interrupted pleasure cycle." Perhaps we had shared a particularly fun day, or were both in an elevated mood for some other reason. When both Katie and I were in good moods, it was often quite natural for me to become physically affectionate with her. I might flirt, touch her playfully, make suggestive comments, and so on.

For a couple who is reasonably well matched sexually, the above would likely lead to more positive interaction and fun, regardless of whether it ultimately led to sex. However, Katie would often cut things short, noting that she had other things to do, or communicating a look of seriousness or anxiety signaling that it was time to cool down. We would stop interacting and retreat off into our own spaces. I would go into a quiet sulking sort of mode, feeling a mix of loneliness and anger; and she would find some project to keep busy with. While I now understand that she was just protecting her authentic self, I was very frustrated at the time. We would likely argue the next time we interacted.

In other words, our significant sexual differences had led me to a very unfortunate habit: shutting myself down when I otherwise would have been having a good time. For me, it was also a consistent invalidation of my nature. I felt kind of like the schoolchild getting struck over the knuckles with a ruler for writing with their left hand—although it feels natural, it's a no-no. Partially due to this, our interactions became increasingly lopsided toward the "chop wood and carry water" aspects of partnership, with decreasing focus on mutually fun and bonding activities to keep things in balance.

I believe that over time, this "rationing" of sex, alongside learning to shut myself down as I started to feel good, contributed to me further decreasing my spontaneity and expression of desire. I had already developed some of these tendencies while growing up, so I don't entirely blame the sexual differences, but I think they exacerbated things. If I felt like I had already gotten my sexual allowance for a given period but wanted more, I would often mope. In my next relationship with Sophia, even though she was more enthusiastic about sex, it took me a while to reprogram my habit of holding back when I wanted to be playful or have fun.

Relax, enjoy, & stop feeling like a time burden

Sexual guilt surfaced in another way in my mixed-orientation relationship. While she was very generous in many other ways, Katie understandably often wanted tighter time limits on our intimate time than I did. The irony was that during sex, if I felt time pressure, I would feel guilt and shame for taking up too much of her time. Then I would have a difficult time relaxing, and it would take me even longer to climax. This created additional stress and tension between us.

I carried some baggage from this into my next relationship. I found myself feeling defensive when Sophia signaled that she needed to move on to something else. This happened even when she let me know in advance that she had to go at a certain time, and it didn't even start out with sex. It started out with things like phone conversations.

It soon translated to sex. Even though Sophia often truly enjoyed extended sessions of lovemaking, it took me a while to believe that she did. This affected our interactions in a few ways. First, because I was still putting time pressure on myself, it often still took much longer than I wanted to climax. Second, partially due to my past experiences with Katie, and partially due to being taught that women rarely enjoy sex as much as men do, I didn't believe that Sophia could actually enjoy having intercourse or giving oral sex. Therefore, I initially spent especially long periods of time pleasuring her. While I usually enjoyed this a lot, it sometimes went beyond the point of being driven by desire, and into the realm of being driven by insecurity. I sometimes felt I had to go the extra mile so that she would still be willing to give me the time and attention that I wanted. I worried that any activity involving stimulation of my penis was relatively unexciting for her. It took a while before I was comfortable receiving even when I didn't give quite as much.

Learn to say "yes" enthusiastically

One morning, Sophia asked if I would like to set aside some time for lovemaking after she returned home that afternoon. I was very excited to hear this, as that week had been busy and emotionally challenging. We hadn't had sex for a week, which was a longer gap than either of us usually preferred. However, I responded in a rather lukewarm way: "That sounds good. I might be doing some other things, but yeah, let's see where we're both at when you get home." She kissed me and said she looked forward to it.

As I got out of bed, I found myself reflecting upon why I had not expressed my true level of excitement. I realized that it stemmed from a few possible places:

➢ While I was with Katie, I had habituated myself to not getting my hopes up too much. I didn't want to make myself vulnerable by admitting to myself and Sophia that I wanted sex. I still hadn't broken out of that habit entirely.

➢ I still felt a bit of guilt over abandoning Katie and Charlie for seemingly superficial reasons. There was still a part of me that didn't feel I deserved joy.

➢ I worried that if I wholeheartedly committed to sex, I'd need to be incredibly horny and ready to perform at a certain level right after Sophia got home. I was creating unnecessary pressure and performance anxiety. This stemmed partially from habits I had developed in my previous relationship, such as worrying about whether I was making it good enough for my partner to enjoy it, and whether I was taking too long to get my needs met.

Following these realizations, I went downstairs, naked, to catch Sophia and hug her before she headed out the door. I let her know that I was quite excited that we would be having some connective time that afternoon. I let her know that I had allowed some of my internal "stuff" to mask my true level of enthusiasm. While she seemed very happy to hear this, the most important thing from my end was that I was honest about my desires.

If your partner is sometimes willing to offer sex, notice the level of enthusiasm with which you respond. If your response is lukewarm, ask yourself why. Is it due to reasons similar to those just above or in the previous sections? Next time, allow yourself to respond more enthusiastically, and observe what happens. Is there any change in your partner's behavior? Regardless of your partner's response, is there any change in your internal state?

Learn to respond to "no" more lovingly

With Katie, there were occasions where I was hoping for sex and hadn't explicitly voiced it yet, but discovered that she probably wouldn't be in the mood. Not surprisingly, this type of occurrence didn't disappear with a sexual partner—it sometimes happens in any relationship. Just before I'd ask for sex, Sophia might say that she was very tired, wanted to read or take a walk, or something similar.

In such cases, I'd often not verbalize my desire or the accompanying disappointment at all. I feared that it would be insensitive or even manipulative. After all, part of me would hope that she'd still say "yes" despite it being an inconvenience for her. "How dare I not respect a woman's right to say no, to control her own body!" chided my inner moral critic. On occasion, she would suggest that I was being insensitive when I expressed disappointment. This simply confirmed my fears.

For a while, I felt that Sophia was being hypocritical. Sometimes when I complained that she was acting disappointed with me, she opined that such expression was a normal and healthy thing. Why was it okay for her to express disappointment, but not me? Soon, however, it became clear what was making both of us upset. It was *how* we were expressing disappointment. For both of us, disappointment sometimes triggered a real or perceived withdrawal of affection—just as described under "Stop depriving yourself & others of pleasure."

After feeling desire and getting a real or perceived "no," I would experience guilt and shame, almost as though I had committed emotional rape. I judged myself as insensitive, worrying that I had violated my partner or crossed a boundary simply by wanting something sexual when she didn't. Afraid to express my disappointment, I allowed it to turn into anger and frustration. I would then emotionally withdraw, not expressing desire again until it was very clear that Sophia was receptive.

When I didn't express my disappointment and desire verbally, the energy didn't automatically disappear. And Sophia could feel it. Whether subtle or blatant, the withdrawal was clear to the other person. We sometimes observed in each other removal of eye contact, frowning, terse speech, removal of touch, and turning away of the body. Sometimes there was an explicit verbal expression and sometimes there wasn't.

The conclusion: It's often healthier and more loving to express desire and disappointment with words rather than withdrawal. But it has to be done kindly. Here are a few tips for such expression:

➤ Realize that there's probably no reason to feel guilt or shame for your desires. The timing of sexual desire can be unpredictable. The more compassionate you can be with yourself, the more compassionate you can be with your partner.

➤ Start by letting your partner know that you hear and understand how they feel. For example, "I hear that you're tired . . ." or "I hear that you've had a long day . . ."

➤ Continue by expressing your desire in a vulnerable way using "I" statements. For example, ". . . at the same time, I really love and desire you, and I was hoping we could have sex before going to sleep." Note the difference from a non-vulnerable way that uses "you" statements, such as, "Oh, so you're probably not available for sex then" (followed by sigh of exasperation).

➤ Let your partner know that you're not trying to manipulate them and that you still love them, even if your needs are not aligned in that moment. For example, "It's okay if you say no, but I wanted to share where I'm at just in case you might be in the mood."

➤ If you wish to take other actions to partially satisfy your urge, let your partner know in a gentle way, reminding them that it doesn't replace your love and desire for them. For example, "So that I can sleep better, I'd like to masturbate. That will probably mean I won't be in the mood for sex first thing in the morning, but I'd love to connect with you soon when it works for both of us." We'll cover this more under "Revisit Porn & Masturbation."

> Attend or host facilitated touch-positive events like snuggle parties, where you can practice saying and hearing "no." We'll discuss such events under "Expand Your World of Physical Intimacy."

The above strategies are obviously easier to implement when your partner is willing to say "yes" some of the time, even if it's not quite as often as you would like. If your partner continues to express little or no sexual willingness, to the point where it's difficult to contain your frustration, then it's probably time to seek additional support and consider other options.

Reintegrate sex with other aspects of your being

Sexuality may naturally express itself through many activities in your life when you are being yourself fully. This might include an artistic hobby like writing, music, or painting. Maybe you like to dance in a sexual way or tell dirty jokes from time to time. Maybe you used to act silly and spontaneous when feeling sexy. The sexiness may appear in other activities overtly, or it may be an underlying creative and energetic force.

During a relationship with someone who is asexual, you may have squelched much of your sexual energy to avoid making your partner uncomfortable. This is in addition to ways you may have already divorced sexuality from other parts of yourself, due to social shame dynamics discussed earlier.

Katie and I enjoyed much wonderful music together, and we often shared it with each other in different ways. However, it rarely had sexual overtones. We usually got into arguments when I wanted to dance in a sexy way, even in settings where other people were doing so. It embarrassed Katie. Because of this, we often missed out on opportunities to enjoy dancing together, even though both of us had previously loved to dance.

Related to this, Katie sometimes worried that I had "gayish" mannerisms, such as bending my arm a certain way while holding her hand, dancing in an effeminate fashion, or not seeming to show enough affection toward her in public. She explained that she didn't doubt I was heterosexual, but feared that other people might think she was dating a gay man. I agreed that I was not a "macho" male, and I explained that I sometimes enjoyed expressing myself in ways not limited by traditional sex and gender stereotypes. I also recognized that I hadn't been doing a great job of showing affection in public, so agreed to work on that. At the same time, I had difficulty fully understanding her discomfort, especially because she had always been so open-minded and accepting of people with different orientations.

After we realized that Katie was asexual, however, I had more empathy. She might have already felt insecure about her lack of attraction to me, and my behaviors might have been magnifying this. I can only imagine how uncomfortable she must have felt. I appreciated the occasions where she had attempted to dance in a sexy way, even though it must have felt unnatural. I also appreciated her previous efforts to bring us together through dance in other ways. For example, knowing that I enjoyed hip-hop dancing, she once enrolled both of us in a class as a gift.

Sophia's dancing preferences were different. She often enjoyed sexy dancing together, both at social events and in private. One night she put on a playlist of sexy music at home and began to dance for me. She was beautiful and fun to watch, but even more exciting was the sense of feeling understood. Since my teenage years, music and dancing had tapped into a range of deep emotions including sexual energy. I knew that Sophia got this, as she had experienced similar emotions. This more sexual connection wasn't necessarily more profound overall; it merely enabled me to tap into different parts of myself that I had missed.

I realized that over the years, I had begun to squelch my sexy side. This became more apparent as I attended events where both women and men expressed various aspects of their sexuality very openly, through dance, music, and other arts. This expression sometimes occurred through conversation, such as discussing the connections between sexuality, sustainability, and spirituality. I even attended the nation's first sex-positive theater festival. Parts of me that had not been fully alive for a while lit up again. (No double entendre intended.)

Getting yourself back on track may involve recognizing sexually integrative activities in your life, and reclaiming them. Surround yourself with people who can inspire you to do this. I'm not suggesting that you need to seek out blatantly sex-oriented gatherings or venues unless that excites you. Simply going to groups where people are talking openly about sex and relationships may be a step forward.

Sex as relationship test paradox

One common aspect of dating rituals can inadvertently increase sexual shame and confusion. When taken too far, it can also increase the likelihood of sexually incompatible couples ending up together.

People often employ sex as a relationship commitment test. One's ability to be "patient"—often translated as a willingness to forgo sex for a lengthy time—is still often seen as a key indicator of worthiness as a long-term mate. This practice weeds out people who aren't willing to put in a lot of effort to obtain sex. This, in turn, supposedly translates into someone who will stick around for a long-term relationship after they have sex.

A wait-to-have-sex strategy makes sense for many reasons. Sex bears certain physical risks and vulnerabilities, especially for women in heterosexual relationships. This is true even in the era of more reliable birth control and safer sex methods. Additionally, sex is a very emotionally vulnerable act that triggers many bonding mechanisms. In fact, in both of my long-term relationships, I was hesitant to jump into full-on sex until I got to know the person fairly well.

At the same time, however, taking the waiting approach too seriously can set up a few dynamics that are paradoxical and tricky to navigate. This is especially true given that "waiting periods" can last anywhere from a few dates to a few years.

As you become interested in another person, you may want reassurance that they want sex from you. You may want them to show signs of strong sexual interest. If they don't act interested enough, you may doubt that they are passionate about you. Do they want to be more than just friends?

At the very same time, you may want almost the exact opposite: You want them to be willing to wait for it, and not too easy or willing to give, either. Their willingness to sacrifice sexual joy for a while shows that you must be worth it to them, and that they are wholesome. If they seem too persistent about wanting sex, you may doubt that they love you—particularly if they are male. They might not respect you. It may be just lust. If they seem too eager or willing to give sexually, you might judge them as being a "slut"—particularly if they are female.

These nearly opposite expectations can be difficult to manage. They also make it more difficult for us to view sex as an integral part of love.

Additionally, when holding off on sex altogether until you have established a long-term commitment of some type, you may find out that you are indeed sexually incompatible. Unless you've already talked about sex extensively, you are starting from square one in terms of learning what the other likes and dislikes, what you are and aren't comfortable doing, and so on. While this may be in line with many people's religious or ethical beliefs, the risk of incompatibility is real. If one or both people have very limited prior sexual experience, the odds of confusion about orientation also increase.

Katie and I both had limited prior sexual experience when we met, and we waited several months before having sex. Outside of brief visits when we had sex a few times each year, we agreed to forgo any sexual activity for two years, while we dated long distance. This was not always easy for me, but surviving a long-distance period gave me more confidence in our relationship. It made it clear that we were important to each other. However, at the time I had no idea that Katie was asexual. She was still figuring things out, too. Our lack of sexual experience likely postponed the discovery process.

6. Put Things into Perspective

• • •

Your partner is still largely the same person

Being in a relationship where physical intimacy is on the back burner can be tough. It has been said that when sex is working in a relationship, it accounts for less than 10% of the relationship; but when it is not working, it can feel more like 90%. If you are highly dissatisfied with your sex life, you can spend a significant amount of time arguing with your partner about it, quietly stewing, giving each other the silent treatment, moping, lying awake at night, or just feeling anxious and stressed.

When you are not getting basic needs met, it becomes easier to pigeonhole your partner as an obstacle to meeting those needs. As tough as it may be, try your best to avoid reducing your partner to that. You likely still love other things about your partner. There are many things about Katie that I didn't truly appreciate until months after we had separated.

True, things might not work out with your partner. You may sense a decreased connectedness when you look into their eyes—like you don't know them as well as you had thought, or like they just don't understand you. After all, there is this big thing you had assumed about them—that they also liked sex—and it turns out you were wrong. You may be questioning your ability to "read" another person, and you may be wondering whether you can trust your partner in other ways.

Rather than trying to understand this person with their added layer of complexity, it may seem easiest to reject them altogether without further effort. Depending on your specific situation, that could be the case. Regardless, keep in mind that your partner is still largely the same person you have loved. Chances are, despite the pain and anger you may currently feel, you still have some important things in common with them. While your partner might have been dishonest with you, it is also possible that they simply didn't (and perhaps still don't) understand their sexuality.

While you will likely need to seek additional supports, you and your partner may still be able to serve as supports for one another. This is true even if your relationship takes on a very different form—for example, if you ultimately separate. The various life struggles through which you have been teammates, the countless hours you have spent building your relationship, don't suddenly vanish following your partner's revelation—unless you choose to make them do so.

Even if you haven't had a fully honest connection on the sexual front, review the ways in which you *have* been connected to your partner, and may continue to be. As we'll discuss a bit later, there are many forms of giving and receiving, and several forms of intimacy. Sometimes partners lose track of such signs of commitment when they are upset with each other, so you may need to look back in time a bit. The chances are good that you will find some things. If you genuinely cannot, then your differences may span well beyond sex.

Every asexual-sexual relationship is unique

While you may see many commonalities between my experiences and your own, each relationship is different, just as sexuality is expressed differently for each person. In the AVEN website's "For Sexual Partners, Friends, and Allies" forum, sexual partners describe a broad range of situations. For example, one couple might have stopped having sex altogether on their honeymoon, while another still has sex regularly but with the knowledge that one partner never really wants it. Behavior and understanding can vary greatly across couples.

The overall umbrella of physical touch is extremely broad. Even within the area of more physically intimate or sexual touch, there are numerous activities in addition to genital-to-genital friction. Just a partial list of physically intimate activities: hand holding, clothed massage, naked oil massage, vaginal intercourse, oral sex, anal sex, cuddling, gazing into each other's eyes, bathing or showering together, closed mouth kissing, open mouth kissing, bodily kissing and nibbling, licking, role playing, spanking, eating sensual foods off each other's bodies, gentle or rough scratching, tickling, pulling or playing with each other's hair, g-spot and clitoral massage, prostate massage, playing with toys, mutual masturbation, and watching or reading erotica. That's a lot of possibilities. A given person, whether sexual or asexual, may be comfortable with—and even excited about—some of these activities but not others.

As the sexual partner, your sex drive and preferences likely differ from that of other sexual partners in asexual-sexual relationships. Maybe you like sex at least four times a week, and enjoy a range of positions and toys. Your relationship dynamics will differ from those of a couple where the sexual partner is content with having intercourse twice a month, always in the same position, with no toys.

You deserve happiness & the world needs it

You deserve to live a happy and fulfilling a life. While that may sound trite and clichéd at first, it's important to remember that the pursuit of happiness isn't entirely selfish. When your own cup is overflowing, you can bring more positive energy into the lives of those around you.

If you and your partner are unable to find a way to accept and live with your differences—either by making significant shifts in your relationship or by transitioning out of it—it will adversely impact the way you show up in the rest of your life.

For example, if you go into work every day with a sense that you are unattractive, unloved, and desperate for affection, you'll probably be less productive. You might work longer hours in an attempt to distract yourself from your home life, and in an attempt to make up for your lower productivity. But does that help you or anyone in your family?

Or you may have a harder time relaxing with your friends because you are tired of hearing about the ways in which their relationships seem better than yours. If you are not often fully present or are frequently feeling blue, it will eventually impact your connection with them.

As mentioned earlier, if you have kids, and they are having a stressful day that requires your grounded presence, you may have a harder time showing up for them if you feel stressed and unloved by your partner. If sex is an important part of your overall well-being, then you are likely doing everyone around you a disservice by trying to suppress it.

You may feel like you're not living up to the value you place on loyalty by giving up on the relationship. However, the value of loyalty decreases if you're not able to exercise it without resentment. If you feel that you are staying with your partner out of obligation, and not by conscious loving choice, nobody wins.

Just doing it may not be enough

Several sex experts recommend that the lower sex drive partner needs to "just do it" and occasionally initiate, even if they don't feel the urge. One argument for this is that it will make their partner (you) feel loved and content, thereby enhancing your interactions outside of the bedroom as well. Another argument is that at least some of the time, they will end up finding the interaction pleasurable, and will be glad that they initiated.

Several spouses on one relationship forum—mostly women— described agreements to have sex more often with their partners, even when they didn't initially feel like it. It became more enjoyable for them and they started to crave it. This may work for many couples, assuming that the potentially asexual partner still feels some desire for sex.

But such results could be less likely with an asexual-sexual couple. If one person never experiences sexual attraction or desire, things may be a bit trickier. They may still experience some pleasant sensations including orgasm, but no matter how good you are at tuning into their needs and stimulating them, they might never find it any more exciting than self-stimulation. Some asexuals still desire sex. For others, the presence of another person is not needed, and perhaps not preferred.

As mentioned earlier, an asexual partner may be willing to have sex because they love you in other ways and want to maintain the relationship. I was fortunate on this front. Until our last few years together, Katie was generally willing to have sex when I requested it at reasonable times. As I read over some of the sexual spouses' stories on AVEN, I saw that many individuals are not so fortunate. However, while I had long known that Katie wasn't as enthusiastic as I was, I didn't initially realize that she had rarely desired sex. Once she made this clear, I wondered whether my desire had been a large burden on her.

Alongside love, you partner's willingness could also be driven by complex feelings of obligation, guilt, fear of upsetting you, or fear of ending up alone. That's obviously not as fun as doing something because it feels good. You may have a strong need for a partner who mutually wants you at least some of the time. In addition to receiving, you may also want to know that you are giving something to your partner. We'll talk about this more in the next section. Only you and your partner can determine what is true for you, through open and direct communication.

A few related dynamics may further complicate the "just do it" approach for asexual-sexual couples. Some asexual partners become anxious in anticipation of sex partially because they know that their partner wants them to want it, too. They recognize that their sexual partner has a desire to feel needed sexually, and they experience shame and regret that they cannot provide this. So in addition to having little interest in sex in the first place, they also fear that they won't perform up to their partner's expectations, and that their sexual partner will be dissatisfied anyway. Not much to be excited about!

When your partner just isn't into sex, it can create an additional frustrating dynamic when you attempt sex, regardless of how much they are willing or able to pretend. (And you might question the sustainability and efficacy of asking someone to "pretend" all the time anyway.) If your goals include orgasm, it may take longer because you're not perceiving much energy from your partner, or because you feel pressure to "hurry up and get it over with." You might also experience resentment that you are unable to give back to your partner on an equal level, or guilt that you're taking more than giving. Taking longer to have sex, of course, only further frustrates a partner who isn't that interested in sex. I sometimes experienced this myself, and I have seen similar dynamics discussed on a few marriage and relationship message boards.

These dynamics are not impossible to deal with, but doing so can require significant compromise and a willingness to alter your expectations. One sexual member of AVEN discussed such a compromise that they developed with their partner. Essentially, they came to accept that their partner was never going to initiate sex. They also accepted that their partner might never experience a physical or emotional reward from sex that came anywhere close to their own. However, their asexual partner would respect that they still needed this—even if not as often as would be ideal—and both would still seek to maintain intimacy in their relationship in other ways.

Wanting to be wanted: A complex thing

Over time, I've come to appreciate how many different types of satisfying sex there can be, and how the elements that seem most important to us can shift over time.

When I was with Katie, for some years it didn't matter to me that she wasn't incredibly enthusiastic about sex. Because I felt safe, loved, and securely attached, her mere presence and moderate enthusiasm was enough. Over time, though, I began to crave more of a spark. But because Katie was already compromising a lot just by making herself available for sex, such a spark probably would have been too much to ask.

In the CBS sitcom *Two and a Half Men*, Walden struggles with the fact that his new girlfriend doesn't seem to enjoy having sex—or even using sexually explicit words—as much as he does. It's not enough for him that she's simply willing to do these things. In "The Duchess of Dull-in-Sack," we later learn that Zoey is simply a bit uptight with men until they have earned her trust. However, their conversation likely echoes an ongoing struggle for asexual-sexual couples.[60]

Zoey: Is something wrong?
Walden: No, why?
Zoey: Usually at this point in the evening, you start getting frisky.
Walden (in a mocking tone): Frisky?
Zoey: Randy.
Walden (again, in a mocking tone): Randy?
Zoey: All right—horny!
Walden (laughing): Made you say it. Was that an invitation to get frisky?
Zoey (after a short pause): If you want.
Walden: If YOU want.
Zoey: Well, I want if you want.
Walden (frustrated): I want you to want because YOU want, not because I want.
Zoey: Okay, I've lost the thread now. Are we gonna do this or not?
Walden: Only if YOU want.
Zoey: Walden, why are you making this so difficult?
Walden: Because it's not fun for me unless *you're* having fun.

Katie and I both chuckled and nodded knowingly as we watched this because it struck a chord of reality. The AVEN discussion boards echo related struggles from both asexual and sexual partners.

But isn't it enough just to have a partner who loves you enough to be willing to have sex? Is it necessary for them to want it, too? If they have been willing to have sex with you despite their lack of attraction, could that be viewed as a particularly generous sign of love and commitment? In other words, while you are partially driven and rewarded by hormones, your partner consciously chooses to be with you even without such biological support. I remain grateful to Katie for that.

Sometimes we gain perspective only through contrast. When I first met Sophia, having someone who was enthusiastic about sex felt wonderful and exciting. I felt loved and nurtured in a different way. It seemed impossible to have anything other than excellent sex. But over time, as more of our differences surfaced, I realized that even when I physically crave sex, it sometimes doesn't feel that good if I don't feel safe and loved. If I still feel distant because we haven't worked through something, it's difficult to open up fully. The first few times that happened, I missed the longer-term familiarity I had experienced with Katie. I realized that it would simply take time to rebuild this with another person.

As a few sexuality experts have noted, a connection that blends both sexual intimacy and deep emotional intimacy depends on a range of factors that sometimes seem at odds with one another. These include safety, familiarity, and predictability on one hand, and mystery and novelty on the other hand.

Intimacy is a dance of connection and autonomy, so that neither person is overly enmeshed in the relationship, and neither person is overly independent and detached. Both people are *interdependent* while also being sufficiently differentiated or able to hold onto their own identity.[61]

When your partner doesn't seem to want you in return, it can feel like a threat to both your connection and your independence. This is because one-sided attraction can impact the give-and-take balance in a relationship. In most relationships, your partner has qualities and ways of giving that you highly value, and you have qualities and ways of giving that your partner highly values. These characteristics or activities may be quite different for both of you, yet complementary.

For example, perhaps you enjoy giving to your partner by cooking special dinners and by keeping her favorite area in the backyard nicely landscaped. She highly appreciates that you usually do these things, especially because she doesn't like doing them herself. She enjoys giving to you by planning many of your long weekends away together and by keeping track of the finances—two things you appreciate because you're not as good at them. In other words, in different areas of life, one of you may usually be the "giver" while the other one is usually the "receiver." As long as the two of you perceive the overall workload as being relatively equally balanced, all is well.

However, in the realm of sex and physical intimacy, you might not want to feel like you are always the one wanting and receiving. Sex is an area where many sexual people want to receive *and* give pleasure to feel connected. They want to know that their partner is also enjoying the experience to a reasonable extent. It may not be as fulfilling to have sex with someone you believe is doing it mainly because they appreciated that you mowed the yard.

Granted, even in relationships between two sexual people, there will often be times when one partner is willing to have sex mainly because their partner wants it, and not because they desire it themselves. Sometimes I'm not in the mood for sex when Sophia is. However, such disconnects can become an issue if they happen consistently.

I found the following analogy useful in explaining my asexual-sexual relationship conundrum to close family and friends. The last paragraph refers to our experiment with an open relationship:

> Suppose that you have a very good friend, Pat, who would do almost anything for you. Because you love going to the movies, they willingly accompany you to see a movie every weekend. In fact, they've been doing this for the last 10 years. One day, you learn that Pat really doesn't even enjoy movies, and never has. They've been going mainly because they know that seeing a movie together is a very intimate thing for you, and they appreciate the intimate connection that you seem to share.
>
> Pat sometimes falls asleep during the movies and doesn't seem too enthusiastic while talking about them afterward. This bothers you a lot. In an attempt to make things more fun for Pat, you try various genres of movies. You try sitting in different spots in the theater, going at different times of the day, watching movies both with and without snacks, and attending different theaters. You want Pat to have fun because it otherwise feels like they're just doing you a favor. You need to know that the person

next to you is also enjoying the movie. But nothing you've tried seems to help.

After a while, you suggest that perhaps other friends can go with you to the movie, and Pat needs to come along only some of the time. However, Pat doesn't like this idea out of fear that you'll lose your intimate connection. Also, they have concerns that they'd be failing you as a friend if they were unwilling to go along. Additionally, other friends might judge the two of you and begin to question your relationship as well.

Pause for a few moments to consider the above analogy, where going to the movies symbolizes having sex. How would you continue, alter, or end your movie watching relationship with Pat?

As the sexual partner, I eventually began to resent that I was unable to give to Katie because she was unable to receive as much pleasure. I began to worry that she was usually doing me a favor, rather than it being a mutually pleasurable experience with equal give and take. I not only felt like I had lost an important way of connecting with her, but I began to worry that I had to continuously "earn" my sexual connection in other ways. I sometimes also felt lonely, even when we were sharing life in other ways, and even when I knew she was probably doing her best to be available.

A source of loneliness: Not being understood

"Wanting to be wanted," sexually or otherwise, may be driven by a slightly deeper need: the desire to be understood, so that we don't feel lonely.

As Carl Jung puts it:

> "Loneliness does not come from having no people about one, but from being unable to communicate the things that seem important to oneself, or from holding certain views which others find inadmissible."

We are never truly alone—for most of us, the vast majority of the time, another person isn't very far away. Even in the middle of the forest, we are surrounded by various forms of life. If you believe in some type of higher power or life on other planets, the concept of being alone seems absurd. However, you can still feel lonely, whether you are standing in the middle of the forest, or while you are lying naked in bed right next to another person.

Even two highly sexual people are going to be somewhat different in how they experience sex, both emotionally and physically. It may vary by encounter. One day, two individuals could have sex that seems to have a lot of meaning for both of them; and the next day, it could simply feel good or seem rawer and more animalistic. As one therapist at a sexuality training said to our breakout group, "Sometimes a fuck is just a fuck."

Despite this, two sexual people usually know that they share at least some level of firsthand understanding. They both know what it is like to have that primal attraction. Each knows that their partner has at least a reasonable degree of empathy for what they are feeling.

An asexual-sexual couple, on the other hand, may not be confident that they share at least this basic understanding. One source of loneliness in my relationship with Katie was that we had such different experiences of what many couples share as one of the most profound ways of connecting.

Intimacy expert David Schnarch explains the concept of mind mapping, the ability to form a mental map of another person's mind. This includes knowing a person well enough—their preferences, values, and reactions in past situations—to predict how they are probably going to respond to your behaviors. [62] You can derive a sense of joy and connection from this, as can your partner, especially when you use the knowledge to bring each other pleasure. It can enhance the sense of knowing and of being known. If you and your partner frequently struggle with this ability to understand and predict each other, perhaps because you are *too* different in certain ways, it may create distance.

Add to this the lack of understanding that society has about asexuality, and social pressure to avoid talking about one's sex life with other friends and family, and it can feel even lonelier yet. At one of the times when you are already feeling the most misunderstood and disconnected, you may feel pressure to keep your struggles largely to yourself.

Neither partner may be to blame

If your partner wasn't open with you about their sexual differences from the beginning, you may be wondering, "How could they not have realized this sooner?" or "Why couldn't they tell me this before?" You may feel deeply betrayed and angry. When Katie came out to me, I experienced these emotions pretty intensely.

On one hand, it is possible that your partner knew from the beginning that they rarely or never desire sex, and they weren't totally honest with you about this. Even some individuals who are clear about their asexuality wrestle with how soon they should "come out" to a sexual partner on a date.[63] But even if your partner did deceive you, try to picture yourself in their shoes for a moment. I know firsthand that this is difficult to do, especially at a time when you may still be feeling angry, hurt, and confused.[64]

For just a moment, though, imagine the fear of identifying as *asexual* in a world where the vast majority of people base their most intimate partnerships largely upon sexual attraction. Imagine wanting many of the same things that most people want from intimate relationships, except sex. Imagine fearing that you might be "out of the running" with a potential partner if you come out to them. Imagine fearing never being able to find a partner who is compatible, because you have no idea how many others similar to you even exist. Imagine fearing the judgment of everyone around you, worrying that they will think you are broken in some way.[65]

Perhaps your partner assumed that they would become more attracted to you as time went on. They, like you, heard society's constant messages about how sex is one of the most amazing bonding —and even spiritual—experiences. They longed to experience that, too. They also came to love many other things about you. For these reasons, they were willing to take the risk of committing to someone to whom they didn't feel physically attracted.

On the other hand, perhaps your partner knew something was different about them, but had never heard of asexuality or didn't think it was a real thing. Our culture is still not supportive of open and in-depth discussion about sexuality in general, especially among youth. So we end up having to figure out a lot of things on our own, and it may take us until later in life to do so. We are all victims of this silence. Sex is discussed on the surface, and its imagery surrounds us every day, but more in-depth discussion is still limited.

Even prior to getting married, there are no standard requirements for engaged couples to discuss their sexual preferences and expectations in detail. Many churches recommend premarital counseling to ensure that couples have discussed some of the most important topics. But the requirements can vary greatly, and many people don't even get married through a religious institution.

Long-term romantic relationships, particularly marriages, create confusion about sex because people often view them as predefined boxes where the most important parts of the agreement are already in place. They enter into an arrangement with someone they love, feeling secure that it will automatically ensure they get most of their needs met. The problem is, without conscious dialogue, they likely have little more than a basic framework, highly open to personal interpretation.[66]

Two people can have very different expectations about what their sexual rights and responsibilities are once they enter a long-term committed relationship. While most people anticipate sexual intimacy with *some* degree of regularity, *how often* is open to debate. One person may hold the unspoken expectation that they will enjoy sexual intimacy with their partner at least once or twice a week. The other may look forward to settling into a once-a-month or less pattern of lovemaking. These expectations stem not only from each person's sex drive, but from messages they've picked up from their parents and family, friends, and media.

It is probably safe to say that most decisions to enter intimate relationships are driven by some combination of love and fear, alongside imperfect understandings of oneself and one's partner. Often, this prevents people from consciously clarifying some of their most important desires and expectations early on. Asexual-sexual relationships are not immune from this dynamic.

The only way to know your partner's truth is to ask for it, from a place of non-blaming curiosity. However, you may still be too tender and hurting inside to hear it. And your partner may or may not have the courage to share it. They may fear losing you altogether, which is a possibility. Even though you have a right to experience your own anger, sadness, and frustration, they may fear that you will express this energy in a way that could hurt them. Only when you create a safe environment for honest dialogue is it possible to open up.

The next piece is even more difficult than putting yourself in your partner's shoes, but it is very important. Consider that it takes two to tango. Not only did your partner choose you, but you chose them. You both played an active role in creating the relationship. Without being fully conscious of it, you might have *chosen* someone for their asexual characteristics.

"What?" you exclaim, "Why on earth would anyone do such a thing?"

Shame or fear about sexual desires, driven by dynamics like the Madonna-whore complex, can be very powerful. An asexual person might feel safer and more wholesome to you, and they might make you feel safer and more wholesome. Alongside this, you might be intimidated by things you strongly desire, taking a safer route to avoid potential loss of control. I believe that both of these dynamics help to explain how I ended up with an asexual partner, despite my having a relatively high libido.

I met Katie through a chance encounter with Kelly, a woman to whom I was even more strongly sexually attracted. Kelly and I crossed paths in the middle of the woods, an hour and a half from where I lived. I was volunteering on a trail restoration project, and she was hiking with her dog. We began talking and discovered that we lived on the same street, just a few blocks from each other. Kelly invited me to a block party where I met Cindy. Cindy invited me to go out with her and her roommate, Katie.

My first experience with Cindy and Katie opened my heart on many levels. Katie worked with individuals with limited physical mobility. Although it wasn't part of her job description, she wanted to spend her Saturday taking a client, Linda, swimming at the beach and dancing at a local club. I had a wonderful afternoon and evening with the three of them, and felt incredibly at ease around Katie. I was impressed with her kindness, patience, nurturing instincts, and generosity. We agreed to get together again soon.

As I got to know Katie, I also saw Kelly several more times. Despite some opportune moments, I refrained from becoming romantically or sexually involved with Kelly. Part of my hesitation was due to my deepening friendship and budding romance with Katie. I loved, admired, and appreciated many things about her from the very beginning. However, there was an additional reason for my hesitation with Kelly that I didn't grasp until years later: Because I felt such a strong sexual attraction to her, I feared loss of control in a relationship.

So I chose someone to whom I still felt attracted on many levels, but less intensely in the physical realm. Katie and I began to create a "safe" relationship based upon strong friendship and mutual commitment. These are, of course, very important things; and as a result, we had an extremely loving relationship that I deeply cherished for many years. I even became more physically attracted to Katie as we grew closer in other ways, and I still miss many aspects of our partnership. However, it was never that physically intense.

Later in our relationship, focusing so much of my energy upon Katie's sexuality sometimes distracted me from personal issues I could have been spending more time on. For a while, it was easier to focus on how she was potentially "broken" rather than upon things I needed to examine and change within myself. As I gained courage to look at myself more deeply, we stopped arguing as much. I began to explore other topics on my own and with a coach and therapists. For example, I realized that I wasn't happy with where my career was, and that I wanted to do some more creative work including writing a few books. I realized that I sometimes leaned on Katie too much for nurturing and emotional support. I had to learn to manage some of my stress on my own more effectively. I needed to explore some of my own attitudes and behaviors around sexuality. These topics weren't comfortable for me to explore at first—it had been easier to focus on the sexual differences and to blame Katie's asexuality for most of my frustration. The reality was that her asexuality was just a piece of it. Some realizations didn't occur until well after we had separated.

Is it possible that, on some level, your sexual differences and sex-related arguments with your partner have provided emotional distractions for you? Are some of your self-growth needs fueling part of your frustration? This may or may not be the case, but it's worth considering.

Stopping the blame game doesn't mean letting go of your anger and sadness overnight. It's important to give those emotions space to be felt, expressed, and heard. At some point down the road, however, it's in your best interest to forgive your partner as much as possible. This is the case whether you remain with your current partner or pursue a new relationship. Putting yourself in your partner's shoes, and exploring and admitting your own role in the situation, may help with this. Also, be compassionate and forgiving toward yourself—even if you chose an asexual partner, and even if you confused other sources of frustration with sexual differences, you probably weren't conscious of these things at the time. You and your partner were probably trying your best. Later we'll talk more about forgiveness, including additional ways to develop it.

Math and logic don't apply to sex

Even if you had sex every other day, for 45 minutes each time, it would add up to 2.25 to 3 hours per 168-hour week or less than 2% of your time. Chances are, you spend close to this amount of time being unhappy and butting heads with your partner due to lack of sex. As noted earlier, sex-related conflict may consume a significant percentage of relationship energy when things are not going well.

Given these considerations, the most time and energy efficient solution for both partners may seem obvious: Just have sex, even if both people aren't really into it. After all, you will probably spend much less time *doing* it than you would otherwise spend thinking and arguing about it. Furthermore, don't relationships always involve tasks and chores that aren't necessarily pleasant for both people? Mowing the lawn, washing baby bottles, and doing laundry are just a few examples. In the bigger scheme of things, a small proportion of your time can go a long way toward creating a happier relationship.

Regular logic doesn't always work with sex, though, because it is such an intimate and powerful act. First, given anticipation and foreplay, its energy spans well beyond the bedroom and the amount of time that sex itself takes. As a sexual being, you are likely doing things to remind your partner that at some point, you will want them to spend some time having sex. This is true even if you have agreed upon specific days and times of the week to help you respect each other's schedules. Second, sex cannot be compared to chore-like activities because neither partner is *expected* to enjoy mowing the lawn or washing the dishes. During sex, on the other hand, most people would like their partners to seem like they are enjoying things. In line with the movie analogy described under "Just doing it may not be enough," this can trigger your partner to feel more pressure.

Your brain may plummet into a negative spiral: "If my partner loves me, why aren't they more excited about this? Is it more difficult or even less enjoyable to have sex with me than it is to mow the lawn or wash dishes?" The truth is that your partner's ability to love and care may have absolutely no correlation with their sex drive or physical attraction to you. As one example, Katie volunteered with an emergency response organization for a few years, often getting out of bed at 2 or 3 a.m. She would often awaken early the next morning, either for work or athletic practice. I was impressed with her ability to function on far less sleep than I usually needed. However, things were different for sex: Tiredness often seemed to be a barrier, under a range of circumstances.

I deeply admire the love, dedication, and selflessness Katie showed in many ways, toward other people as well as me. However, I was confused and even jealous for a long time. How could she show such a tremendous capacity to love, yet struggle to connect with me sexually? Only when I finally understood that Katie simply experienced love in very different ways, and I understood that the normal rules of logic didn't apply, was I able to let go of some of the resentment.

Another point on the topic of math, logic, and sex: Don't get too hung up on statistics regarding the average number of times per week couples have sex. According to one research group, U.S. married or cohabiting adults aged 18 to 60 report having sex one to two times per week on average.[67] They also note declines in the frequency of sex reported over the last 20 years.[68] However, getting people to report accurate data on sensitive topics such as sex can be challenging. This may be one reason they state that some of the findings are difficult to explain. Also, statistics can vary across cultures and countries; and culture, politics, and religion can impact sexual research. Furthermore, averages don't tell you anything about the range of a group. If a group of 3 people has sex 1, 7, and 16 times per month, their average comes out to 8 times per month. The average alone doesn't tell you that one has significantly more sex and one has significantly less.

Because sex drives and relationships vary a great deal, only you know what frequency will make you happy. Each person has their own preferences regarding quantity versus quality.

Also know that increased frequency of sex alone doesn't necessarily make a couple happier. In a Carnegie Mellon University study, researchers randomly assigned married female-male couples to one of two groups. One group was asked to double the frequency with which they had sex, and the other group received no specific sexual instructions. At several points over three months, subjects answered questionnaires about their health and happiness levels.

The results: Those told to have more sex did have more sex, but they reported slightly decreased happiness, lower sexual desire, and less enjoyment of sex. However, the increased frequency of sex itself didn't seem to be what made it less enjoyable and desirable. The shift seemed to be caused by subjects being asked to do it as an assignment or requirement, rather than having the opportunity to initiate it on their own.

Tamar Krishnamurti, one of the study's designers, offers this thought:

> "The desire to have sex decreases much more quickly than the enjoyment of sex once it has been initiated. Instead of focusing on increasing sexual frequency to the levels they experienced at the beginning of a relationship, couples may want to work on creating an environment that sparks their desire and makes the sex that they do have even more fun."[69]

Drawing from the above, it becomes easier to see how your partner's happiness—and indirectly, yours—may suffer if they feel they are having sex only because they *have* to, and rarely because they *want* to. If they are continuing to have that perception, you are going to feel it as well. Simply focusing on the numbers or agreeing to do it more often isn't likely to improve things. Even if you are always the one initiating, can your partner help you brainstorm low-effort ways to create a setting that makes things more fun for them? They may or may not be willing to do this, but you won't know until you ask.

The Devil's Pact usually fails

Sex therapist David Schnarch refers to an agreement that couples often make as the *Devil's Pact*.[70] In the following example, Hiya is the partner with higher sexual interest, and Lowya is the partner with lower sexual interest. It goes something like this:

➤ Hiya complains that Lowya never initiates sex.

➤ Lowya says that they never have the chance to initiate because Hiya always initiates.

➤ They agree that Hiya will stop initiating so that Lowya will have the opportunity to initiate.

➤ Hiya becomes increasingly frustrated over time as Lowya still doesn't initiate.

> Lowya senses Hiya's growing frustration, feels even more pressured by that, and uses this as a justification to avoid initiating.

According to Schnarch, the couple is likely to remain in a state of emotional gridlock until they are both willing to be extremely honest with themselves about who they are, and about what they really want from sex and from the relationship. Whether or not you have already attempted the Devil's Pact with your partner, you may be ready for a higher level of honesty and authenticity.

7. Begin to Accept Past, Present, & Self

• • •

Know the stages of grief

If your partner is truly asexual, it may take a while to accept that they are a different person than you—and possibly they—originally thought. You are essentially grieving a loss. As you continue to heal, it can be helpful to know some of the types of emotions to anticipate. The "Five Stages of Grief" model, created by Elisabeth Kübler-Ross, offers one way to understand the range of emotions that most people cycle back and forth through on their way to acceptance. The emotions don't necessarily occur in neat and separate stages, in the order listed. It is possible to experience two or more of the emotions simultaneously, or to bounce back and forth between several stages for a while, before finally reaching acceptance. The emotions may include the following:[71]

Denial

You may deny that your partner is asexual, or that asexuality even exists, even if they decide that this label seems to describe them. As mentioned earlier, it is important to maintain an open mind and hope for a while, given that there are many causes for lack of interest in sex. But if, over time, there's no sign of change in your relationship, or your partner states that they don't want to change or can't change, then it is important to accept this reality eventually.

Anger

You may feel intense anger, now and as you move forward. If it is there, find people to talk to about it. Uncover what specific feelings and fears are beneath the anger, as bottling up those feelings isn't going to make them go anywhere.

Part of this anger may stem from a feeling of loss—a loss of past possibilities as well as future hopes and dreams. You may consider all the ways in which your life could have been better in the sexual realm, and beyond that as well. If your partner is asexual, you may lament that you made important life decisions, and invested significant personal resources, based on incomplete knowledge about your partner. You may have assumed that you would be growing old together no matter what, and now you may be having doubts. You have been powerless to solve certain relationship issues, as there has been at least one important underlying cause not known to you.[72]

Bargaining

At times, you might wish that your partner were different, or that your past or present life were different. You might attempt to bargain with the universe or your higher power to change things, and you might blame yourself for things not being different. For example, you might wonder, "What if I had been more mature a few years ago? Perhaps I wouldn't have gotten together with my partner." Or, "If only God could make my partner desire me, I'd agree to be the most loving person possible."

While it's natural to wonder about what could have been or should have been, obviously this does not honor reality. Also, blaming yourself can lead to shame and isolation, the exact opposite of what you will ultimately need—stronger connections with other people for emotional support.

Depression

If you are suffering a profound change or loss in a very important relationship, you may feel deep sadness that lasts a while. It may or may not correspond to the definition of clinical depression. If your sadness does last a while and affects your overall functioning, consider seeking professional support. The loss of sex itself might also be a contributor, as sex helps to reduce stress, enhance mood, and improve sleep.[73]

Acceptance

The amount of time taken to gain full acceptance of a profound loss or change varies by individual. It usually increases slowly over time rather than happening all at once, and could take several weeks or months, or a few years. This is the point at which you are no longer caught in a cycle of wishing the past or present were different, and are able to move forward in your relationship. This might be with your current partner, or with a different one.

Gradually move toward forgiveness

Developing forgiveness is often a gradual process. It may take several years, along with conscious effort. It cannot be rushed overnight. Nor should it be, as it's also important to acknowledge any loss, sadness, and anger you are experiencing. At the same time, forgiveness is important for your happiness, and for the health of your relationship, regardless of your current and future situation. It is closely related to acceptance, the fifth stage of the grief process discussed earlier.

It's no accident that major religions and spiritual traditions emphasize forgiveness and acceptance among their key principles. When you have not yet forgiven someone or something, you may continue to put significant time and energy into it, wishing things were different. You may experience resentment. This means less space for positive emotions and experiences, including development of intimacy and connection. When you have not yet forgiven, it can be difficult to fully open your heart to others. This includes establishing trust and emotional connection.

Consider the analogy of a child who has their fist closed around a stale cookie crumb that they refuse to release. Because they are unwilling to open their hand, they miss out when someone offers them a large, fresh cookie. Is your fist closed around past resentment? Do you want to miss out on opportunities to have a better relationship? One of my counseling mentors refers to the dysfunctional practice of "allowing someone to rent space in your head." That is what you are doing when you spend time and energy resenting someone, being angry at them, or wishing they were different. I am not fully immune from this habit. When I do it, I generally feel worse. It usually doesn't help me to accomplish anything. How much of your precious head space do you rent out to unhelpful energy and thoughts?

If you plan to remain in a relationship with your current partner and want to be mutually happy, you will ultimately need to forgive them for any experiences of separation and conflict you have endured. This is true regardless of what they decide about their sexual identity and how they're willing to relate to you. If you are still holding onto resentment about the past, it could affect your ability to be fully present. If you plan to move on and eventually connect with another partner, your lack of forgiveness from your prior relationship will affect your emotional availability in your new relationship.

Studies suggest that forgiveness has a range of psychological, emotional, and physical health benefits: lower blood pressure, reduction in depression and anxiety, fewer physical symptoms and medical complaints, less fatigue, and better sleep, to name a few.[74]

Forgiving someone else can also help you to become more lenient with yourself for similar things. As mentioned earlier, when I began to forgive Katie for taking so long to become clear about her sexuality, I stopped beating myself up so much for my confusion about polyamory when I first met Sophia.

Fortunately, many of the strategies covered elsewhere in this book can also help with developing forgiveness. These include:

➢ talking with others about your situation, either one-on-one or in groups, in person or online

➢ developing closer relationships with others

➢ trying to imagine yourself in your partner's shoes

➤ being honest with yourself about your role in your interactions

➤ reframing your struggles as a learning opportunity, reflecting on what you've learned, how you've grown, and how you are prepared for relating in more rewarding ways

➤ focusing on how you can continue to change and grow, rather than wanting to change your partner

➤ focusing on what you want and how to create that, rather than what you don't want and fretting over that

➤ being more compassionate and forgiving with yourself

➤ maintaining a sense of humor

➤ finding additional options for meeting some of your intimacy needs

Here are a few more tips, not previously mentioned, for fostering forgiveness:[75]

➤ Publicly commit to forgiving your partner, either by telling them directly or by stating your intentions to someone else.

➤ Recall the way it felt for you to be forgiven by someone else you felt you had wronged.

➤ Remind yourself that you have already forgiven your partner when feelings of anger resurface.

Mourn loss of possibilities without idealizing

As noted earlier, you may find yourself mourning the loss of both past possibilities and future hopes and dreams. This is normal. How much more exciting might your sex life have been with someone else up until this point? What might it have been like to have sex with someone who was more enthusiastic about it, and who desired you in return?

If you agreed to be celibate for a while to show your commitment to your partner, this could be a source of resentment. You may feel like you have been subjected to a double standard, as this agreement required self-denial and effort on your end, but no self-denial or effort on their end. It's like making a pact with a friend to support each other in giving up chocolate for Lent when you love chocolate and they don't. You may wonder what possibilities for connecting with others you might have missed during that time. This can make it difficult to forgive your partner, and it can make it difficult to accept the decisions you have made.

As mentioned earlier, I wasn't sexually involved with anyone else while dating Katie long-distance. Although this initially strengthened my confidence in our relationship, after our relationship fell apart, I found myself wondering what I might have missed during those two years. I considered some of the attractive women who had flirted with me, who likely enjoyed sex more than Katie did. I recalled how some of my female friends had complained about their male partners wanting sex less than they did—it seemed bitterly ironic.

As you recount your losses and allow yourself to be angry and mourn them, it is important that you don't idealize the "could have beens." This is particularly easy to do with sex, given all the societal messages we receive on this topic. At times, it may seem like everyone is having passionate sex at least once a day, given the inflated scenes on television and in movies. But that's usually not the case.

I eventually realized that I was probably idealizing somewhat. I had no idea what the sex drives of the women mentioned above were actually like. Perhaps "enough" sex for them would have been a few times a week early on, but only once a week or a few times per month later in the relationship. Additionally, even if some of them had been a closer sexual match for me, we may not have been compatible in other ways. In other words, it's impossible to say what my sex life could have been like. The same probably holds true for you.

Also, watch out for selective perception, which is a natural tendency to notice examples that confirm your existing attitudes. Suppose you already believe that your relationship is dull compared to everyone else's. You will be less likely to notice when Sally and Shirley mention that they have little romantic time together, but you will be more likely to notice when Bob and Nancy imply that they have sex all the time. Chances are, you will later bring up Bob and Nancy—not

Sally and Shirley—as an example when you have a "Why can't our relationship be different?" argument with your partner.

Additionally, you might recognize that some portion of your loss is attributable to your own attitudes or actions. This includes attitudes you learned while growing up, which are important to recognize and take ownership of. Attitudes I learned from my family influenced my choice to be monogamous with Katie while we dated long-distance, even though she and I had known each other for only a few months at that point. I could have asked Katie, "Honey, I love you, but I also don't want either of us to miss out on opportunities to enjoy other connections, given that we can't be together regularly for at least two more years." But I didn't even consider that possibility. Years later, I recalled that my parents had been together ever since they dated in high school. Neither of them had ever talked much about dating, because neither had done much of it. And in the world in which I was raised, once you were sexually involved with somebody, you were monogamous no matter what.

I'm very grateful for most of the things I learned about relationships from my loving family. At the same time, it's now my responsibility to choose which things I do similarly, and which I do differently. I can't blame my family for the attitudes I hold onto, and I can't blame my partner for the choices I make based upon those attitudes. I can no longer blame either of them for taking away my possibilities. This also holds true for you.

Once you have looked at your possible sexual losses in a more balanced way, you might also look at your possible non-sexual losses. If you've been together for a long time, you've probably made many other compromises and sacrifices. For example, I strongly considered a different educational program than one that I attended, but the location would have left Katie with much less to do socially or recreationally. I also wanted to move on a few occasions, but we stayed put largely because of her job. After Katie came out, I felt disappointed that I had made several major decisions based upon incomplete information about my partner.

You may also be disappointed by decisions you have made, which is natural. However, as with the sexual piece, it's important to look at things in a balanced fashion and to avoid idealizing lost opportunities. In my case, Katie also made many sacrifices, and she endured many of my quirks and challenges. For example, when she first wanted a child, I was hesitant, so we delayed parenting for a few years. It can be difficult to quantify the sacrifices each person makes when they believe they will be with their partner "until death do us part."

Keep a healthy sense of humor

As you continue to discover how sexual compatibilities have fueled many other relationship tensions, there may be waves of anger, resentment, and sadness. At the same time, a sense of relief may accompany new insight and understanding. If you can eventually learn to laugh at some of it, it can also help with the acceptance and forgiveness process. I'm talking here about humor that is affirming, mood-lightening, or making light of one's own imperfections—not humor that is insulting, sarcastic, invalidating, or covering up other important emotions.[76] Keeping a healthy sense of humor is not always easy, and it may take time to develop.

For example, Katie and I had a several-year dispute over whether the cat should sleep in the bed with us. Upon realizing that this dispute was probably at least partially due to our sexual differences—I rarely attempted to initiate sex when Fuzzles was in the bed, for fear the movement would inspire him to pounce—I had a new perspective on Katie's motivations. In light of this new information, I was able to laugh about my frustration and start letting go of my resentment.

Additionally, while the exact mechanisms are not yet understood, laughter has been linked to a reduction in stress levels, lower inflammation, and improved blood flow.[77] When used properly, humor can lend greater stability to relationships.[78] Learning to laugh at things (within reason, of course) can also make you more attractive to others: People often cite humor and playfulness as some of the most attractive and important qualities in potential mates.[79]

Rebuild your sexual & overall self-esteem

You may have tried hard to get your partner more interested in sex. You have probably been rejected on many occasions, and your partner may rarely or never have initiated. Even if you've been fortunate enough to have a partner who sometimes still agreed to sex, as I was until the later stages of my relationship with Katie, it may still be obvious that they are simply not that into it.

You've probably often wondered if your partner's lack of attraction has been due to some fault of your own. You may have said to yourself, "Even with all this effort, I'm *still* not desirable to my partner." If you've been in a relationship for years, this pattern has probably replayed hundreds of times. There are likely many things that make you attractive, but you have probably forgotten many of them. Your self-esteem and confidence may need a recharge. Not surprisingly, in online conversations involving asexual-sexual mixed relationships, some people swear they'll never tolerate another relationship that includes a significant libido difference.

Amity Pierce Buxton explains that many heterosexual spouses of closeted gay partners suffer from self-esteem issues. They erroneously believe that a lack of attractiveness or sexual ability is to blame for their partner's lack of interest. As mentioned earlier, they may also over-perform in other areas of the relationship.[80] This may be an attempt to compensate, or to win their uninterested partner's affection. A similar dynamic may impact sexual partners of asexuals.

For example, I often created things to express love for Katie, and she often expressed great appreciation for them. Once while she was out of town for the weekend, I built a small patio in our backyard, working until 11 p.m. with a bright outdoor work light to get it finished in time. The neighbors thought I was a bit crazy, but Katie was excited by it, and that made it even more fun for me. When I built a multi-platform climbing tree for our cat, Katie loved it.

But whenever I tried to incorporate my creativity into enhancing our sexual connection, the same energy wasn't reciprocated. I once spent half a day installing a heavy-duty hanger above our bed for a sex swing, in an attempt to make things more exciting for both of us. I spent a few hours shopping for the perfect vibrator, and I occasionally spent extra time cleaning the house or running errands in hopes that she would be more relaxed for sex. I trained for a marathon, partially as a midlife crisis project, but partially in hopes that if I got into exceptionally good shape, Katie might find my body more attractive.

The results of all this: a few toys that were boxed up after just a few uses, a clean house, and the satisfaction and fitness of having run a marathon. And a large metal hanger above our bed that I told our Realtor was a heavy-duty plant hanger. Even though I knew the truth would have provided an uncommon selling feature for the house. In Katie's defense, the sex swing wasn't all that comfortable to sit in. The fuzzy leopard print material did look sexy, though; and I enjoyed bouncing and swinging around in it.

Katie often expressed appreciation and loving support for my efforts, but it was never attached to sexual energy. I developed a growing frustration that I just wasn't attractive enough.

How can one person's lack of attraction impact our self-esteem so significantly? David Schnarch talks about the tendency of couples to become overly reliant on a "reflected sense of self." This means that you depend on feedback from your partner—the person you are likely with most frequently—to shape your opinion of yourself.[81] With most couples, the feedback starts out mostly positive, as each person strives to make the other feel wonderful. But over time, as the honeymoon phase passes, each person starts becoming more honest with the other about annoyances, faults, and incompatibilities. If you have major incompatibilities, you may remind each other about them frequently, and you may reflect them back to each other in a way that makes them all feel like faults rather than incompatibilities.

Obviously, it's difficult to free yourself entirely from the reflected sense of self, because people are social creatures. I cannot imagine ever being entirely immune from the impacts of my partner's opinions. Most of us learn to depend on others' feedback starting at a very early age, as we look to our parents and other adults for reactions to our facial expressions, sounds, and actions.[82]

Given all of the above, how can you begin to rebuild your self-esteem, sexually and otherwise, if needed? Following are some ideas.

Broaden your sources of feedback

When a person is very close to you, it can be especially difficult to remember that one person's opinion is just that—one person's opinion. But having feedback from more people can help a little bit. Regardless of whether you remain with your current partner, consider how you can bring additional people into your life through socializing and other activities, to broaden your perspective. As I transitioned out of my long-term relationship, I sometimes attended dances and other social events. There, I occasionally allowed myself to flirt lightheartedly and playfully with other women, which is something I hadn't done in years. I found it affirming and energizing when they appeared to flirt back.

This works not only with physical desirability but also with other aspects of yourself that your partner might not appreciate. No partner is ever going to find all aspects of you beautiful or perfectly compatible. However, others may appreciate some of those aspects and may have different opinions. For example, your partner may frequently complain about the way you drive, but you could say to yourself, "The co-workers I carpool with have actually complimented me on my driving, and other members of my family never seem to complain. So I know I'm a reasonably good driver, regardless of my partner's personal opinion." As another example, you may recall how two of your friends enjoy sharing aesthetic and creative intimacy with you, even though you don't click with your partner in these areas. (See the chapter "Enhance Connection Beyond Physical Intimacy" for the 12 types of intimacy.)

Remind yourself of your strengths

Grab a notebook or open up a blank word processing document. Spend just five minutes jotting down things that you believe make you attractive. If you feel ambitious, ask two or three friends to share their opinions. If the word *attractive* sounds intimidating, begin with *interesting.* What are 10 to 20 things that make you interesting, and what do your friends find most interesting about you?

You can even use index cards, writing one thing that makes you attractive on each card. Consider posting them in a place where you will see them regularly, or take the time to review them alongside an already established daily routine, such as eating lunch or brushing your teeth.

You are not alone if you initially feel shy about paying yourself a few compliments. In sessions with my life coaching clients, we often spend time reviewing strengths and successes, because many people have a natural tendency to self-criticize and to focus solely on what needs to be improved. I'm often in that boat myself.

You might be thinking that simply having sex with someone else will help you to get your confidence back. That is possible. However, keep in mind that having sex is just one piece of the puzzle, and it may present other dynamics and challenges. You may still need to cope with rejection eventually, and jumping too quickly and deeply into a new relationship could distract you from healing that you still need to do. I experienced some of this.

Whatever the case, try to act in a way that doesn't compromise your values out of desperation or take advantage of others. If you are looking entirely outside of yourself for affirmation of attractiveness, it may not matter how many other people you sleep with. It will take a bit of time to heal and rebuild yourself regardless.

Reflect on your growth

Consider how you have already become a better, more attractive partner and lover through your struggles. Without sex as a bonding mechanism to rely upon regularly, perhaps you've already gained an above-average amount of practice using other tools to maintain intimacy in your relationship. In an attempt to get your partner more interested in sex, perhaps you've learned about various sexuality and relationship techniques, sex products, and so on. Maybe you've already developed a repertoire of sensuality and romance skills that extend well beyond sex. Such learning experiences and qualities make you more attractive than the average lover. Make a list of them, and revisit it whenever you doubt yourself.

I didn't fully appreciate all the ways I had learned and grown until I had been with Sophia for a few years, as she had also devoted significant energy to studying sensuality and sexuality. While many factors fueled the quality of our intimate experiences, I attributed some of it to the self-growth activities I had proactively engaged in during my asexual-sexual relationship. In the desperation of trying to sort out my relationship with Katie, I read a range of relationship books, tried new activities such as ecstatic dance, joined support and discussion groups, and attended a number of touch-positive events. These helped me to grow in new and often unexpected ways.

How might you continue to evolve, regardless of what the future holds for your current relationship?

Rediscover what turns you on

Another way to rebuild self-esteem is to bring back activities that are important to you. For many people, sexuality is intertwined with playfulness, creativity, spirituality, and other important components of being. However, if you have developed a habit of repressing much of your sexuality, you may also have developed a habit of repressing other vital parts of yourself. You may also have abandoned some important activities and dreams simply due to lack of time, as you invested more time and energy into your relationship.

Earlier I shared how I would often flirt with Katie with attempted humor and playfulness, but then "shut myself off" when she felt I was becoming too sexy. This pattern also occurred with sexy dancing. As a result, I suppressed my sense of humor and danced more conservatively. In fact, I largely gave up dancing for a while. Later, as I began to reclaim my sexuality, I also began to express these other parts of myself again.

If you have pushed aside important activities, rekindling some of them may boost your rebuilding process. It can serve as a reminder of potentially forgotten attractive and talented parts of yourself, and give you a renewed sense of purpose.[83] This might include activities that directly involve sexiness, like dressing sexy more often or dancing in a sexy way. It might include activities that rejuvenate your sexual and creative energy more broadly—for example, perhaps going on bicycle rides in nature gives you a recharge, also boosting your sexual energy. The support of your partner will be helpful, as you may need to decrease family obligations to carve out time for self-exploration work.[84]

One approach to rediscovering yourself involves reviewing your past, going all the way back to childhood to look for long forgotten but favorite activities, friends, games, books, and hobbies. Below are a few related exercises, from the self-help guide *Naked Idealism*.[85]

Exercises for rediscovering what turns you on

Option 1: Create your "peak experiences" timeline

On a large, blank sheet of paper, draw a timeline of your entire life including the youngest age you can remember, your present age, and your death. In between these points, list 5 to 10 major "peak experiences" in your life so far and 5 to 10 more you would like to see going forward. Each experience should have at least one of the following characteristics:

➤ You consider it a major accomplishment.

➤ You have created something very important to you.

➤ You were having a great deal of fun.

➤ You were in a state of "flow." In other words, you were deeply engrossed in what you were doing, time seemed to pass rapidly, and the activity seemed almost effortless.

If you have difficulty recalling those times in your life that were the most fun or the most rewarding, try some of the following:

➤ Dig out any old pictures of yourself and ask family members if they have any albums with pictures of you. Notice what types of activities and play you're engaged in and which pictures bring back the fondest memories.

> If your family saved any report cards or teacher's reports, look at them. For example, I found a few high school reports where teachers commented on how much I loved to talk about psychology.

> Ask your family and old friends what types of toys you played with, and when you seemed to have the most fun. Were there any places you were always begging to go? What types of events seemed to excite you the most?

Option 2: Write your own eulogy

Ask yourself this difficult but thought-provoking question: If you could write your own eulogy, and it could include only three of your activities or accomplishments, what would they be? Why are these things important to you?

Option 3: Consider your favorite topics

Think about topics you just can't stop talking about at social gatherings—topics that may even keep you at events much longer than you had intended. Is there a pattern or commonality that they share?[86]

Option 4: Ask your friends

Ask a few of your closest friends for their opinions regarding your favorite activities—others often see things you may not see in yourself.

Option 5: Ask yourself the billion dollar question

Imagine you awaken tomorrow and discover that you have just inherited one billion dollars—no strings attached. Or two billion, if that's not enough! Earning a living is no longer a concern; all your financial needs are met. Name up to four or five activities you would choose to engage in. Why would you choose these activities?

Once you have rediscovered some your favorite activities, a next step is to bring some of them back into your life, perhaps with the support of existing friends or new friends with similar interests. Enlisting a professional counselor or life coach may also be helpful at this stage.

Rebuild trust in self & others

If you initially thought your partner was much more sexual than they turned out to be, you're probably disappointed that you didn't have more awareness about their sexuality earlier. Perhaps they didn't have clarity about their sexuality when you met, or perhaps they weren't up front with you about any uncertainty they already had. Alongside this, you may be asking yourself two questions: If I was initially so clueless about such a big thing with my partner, how can I trust anyone else to give me accurate information about their sexuality in the future? How can I trust my instincts to select a partner who is a better match?

After discovering that Katie was probably asexual, I began to question the wisdom of my past perceptions and decisions. I recalled that shortly after I met Katie, she very calmly paused me the first time I attempted to kiss her, so that we could talk. She said it was because she was still in the process of transitioning out of another relationship. I had appreciated her honesty and thoughtfulness, but in retrospect, I wondered: Was that the only reason she hesitated? How was she able to remain in such emotional control? Had I failed to see that she wasn't physically attracted to me?

When such thoughts begin to enter my head, I do my best to return to "It probably wasn't anyone's fault." That includes me. I remind myself that I simply need to accept the past and assume that it has prepared me for the future. I ask myself what I have learned, and what actions I can take to correct things in the present and future. For me, this has included talking much sooner and much more openly about sexual preferences with Sophia. That strategy has enabled me to trust both of us more.

If you have repeatedly been in situations where your and your partner's actions seem to be leading toward sex, only to learn that the arousal you feel is not suitable or acceptable, you may have lost trust in your arousal instincts as well. For you, certain activities with your partner, such as giving each other naked massages or spooning each other with few or no clothes, may feel like a precursor to sexual activity. For your partner, such activities may not feel connected to sex at all.

I have seen several online discussions about individuals in asexual-sexual relationships struggling with boundaries. How close can the physical intimacy be without leading to arousal or sex? One conversation revolved around a suggestion of a Valentine's Day bubble bath. It sounded relaxing and connective to the asexual partner, but would it overexcite the sexual partner and set them up for disappointment?

One asexual person expressed fear of being naked around his sexual partner under any circumstances because it often turns her on. A few others shared their desire for hugging and cuddling, and even "sensual groping and stroking," but only if no sex or intentions of sex are involved. Katie and I struggled with boundaries around cuddling while sleeping, because we both enjoyed sleeping naked together. It would sometimes make me want sex, while she preferred to stop at the naked cuddling. Temporary solutions like wearing pajamas didn't address the underlying differences in our needs.

If and when you find yourself with a partner whose needs are more aligned with yours, you may have to remind yourself that you don't need to hit your internal "off" switch every time. You will need to be open to new possibilities with your next partner, without overreacting or jumping to any conclusions—regardless of their level of interest in sex. For example, if a potential lover invites you to sleep over without having sex on the second date, you may be tempted to think, "Oh, no! They're asexual, too!" The truth is that you may not know much about their sexual preferences until you talk openly about it, which may be just before or shortly after becoming sexually involved with them. Unless, of course, they were very open about their preferences in their online dating profile.

It's even possible that your new partner has a higher libido than you do, or may sometimes want sex when you are not in the mood. This role shift may require some learning and readjustment on your part. Because I have experienced this, I provide a few tips on this elsewhere.

Rebuilding trust in yourself and others can extend well beyond sexual partners, and beyond sex. Strengthening relationships and positive interactions with other individuals, like friends and family, can be beneficial following a partner's coming out. Recalling the aspects of your relationship that have been based on truth and honesty can also help.[87] Again, while sex is very important for most of us, it is still just one piece of the puzzle.

Convert envy to action & gratitude

While envy can hold you back, it can also be a useful tool. It may serve as a call to action, an indicator that you need to shift something in your life. As I started to sense that something wasn't quite right with my relationship, I began to resent hanging out with other couples who seemed more romantically engaged than we were. When I saw couples romantically gazing into each other's eyes, kissing, or even holding hands and hugging, I felt envious and sorry for myself.

I eventually started to see my envy as an indicator that I needed to take action. I accepted that something had to change in a major way. After I acted upon my desire and met someone with whom I experienced mutual physical attraction, I was again able to look at other passionate couples with more joy than envy. However, this was not an overnight process. I had developed the habit of feeling sorry for myself over many years. Often when I had started to feel aroused around Katie, I had chosen to shut that arousal off, going into self-pity mode. As I was first getting to know Sophia, this habit created an obstacle to appreciating the changes I was already experiencing.

Determining whether your partner is asexual, and what actions to take if that is the case, may seem like the highest priority. However, your situation may also provide an opportunity to explore and get to know yourself better. Discomfort can provide a reason to venture outside the box of familiarity.

PART THREE:
Broaden Your Possibilities

Part Three Overview

• • •

WE LIVE IN A TIME of unprecedented exploration and change. Technology, knowledge, and our human-created surroundings have shifted at profound rates in recent decades. Amidst this transformation, which can be both exciting and disruptive, we often find solace in our established social institutions and ways of connecting. We usually don't question the ways in which we traditionally define, share, and obtain physical intimacy—such as marriage or the nuclear family structure—until we are deeply embedded in an arrangement that isn't working, or we are otherwise feeling desperate.

This is partly because we don't often engage in explicit conversations about sexuality and relationships. In school, we learn about math, computer technology, and scientific discoveries, opening them up to debate and questioning.[88] However, we have relatively few conversations about how to choose romantic and sexual partners, what specific expectations we have for others and ourselves in long-term relationships, or what our options are when relationships don't work as planned. Instead, we rely on unspoken expectations gleaned from observations of parents and other adults, TV and film plots, music lyrics and videos, books, religious teachings, experiences shared by peers, and media coverage. We often enter relationships largely on autopilot. When life throws obstacles into our route, and we need to take the wheel, we may panic. Situations like having a potentially asexual partner don't fit within the existing boxes.

Part Three provides ideas for navigating your existing route in new ways, as well as additional routes for you to consider. Included are considerations specific to couples with an asexual or low-interest partner. As with the rest of this book, you are not required to try or even strongly consider any of the ideas—I'm not claiming that I would try all of them myself. Simply know that additional options exist. You and your partner have significant power to define your own relationship, if you choose.

8. Expand Your World of Physical Intimacy

• • •

Benefits of branching out

There are many benefits of expanding both your definition and your sources of physical intimacy, whether you have an asexual or sexual partner or are single. Beyond sex, there are many ways for relationships to be more "open." While the term *open relationship* is often associated primarily with sex, only a small portion of *Open Marriage*, one of the earliest books on the topic when published in 1972, was devoted to sex. Much of the book focused on topics such as partners allowing each other to see a movie or to go dancing with another person, rather than feeling that they have to do everything together.[89] While times have changed a bit since then, they haven't changed that much. Many of us would still struggle with allowing our partner just to see a movie or go dancing with someone else, let alone snuggle or exchange massage with them.

Nonetheless, if you are in a relationship with an asexual person, expanding your definition and sources of physical affection can lessen pressure on both of you. First, it may help you to tease different types of touch needs apart from sex. You may learn that some of the touch that you crave doesn't always need to lead to sex. If you can sometimes experience and enjoy connective touch without this expectation, and without feeling disappointment when it doesn't lead to sex, it can open up more possibilities for you and your partner.

Is it just sex that you are lacking, or is it sensual touch in general? If the two have always been closely connected for you, you may lack both. Perhaps your partner is still willing to cuddle and exchange massage, but just isn't into certain types of sex that are important to you. Or, perhaps they lack interest in most of these activities or fear that engaging in any of them may lead you to desire sex.

Even if you are with a sexual partner, there is a good chance that some types of touch you enjoy sharing are not your partner's favorites to share. For example, maybe you love trading foot massages but your partner can't stand trading foot massages. If you have other people to do this with, you will both feel better. You will also be adding connection and joy to other people's lives.

With either an asexual or a sexual partner, practicing a range of ways of giving and receiving touch can also enhance your sex life. While genital stimulation feels wonderful for most of us, adding other types of interaction into the mix can create additional ways of sharing physical intimacy. It can spice up foreplay, sex itself, or physically intimate time without sex.

If you are single and between relationships, or if you are planning to transition out of your current relationship, diversifying your definition and sources of touch can boost your confidence. It can make you feel less "touch needy." Physical touch needs often increase after leaving an intimate relationship.[90] When you know that you can get many of your touch needs met even without a sexual relationship, you will have one less fear-based barrier to leaving your current relationship, if you determine that is what's best.

Additionally, when you are getting some of your touch needs met, you will be less likely to put out a vibe of desperation when you are on dates. Paradoxically, your lower level of neediness will make you more attractive to emotionally healthy potential partners. (Neediness may make you more attractive to certain types of potential partners, but I assume you are not seeking a codependent relationship.) You'll also be more likely to exercise reasonable discernment when choosing your next sexual partner, rather than jumping in just so you can get your physical touch needs met.

Beyond an all-or-nothing approach to touch

Many people take an "all-or-nothing" approach to physical touch that has any degree of intimacy. Either you are in a sexual relationship where you get virtually all of your physical intimacy needs met, or you are in a platonic relationship where you share very little touch with another person, except for the occasional handshake or hug. Activities like snuggling, and often even massage, are reserved for those with whom you are sexually involved—or are pursuing as a sexual partner.

While sex is a wonderful and amazing experience for most people, and there is no direct substitute for it, there is also a broad range of intimate touch you can enjoy with others. To paraphrase snuggle expert, Jas Davis, "There's a lot of ground between a handshake and sex."[91] Sensual touch doesn't have to be sexual: It also includes snuggling, backrubs, foot massages, and playing gently with someone's hair.

Although the extent of this all-or-nothing approach varies by culture, it is very pronounced among American males in particular. This is partially because we tend to oversexualize all types of touch. We are taught that all the other types of touch must lead to sex, or at the very least mean that we're interested in pursuing sex with another person. This, of course, negatively impacts both men and women. Fortunately, there are many ways to approach physical affection.

Options for diversifying physical intimacy

When you are not used to experiencing sensual touch in a setting where it's not intended to be romantic or sexual, it can be difficult and even scary at first. You may occasionally experience a pang of sexual arousal with activities like snuggling, especially if you're with someone you happen to find physically attractive. Or you may fear that a person you are interacting with may find it sexually arousing when you don't at all. However, if done in a facilitated group setting, it can be easier. A group setting provides peer pressure to keep things platonic, reminders that you don't need to act on sexual arousal if it occurs, and practice asking for what you want.

While transitioning between relationships, I found one type of touch-positive event to be a lifesaver. From *The Snuggle Party Guidebook*:

"A snuggle party is an event where participants share consensual, nurturing touch. Everyone is clothed, and the event is non-sexual. The energy is intended to be more relaxing and soothing, rather than arousing or stimulating. Touch might include holding hands, exchanging back, shoulder, or foot massage, light facial touch, holding, playing with hair, or spooning. The importance of open communication is emphasized. This includes stating one's own needs and boundaries, as well as asking for permission. More boisterous activities at snuggle parties can include playful wrestling, puppy piles (many people blissfully snuggled together), and pillow fights."[92]

Attending these events had a range of benefits. It made it easier to tolerate the stress of ending a relationship. It also made me a bit less desperate for touch in my next romantic relationship. While Sophia's sex drive was similar to mine, there were still a few areas of touch where we didn't align. As I love both giving and receiving massage, I was initially excited to learn that she was a massage therapist. Understandably, however, because she gave long massages at work, she often had little or no desire to offer me massage—even if I was willing to initiate. At that point, attending events like snuggle parties was a lifesaver. I found other people with whom I could exchange massage, and I felt much happier.

The snuggle parties had another benefit that I found helpful after being in an asexual-sexual relationship. They provided practice in asking for what I wanted and negotiating touch with other people. This included the concept of *leveling* discussed elsewhere in this book, additional language for communicating wants, and strategies for taking rejection less personally. In my relationship with Katie, I had become accustomed to certain patterns of interaction. My habits initially made it more difficult for me to read Sophia's cues and negotiate physical interaction with her. The snuggle events helped me to remember just how different each person is.

Platonic snuggles aren't the only event option for getting more touch. A number of individuals and organizations offer events that allow participants to explore a range of intimacy. Some include only moderate levels of physical intimacy, while others offer advanced events that may include erotic connection. Such events can allow you to explore in a relatively safe space, and then decide whether you wish to develop further connections and practices outside that setting. A few such organizations are the Human Awareness Institute (HAI) and Network for a New Culture.

If available in your area, check out Kaleidoscope Community Yoga or contact improvisational dance. Pujas, a type of interactive, connective event mentioned earlier, might appear under search terms such as "sacred Tantra" or "spiritual connection." These events and groups can vary a great deal. If needed, contact someone to find out more before you attend. Go with at least one friend or partner if you have any reason to doubt the credibility or safety of a specific facilitator or group.

A few words of caution regarding any touch-positive event are in order. Under no circumstances should you be pressured to do anything involving physical touch that you are not comfortable with. While some events are designed to stretch your comfort zones, you should always be at choice regarding how much you are willing to stretch. Even if others in the group seem comfortable doing something, it doesn't mean you need to be. If you feel that you are being pressured into anything, leave the event and inform others about your experience.

Also be aware that attending such events may help you and your partner in ways you haven't anticipated. It could influence your decisions around staying together or separating. If you are both committed to staying in the relationship, then adding external supports may make it easier for both of you to stay together. If you are seriously considering separating, external supports may give one or both of you additional courage to leave the relationship.

A last option for expanding your touch horizons is paid one-on-one snuggle and cuddle services. This is a relatively new industry where you pay a professional cuddler an hourly rate to cuddle with you. Such services can be useful if you aren't comfortable with group events, and if you want touch that's different from what professional massage therapists provide. A few examples: Cuddle Up to Me, Cuddle Connection, BeSnuggled, The Snuggery, and Cuddle Therapy. There are currently no legal certifications for the profession, so you will need to use your own discretion in determining whether a cuddle business is safe, professional, and legitimate. At the very least, a well-managed cuddling business should provide a written contract explaining what you can and cannot expect from the relationship. It should clearly outline that sexual touch is not allowed, and it should outline the clothing requirements and fees.

The "Additional Resources" chapter has a section titled "Increasing connection, touch, & physical pleasure." It includes organizations that provide event facilitators and facilitator trainings, businesses that offer one-on-one services, and books with tools and techniques.

9. Enhance Connection Beyond Physical Intimacy

• • •

Look beyond sex now, or it may bite you later

And I don't mean *bite* in a playful, sexy way if you are into that sort of thing.

On a cerebral level, you already know this: There are probably many things you appreciate about your partner besides sex. But if you have a sex drive, then you know that there's no replacement for sex itself. As we've already discussed, when you feel deprived of sex, the associated thoughts and emotions can take up a lot of time and energy. It can be easy to forget the other things you appreciate.

If you want to have a lasting *and* fulfilling relationship, you'll probably need to find a way to squeeze it in there at least some of the time—no double entendre intended. However, whether you remain in your current relationship or eventually move on to another one, it is important to try not to focus too much on sex.

"What?!" you exclaim, "How can I *not* be so focused on it when I'm feeling so deprived?"

It is much easier said than done. I know this all too well. When a therapist suggested that I was initially allowing sex to drive my next relationship, rather than allowing sex to flow naturally from the development of the relationship, I bristled, even though I saw her point. After my prior experience, how could I *not* do that?

We'll soon talk about how to avoid focusing on sex too much. In the meantime, here's *why* it's important. People leaving long-term relationships often have this experience:

➤ They meet someone who seems like the perfect opposite of their former partner. In other words, the new person has an abundance of the things they are starving for, but that their former partner could not provide. Or, the new person seems to lack the most challenging quirks of the former partner.

➤ They jump into a relationship with the new person, largely ignoring or blindly accepting other qualities.

➤ They later become disappointed as new incompatibilities surface with the new partner.

In other words, if sex is the number one priority for you, you will likely seek someone who is very sexual. You may initially ignore many of their other traits because you are so overjoyed just to be with someone who is enthusiastic about sex.

But no two people are perfectly compatible. Every one of us has our quirks that any intimate partner will have to tolerate if they wish to remain with us. As time passes, you discover more of your partner's quirks, and they discover more of yours. Dan Savage calls this the "cost of admission." Just as the best movies, amusement park rides, and concerts are usually not free, neither are relationships.

Asexuality might be a cost of admission for your current or past relationship. Only you can decide whether the cost is too high. Just know that a relationship with any other person will have its own unique set of costs. The costs might be much easier for you to tolerate, and perhaps even embrace. Or they might not. Likewise, this new person may share with you additional news about your quirks—things that your former partner didn't find annoying or challenging at all, or perhaps kept to themselves. Some of these differences may present wonderful new learning and growth opportunities while others may turn out to be deal breakers.

Once you are experiencing an abundance of sex again, you may realize that you took for granted other things about your asexual partner, and certain relationship components outside of sex may seem more important to you. You might not be able to see such things until you have experienced an abundance of sex for a while. Over time, the elevated levels of sex and love hormones that provide extra initial "zip" with a new partner will diminish. At that point, you may see a larger picture.

After I had been separated from Katie for some time, I began to appreciate more fully some of the ways I had enjoyed simply being in her presence, even when there was little or no sexual energy. I had often been overly focused on whether and when we were going to have sex again. That had just as much—if not more—to do with my inner dynamics and emotional "stuff" as it did with her sexuality. I didn't realize this until I recognized that I was continuing some of the same dynamics with Sophia, even though she was more sexual.

I had another realization after Sophia and I attended a mutual friend's art show. Sophia shared that she had once been sexually involved with a man we had talked with for a while at the event. Although he was very friendly, and they had dated only briefly, some of my insecurities cropped up. They stemmed from my sex-negative cultural programming. First, I was judging myself and both of them by perceived number of sexual partners. I felt inferior, fearing that I hadn't been desirable or autonomous enough to have the number of sex partners both of them had probably had. I was also jumping to conclusions: While I knew Sophia had had several previous sex partners, I knew nothing about this man's sexual history. Second, the fact that they had been involved only briefly, but had still had sex, made me wonder how much my sex meant to Sophia. I recalled that she had had sex with a number of other people prior to me, and had not maintained romantic relationships with any of them.

This all made me consider whether I had learned to rely too heavily on sex as a primary defining factor of intimacy, connection, and commitment between two people. After all, sometimes people have sex when they know and care about each other deeply, and sometimes people have sex when they know each other very little. Sex alone is not reliable as a measure of commitment or intimacy. Sharing sex may produce a greater feeling of bonding that makes it more emotionally difficult to separate, but it is no guarantee that two people are going to remain together. Even for the same person, sex can mean very different things at different times, depending on their needs, relationship status, and various other factors at that moment.

As I shared some of my insecurities with Sophia, she kindly explained that her experience of sex with me was very different, and in many ways deeper, than it had been with the other man. I appreciated her candid way of sharing this. I recognized that neither quality of sex, nor decision to share sex in the first place, really distinguished our relationship from any of our prior relationships. The nature of our sex simply stemmed from other aspects of our connection.[93] Those aspects included the honest and courageous way in which Sophia shared about her prior romantic life—I didn't take that for granted.

This realization also strengthened my appreciation for my connection with Katie. I had felt that the disappearance of our sex life, followed by her revelation of asexuality, had erased much of our intimacy, or had somehow made it less profound. In hindsight, I saw that I had relied *too* much on sex as an indicator of the strength and depth of our connection. I'm not saying that sex wasn't important to me—it was, and still is. I just hadn't recognized the limits to how much we can judge intimacy or create meaning based upon it.

If you can see beyond sex at least a bit, it can help you to make more broadly informed decisions about your relationships. Such decisions may include whether to stay with a current partner, or whether to become more serious about a potential future partner. Later I'll suggest options for getting some sexual and other touch needs met over the shorter term. This can help to reduce hyperfocus on sex if it exists.

First, we will examine several ways to look at intimacy more broadly, which can improve your relationship with either an asexual or a sexual partner. As you're exploring whether you can make your relationship work on the sexual front, you also want to be aware of other ways you can be present for each other.

The Five Love Languages

In *The 5 Love Languages*, Gary Chapman outlines the following styles that partners use to express and interpret love:

> **Words of Affirmation**, which includes verbal compliments

> **Quality Time**, which includes giving your loved one your undivided attention

> **Receiving Gifts**, which includes the effort to obtain or create the gifts

> **Acts of Service**, which includes performing helpful tasks to ease your partner's burden

> **Physical Touch**, which includes but spans well beyond sex

It is important to understand your partner's primary language(s) and vice versa because it increases your ability to help each other feel loved and understood. If you consistently fail to give to each other in ways that honor your preferred ways of receiving love, you may continue to feel neglected, no matter how hard you try.

Chapman suggests a few ways to determine your preferred languages, one of them being to look at the style in which each of you most frequently gives. Often, but not always, you will prefer receiving in the same way that you most naturally give. There is a free 30-question assessment at www.lovelanguages.com.[94] You can have more than one preferred language, and any balanced relationship is going to spread energy across multiple languages to some extent. What is your primary language? What is your partner's?

Many individuals assume too quickly that physical touch is their primary language because sex feels so powerful. However, they may discover that other factors like praise or attention are just as important for making them feel loved and appreciated.

Chapman's concepts suggest at least one important consideration for asexual-sexual couples. Physical touch can be an anxiety-provoking topic because you're wired to connect touch with arousal and sex at least some of the time, while your partner is not. So if physical touch is a preferred language for one or both of you, your relationship may be even more challenging. Therefore, it's even more important to communicate openly and honestly about your boundaries, expectations, and needs.

An AVEN website poll asked users to report the results of their love language test.[95] Among 112 respondents, quality time was the most popular language (46%), followed by words of affirmation (21%) and physical touch (20%). While some of the responses might be from sexual members, the poll suggests that at least some asexuals do indeed connect best through physical contact.

Ten ways to give & receive

Why Good Things Happen to Good People covers even more ways that you can give and receive, some of which overlap with the Five Love Languages.[96] I find it odd that it excludes physical touch, but this is likely because the book's focus is much broader than romantic relationships. Here are examples for each:

➤ **Celebration** might include writing a thank-you note to your partner or throwing a birthday or anniversary party.

➤ **Generativity** involves nurturing others in a way that enables them to develop and grow. You might offer to accompany your partner to a couples retreat.

➤ You might show **forgiveness** by getting out of the habit of bringing up your partner's past wrongdoings.

➤ **Courage and confrontation** could include directly addressing your partner about an issue that is affecting your relationship.

➤ You might provide **humor** by learning to laugh at your partner's quirks that sometimes frustrate you, or by offering lightheartedness when your partner is having a rough day.

➤ You can give **respect** by treating your partner as your equal.

> **Compassion,** which Post describes as "love's response to suffering," can be given in many ways. This could be as simple as giving your partner a hug when they are feeling down.

> You can give **loyalty** by doing your best to make your partner a priority when they need you by their side.

> **Listening** could simply entail providing your undivided attention over dinner as your partner tells you about their day.

> You can give **creativity** by baking a batch of your partner's favorite cookies for them, or by building a shelf for their beloved porcelain pig collection. There are many possibilities here.

As with the Five Love Languages, the above may be useful for assessing and strengthening your relationship beyond sex. As a sexual individual, you may find that sex is a way of expressing celebration, forgiveness, respect, compassion, loyalty, or creativity. If you have repressed much of your sexual energy, you may have inadvertently squelched some of these other ways of giving to your partner. How else do you already give, and how else does your partner already give?

Again, there's no direct replacement for sex, especially given that sex is a form of intimacy that distinguishes many partnerships from others. For sexual people, this includes spouses, girlfriends, boyfriends, and lovers. Nonetheless, sex is still just one of many options for creating intimacy with your partner.

Twelve types of intimacy

In *The Intimate Marriage* (1970), Clinebell and Clinebell proposed that there are at least 12 types of intimacy:

> **Aesthetic Intimacy**: experiencing beauty together

> **Conflict Intimacy**: struggling with differences

> **Creative Intimacy**: constructing or co-creating things together (and not attempting to reform each other)

> **Crisis Intimacy**: bonding through coping with problems and challenges

> **Commitment Intimacy**: mutual support of each other's self-interests

> **Communication Intimacy**: affirmation, empathy, and mutual understanding

> **Emotional Intimacy**: being on the same page with one another

> **Intellectual Intimacy**: sharing thoughts and ideas

> **Recreational Intimacy**: experiencing play and fun

> **Sexual Intimacy**: sharing physical passion and connection (I might personally rename this one "Physical Intimacy" to cover the full range of physical and sensual touch.)

> **Spiritual Intimacy**: sharing expression and connection with a higher sense of meaning; may or may not be formally religious

> **Work Intimacy**: sharing common tasks or chores

For example, if you and your partner have supported one another through major problems and challenges, you've likely built intimacy, trust, a strong bond, and interdependence that you can't replace overnight. The challenges of caring for a child developed additional crisis intimacy between Katie and me. But if you don't have sexual or recreational intimacy—that is, if you don't have much fun—then you're still going to have difficulty being happy together.

For a given person or couple, different types of intimacy may feed into one another. For example, you may find that you have an easier time being emotionally intimate with your partner when you're also regularly sexually intimate with them. Or, you may experience deeper recreational intimacy with them after sharing some work intimacy. For me, sex is a form of fun and play, so sexual and recreational intimacy overlap.

Some types of interaction span several types of intimacy, including sexual intimacy. If you and your partner are on very different pages regarding sexuality, it will affect the overlapping areas. As just one example, I enjoy sexual humor, including double entendres. For me, sharing such humor spans recreational, intellectual, and sexual intimacy. So whenever Katie didn't appreciate my witty (at least from my perspective) humor, I felt misunderstood and disconnected on a few levels.

The 12 Types of Intimacy model can help you and your partner to clarify the following:

➢ where you share commonalities in your bonding styles

➢ where you have difficulty meeting each other's intimacy needs

➢ where to focus your energy to strengthen your bonds

➢ where you may need other friendships to fulfill certain intimacy needs

Clarifying your intimacy needs and overlaps can also help you to determine the likelihood of finding mutual happiness with your partner if you remain together. You may realize that you share more types of intimacy than you had previously thought. Or, you may realize that your intimacy incompatibilities extend well beyond sex.

Keep in mind that it's very difficult for any one person to fulfill all of another's intimacy needs. At the same time, you need to have enough in common to make it worthwhile for both of you. An acquaintance shared that after she had been with her prior partner for some time, she had difficulty identifying what they had in common beyond both liking oatmeal for breakfast. Not surprisingly, that wasn't enough to keep them together. "You need more than oatmeal," she emphasized.

View love & intimacy in a more empowering way

"What's love but a second-hand emotion?" sang Tina Turner in her 1985 Grammy-winning hit, "What's Love Got to Do with It?" A few decades later, here's my response for Tina: Love can be much more than an emotion. As mentioned earlier, when we are with a new sexual partner, a flood of hormones and love chemicals gives us an enhanced emotional boost. These emotions are an important and powerful part of attraction for most of us, so they're often confused with love.

However, they account for only a portion of what may develop into love and deeper intimacy.

There is a more holistic and empowering way to define love and intimacy: as a series of ongoing choices you make about how you include other people in your life. Let's say you have met someone named Pat, with whom you are developing a relationship. In any given moment, regardless of whether you are with Pat, you can choose to think about them lovingly, not so lovingly, or not at all. Similarly, when you are with Pat, you can choose to interact with them in a connective and bonding way, in a distancing or conflict-oriented way, or not at all. An example of this last case would be sitting on the opposite side of the room and surfing the web on your smartphone.

On any given day, the level of love you experience with Pat will depend largely upon the moment-to-moment choices you make about how you think and interact. In any given instant, you can shift the amount of love you are experiencing—not just related to physical intimacy, but to other types of connection as well. Looking at love and intimacy in this way can remind you of your role in proactively creating these states. You're not simply being a passive bystander as emotions come and go.[97]

Five frequent phrases from a long-term couple

I appreciated a Valentine's Day radio story about a couple married for more than five decades. They followed the five frequent phrases of successful marriage spotted on a sign along the road:[98]

➢ "You look great."

➢ "Can I help?"

➢ "Let's eat out."

➢ "I'm sorry."

➢ "I love you."

These rules are beautiful in their simplicity, as they touch upon so many levels of a relationship. Using these phrases regularly can probably benefit most couples. But when sexual compatibility is an issue, they may require a few adjustments and considerations.

If your partner doesn't experience physical attraction, the first phrase may sometimes cause disappointment. I often wanted to feel that Katie found me sexually attractive, and I wanted to express similar sentiments to her. I also wanted to feel that my compliment had been acknowledged and validated. However, after we became clearer about her asexuality, I knew that a "You look great" from her still meant she found me attractive, but not in a sexual way. It was still nice to hear, as long as I didn't expect it to have an erotic charge. I would still frequently tell her she looked nice, but if I said it in a sexual context, her expression of gratitude would be relatively flat. So I learned to vary the settings in which I expressed it, and I adjusted my expectations of her reactions.

As for "I'm sorry," making up requires discussion and behavior that addresses underlying the issues at hand. At the same time, sex can help with making up and diffusing tension. Some relationship experts suggest that it works the other way as well: After a bit of apologizing and verbal reconnection, the remaining energy from prior tense interactions can fuel some powerful sex.[99] But that's the case only for a sexual person—with Katie, I found that after an argument and make-up, I was sometimes amped up for bedroom play, while such activities were still not on her priority list. At least we were both good at apologizing, though.

"Let's eat out" is great if you have a mutual understanding about what may or may not be desired following a night out—be it eating out, seeing a movie, dancing, or otherwise. I had to communicate clearly about this even with Sophia, particularly when we expected to return home late from a film, performance, or social event with romantic or sexual overtones that might get one or both of us charged up. That way we were at least on the same page, and we were less likely to be disappointed or frustrated at the end of the evening.

"I love you" is important in any relationship. However, there may be differences in the settings where it comes more naturally for each of you. For me, "I love you" has always seemed natural in the bedroom.

But as Katie and I came to understand our sexual differences, I observed that she rarely said it during or right after sex except as a response to my saying it. This was in contrast to her frequent expression in other settings, such as ending each phone conversation or quick morning goodbye kiss with "I love you." Each couple will be different. The important thing is that you each communicate your appreciation in a way that feels authentic.

"Can I help?" is still key, even though the Pew survey noted earlier suggests that quality sex is highly important for more couples than is sharing chores. Regardless of your partner's sexuality, pitching in will generally enhance appreciation and good will within your relationship. Helping also has an interesting two-way relationship with sex. Offering to help a low-interest (but sexual) partner with household chores can sometimes improve interest in sex. Conversely, if a high-interest partner seems distanced and uninvolved, a roll in the sack can make them more helpful almost instantly.[100] This approach often works with me because I feel more loved and appreciated by my partner when we have quality sex. While you don't want to take this overboard and exploit anyone, it can provide another way for sex to perk up the relationship for both of you.

10. Think Beyond the Binary Relationship Box

• • •

You have many options

If you have determined that you and your partner essentially have different orientations, some major decisions lie ahead. However, it's not a simple "either/or" matter of either keeping the relationship as it currently exists or ending it altogether. While those are certainly options, there are also many shades of gray in between—ways of modifying your current relationship in small or major ways.

If you're mutually unable to keep key elements of the agreement in an amicable way, you have several options:

a) Find a way to be happy with the current agreement as you both understand it.

b) Modify or clarify the agreement to arrive at a mutually acceptable understanding.

c) Pretend to follow the agreement, but break it behind your partner's back.

d) Leave the agreement.

You have likely already been unsuccessful with option (a), and option (c) isn't likely to lead to lasting happiness. That leaves the options of (b) modifying or clarifying the current relationship, possibly with the support of a counselor or other professional, or (d) setting each other free.

We often limit the possibilities around (b) when it comes to modifying a relationship. In our culture, we tend to think of intimate relationships in a binary fashion. Either they work as we originally expected them to, or we end them. On top of that, once we've been sexually intimate with someone, and we decide to end that part of our relationship, we often believe we must terminate our connection with them altogether. Even if we don't believe that ourselves, our next romantic partner may want us to sever the connection. That results in a great deal of loss, as we then give up all the other forms of intimacy and support we've developed over time with our previous partner.

Is any of this necessary? An acquaintance explained that she viewed her prior relationship as having "evolved," rather than having "ended." She and the father of her child still share a connection and see each other regularly; it's just a very different relationship, with different levels and types of intimacy.

Sure, in some cases, continuing a connection may not work, even after attempted modifications. It may make sense to minimize contact for at least a while. Following a significant shift in how two people relate, it may take time and distance before they can reconnect in a mutually enjoyable way. If two individuals don't allow the space needed for healing and forgiveness around certain tensions, incompatibilities, anger, and unresolved issues, it may affect not only the two of them, but also their new partners.

In some cases, however, asexual-sexual relationships may provide a better-than-average opportunity for continued connection. This is because only one partner experiences the tension that stems from lingering sexual desire following a romantic separation. So if the sexual partner can fully accept their partner's asexual identity, and can be content with a more platonic relationship, then the connection may stand a better chance of surviving in a different form.

Fortunately, the traditional nuclear family is far from the only option today. Other relationship arrangements are gradually becoming more common and socially accepted. These include the following:

➢ co-parenting arrangements where parents are not romantically or sexually involved

➢ arrangements where biological parents share custody even after forming relationships with new partners

➢ households with more than two adults, some or all of whom may share romantic and sexual connection

Given that nearly half of traditional marriages in the U.S. end in divorce, the increase in such arrangements is not surprising. In *Psychology Today*, one sexual woman chronicled how she and her asexual husband decided to "divorce differently." After accepting that they were sexually incompatible, they divorced, but they remained living together as friends and co-parents.[101]

Ethical non-monogamy: Basic definitions

Some asexual/sexual couples find a way to keep much of their existing relationship arrangement intact, compromising to deal with their differences. Others find their differences too great, and eventually choose to part ways altogether. Still others toss aside the "traditional" relationship box and create a customized arrangement that works for them. Ethically non-monogamous relationships are one possibility.

Depending on the arrangement, the presence of one or more additional adults can lighten the workload with household and parenting tasks. In some polyamorous families, children get more attention and exposure to a broader range of knowledge.[102] So whatever your family situation, such options may be worth examining.

While I can't cover all forms of ethical non-monogamy here, I'll briefly describe some of the relationship types to give you a sense of the possibilities. Some of the books in the "Additional Resources" section have much greater detail, and I'd strongly recommend reading at least a few of them before attempting a new relationship structure. Some of the definitions that follow are adapted from the "Glossary of Poly Terms" by Franklin Veaux.[103]

As mentioned earlier, *open relationship* is a common term often used to refer to any relationship that is not sexually monogamous. Some people also use *ethical non-monogamy* to refer to such relationships, as they involve honest communication. This stands in contrast to affairs and cheating, where partners *don't* tell each other about their involvement with others.

Some people use the term *open relationship* synonymously with polyamory, but that's not technically correct. The umbrella of open relationships also includes practices like swinging, but polyamory doesn't always involve sex. *Polyamory* means having a committed loving relationship and ongoing emotional involvement with more than one person.

While polyamorous relationships are often romantic and sexual in nature, they don't need to be. A person could be polyamorous but be sexual with only one of their lovers, or they could be polyamorous without being sexual with any of their lovers at all. Of course, they may still enjoy sensual but non-sexual touch with more than one person, making them *polysensual* but not *polysexual*.

Technically speaking, nearly everyone is polyamorous—for example, if you love one or both of your parents as well as your best friend, you are polyamorous. Even if we limit the definition to romantic and sexual relationships, most of us are still polyamorous if we've had more than one such relationship—it's just that most of us have had multiple relationships serially rather than simultaneously. But emotionally, there's still often a simultaneous aspect to it. Chances are, even when you enter a new relationship, you never *totally* stop loving your ex-partner—at least not if you are completely honest with yourself. Even if you are glad to be done with the relationship, you probably still love and miss some things about your previous partner.

People begin some polyamorous relationships with an intent to be egalitarian, where several people get equal say in most or all aspects of the relationships. This might be the case if several people who know, love, and trust one another decide to live together as life partners and lovers.

Some polyamorous arrangements are hierarchical in nature, where one's relationship with a given person takes precedence in many ways over one's relationship with other people. Suppose that you and your current partner of several years, Amadi, decide that one or both of you can date other people. However, you and Amadi will continue to prioritize each other in many ways. You agree upon certain rules and boundaries to help protect the relationship between the two of you.

You also let other people you are dating know that you intend to do this, and you explain how it will impact your connection with them. Amadi, the person who gets the highest priority, is your *primary partner*. Others are *secondary partners*. More informal terms like *sweetie, sweetheart, lover,* and *girlfriend/boyfriend* can refer to a range of relationship types, including a secondary partner or primary partner.

Swinging is the practice of having multiple sexual partners outside of one's committed relationship, usually with the intent that these other connection will be primarily sexual in nature, and will not involve any ongoing emotional or romantic commitments. Note that I said *intent*—people vary in their ability to minimize the formation of strong emotional attachments after having sex. Polyamory and swinging are often confused; I hope that the above clarifies their differences.

Another common arrangement is *polyfidelity*. This refers to a relationship that is usually romantic and sexual, involving more than two people, where all agree to refrain from seeking outside partners without the consent of everyone else in the group. If you maintained a relationship with your asexual partner alongside an ongoing relationship with one sexual partner, and you all agreed to seek the consent of the other two prior to becoming romantically or sexually involved with anyone else, that would be polyfidelity. I mention this to dispel the myth that polyamory means indiscriminately hooking up with other people or throwing one's discretion out the door.

Some couples adopt "don't ask, don't tell" arrangements, where one or both partners are free to see other people, but they do it discreetly and don't discuss the details with each other. They may still agree to certain guidelines such as following safer sex practices and not seeing other lovers during certain priority times. Because the imagination can create scenarios scarier than reality for some people, a "don't ask, don't tell" approach won't work for everyone.

It should now be clear that ethical non-monogamy can take a range of forms, and that such arrangements can provide a way for an asexual-sexual couple to stay together while each person still gets their fundamental needs met. However, it's not a simple walk in the park. In the remainder of this chapter, I address a number of considerations for anyone considering ethical non-monogamy. Some are pertinent specifically to asexual-sexual couples.

Again, this chapter touches only the tip of the iceberg. If you decide to explore any of these options more seriously, consult a few of the works under "Additional Resources." They describe the various forms that open relationships can take, the pitfalls to look out for, and considerations for creating and maintaining such connections.

More on my polyamory learning experience

As I described earlier, after I did much reading on ethical non-monogamy, Katie and I agreed to try it. Later, even though I was sexually monogamous with Sophia, we agreed that she could be polyamorous while we were first dating. I learned important things from my poly-related experiences with both of them.

While trying an open relationship with Katie, I met someone with whom I resonated in new and different ways. Katie also became more confident about her orientation and preferences. Our experiment helped us to decide that separating was ultimately the best next step. I realized what I had been missing sexually, and Katie became even more confident that she had no desire to engage in sexual activity with any regularity. Even if we tried to remain together in an open relationship, I would need to rely completely on non-sexual means of maintaining my bond with Katie.

With Sophia, I found it difficult to manage jealousy, and I found my preferences at odds with those of her other current and recent lovers. During that time, we devoted significant time and energy to processing my emotional triggers around her other connections. It often felt like we had little energy remaining for each other.

It became all too clear that polyamory was far from a free pass to have sex with more than one person. I learned that it's important to get to know a person well and to develop a deep foundation of trust before bringing in other romantic and sexual partners. If you are trying to hop into a multi-person dynamic, particularly after transitioning out of a long-term monogamous relationship, things may get complicated quickly. You'll need to talk about challenging topics, such as how to handle safer sex practices when additional people are involved. That's just the tip of the iceberg.

Open relationships take a great deal of communication so that everyone is clear about expectations and boundaries. Partners must be on the same page, and a commitment to processing emotions together regularly is important. With each connection you maintain, another person's needs, opinions, and emotions will be involved—and you will have more processing to do with your primary partner. Ethical non-monogamy may be especially challenging if you are very sensitive to energy from other people's moods, or if you already have difficulty establishing and maintaining emotional and time boundaries.

My opinion is that polyamory in and of itself is neither good nor bad. It works for some people. When it doesn't work, it's not necessarily the practice of poly itself that creates issues. All of the following can also influence the trajectory of the relationship:

➤ how the people involved manage it

➤ how compatible their styles are

➤ how their priorities and values match up

➤ where they are at in their developmental processes

➤ how stable their relationship is before attempting to open it

I haven't completely ruled out the future possibility of an ethically non-monogamous relationship in my life; I just know that the timing and circumstances weren't aligned when I previously tried it. If I ever try it again, it will be in a different way.

Sexual-asexual open relationships: Unique challenges

Some AVEN members have reported success with different forms of open relationships. There are many possibilities, as involvement with additional partners may involve primarily sex, relatively deep intimacy and friendship without sex, or both. As just one example, you might wish to have a secondary partner whom you see primarily for sex once or twice a week, while your primary partner has a secondary partner with whom they engage in non-sexual but emotionally intimate activities each weekend.

The basic idea is that you and your partner love each other, provide each other with happiness in many ways, and wish to remain together. At the same time, you acknowledge that you can't meet all of each other's needs. You love each other enough that you're willing to go through the extra work it takes to bring additional people into the mix, in an honest fashion.

In cases where two individuals have a strong relationship and also share a mutual attraction, the freedom and excitement of being with others can enhance their bond. While one or both of them get energy from being with others, they still get a mutual charge from being with each other.

However, in a case where only one partner experiences sexual attraction to the other, a different dynamic exists. An outside sexual partner offers a powerful connection that your primary partner may be unable or unwilling to offer at all. Therefore, the sexual partner may present an especially stark contrast to your asexual partner. Even if you do your best to avoid comparing your asexual partner to your sexual partner(s), some of this energy may still come across. Because of this, opening up a relationship with a potentially asexual partner may require additional considerations.

This is especially true in the early stages of a new romantic or sexual connection, where "new relationship energy" (NRE) is present. For several reasons, navigating this phase with any primary partner can be challenging:

➢ A flood of hormones and natural chemicals makes you feel euphoric and infatuated, always wanting to be with the new person, even though you may not know them that well yet.

➢ During this honeymoon period, a new partner will be flooding you with compliments and attention, and vice versa.

➤ You and your new partner are both still showing the most positive aspects of yourselves. You haven't yet discovered many of the aspects that are less compatible or potentially challenging. So you have an idealized view of the other person, compared to the "warts and all" view of your longer-term partner.

NRE is challenging enough for couples who can regularly confirm their bond through mutually connective lovemaking. For couples who cannot, it may take even more effort to manage, and may rely more upon bonds established through other types of intimacy. Many asexuals on the AVEN website have discussed the pain of being unable to provide their partner with what they want. Many such comments aren't even in the context of open relationships, where jealousy, insecurity, and comparison take consistent efforts to manage.

Jealousy management may be necessary for you, too, if you are relating to someone who also wishes to have one or more other partners. If your sexual self-confidence has been wounded by your primary partner's lack of attraction, getting involved with someone who has other partners may deepen your wound. This is one reason I had difficulty managing jealousy and insecurities around Sophia's other lovers.

Don't assume that an asexual partner will automatically accept an open relationship just because they don't want sex from you. While sex may not be a key component of intimacy for them, they know that it is a key component for you. They may fear that once you find someone who is more sexually compatible, they will also lose other types of intimacy with you. You might even choose to leave them altogether. Even if your partner doesn't want sex, they may fear others' judgment of your open relationship, and of them. They may fear being seen as an inadequate or sexually stingy partner, or as a weak victim clinging to an unfaithful partner.

In the beginning, your asexual partner might enthusiastically support—perhaps even encourage—your finding other sources of sex, hoping that it will relieve them of pressure to have sex with you. However, they will still expect you to show up for them in other ways, even as you are bonding with someone else. This may or may not be something that you can do in a way that meets their needs. Additionally, as your relationship with a more sexual partner gets your sexual energies flowing more freely again, you may also crave your asexual partner even more—and that can lead to further frustration. As you may recall, this happened with me.

Know that your primary partner might wish to explore with other people, too. Even if it's not sexual, they may still want to go on romantic dates and spend significant time with others. They may enjoy doing things with another partner that they have never enjoyed doing with you. Also be prepared for the slight possibility that they will want to explore sex with someone else, even if they rarely or never want it with you.

If your existing relationship is on shaky ground, then opening it up could motivate you and your partner to end it. This may or may not be a bad thing, depending on your specific circumstances and desires.

Questions for assessing non-monogamy readiness

If you're seriously exploring an open relationship, and you believe that your partner is asexual, here are a few important questions to ask. You may not know the answers to some of these until you've tried an open relationship:

➢ How well are you and your partner connected in other areas of intimacy and giving/receiving outside of sex? An open relationship probably won't help if the relationship is weak in many other areas.

➢ How well can you continue to prioritize your partner in the ways that they wish, even while experiencing the strong emotional bond that can accompany having sex with someone else?

➢ How will the two of you handle jealousy? Some books on open relationships treat jealousy as inevitable—it may lessen substantially over time, but can be very strong in the beginning.

➢ Even if you're getting some sexual needs met with another person, how often do you still need or want sex with your primary partner to continue feeling connected to them?

➢ What if sex with another person(s) causes you to desire your primary partner even more? While a sexual primary partner may appreciate this, an asexual primary partner may not.

➢ What safer sex and etiquette guidelines does your partner want you to follow?

➢ How much time are you willing or able to devote to outside relationships, while continuing to provide your primary partner with the time and energy they desire? For example, are you looking for someone to see a few times a week for just an hour or two at a time, or someone with whom to spend weekend overnights?

➢ If you have children, how do you and your partner believe that non-monogamy may affect your parenting roles and relationships with your kids? What potential resources and challenges do you believe that an open relationship may offer your family?

Some of the open relationship books listed under "Additional Resources" include more in-depth self-assessment questions.[104]

Everyone's needs are different

A few authors on open relationships make a point that is particularly pertinent to asexual-sexual couples: When negotiating the boundaries of your open relationship with your partner, don't get caught up in trying to make everything equal. The types of activities that meet your needs may not meet your partner's needs. For both of you to be happy, you might agree to let your partner do some things that they may not be comfortable allowing you to do, and vice versa. For example, your partner may be fine with you having sex with someone else frequently, but may not ever want you to stay overnight with them. You, on the other hand, may be fine with your partner sometimes spending entire weekends with someone else, as long as they're not having sex.[105]

It is important to consider the intimacy vs. autonomy preferences of you and your partner(s).[106] For example, if you need a lot of independence and alone time, then it may difficult to juggle more than one time-consuming relationship at a time. You might function best with a secondary relationship involving just a few hours per week. On the other hand, you could find that you all enjoy hanging out together frequently, making things easier to manage.

Testing the waters with polysensuality

If the considerations in this chapter seem overwhelming, you might first explore being more physically intimate with others in non-sexual ways. In other words, you can test the waters by being polysensual but not polysexual. Consider some of the activities under "Expand Your World of Physical Intimacy."

PART FOUR:
Improve Your Sexual Abilities

Part Four Overview

• • •

REGARDLESS OF YOUR partner's level of enthusiasm for sex, you have the power to choose how you care for yourself and how you show up. This is important whether you remain in your current relationship or form a new one. Prior chapters have already offered suggestions and concepts intended to help you in the sexual arena, both directly and indirectly. Part Four takes things a step further.

If your asexual or otherwise low-interest partner is still willing to have sex sometimes, improving your practices may help them to be more excited and receptive. If you are seeking a new relationship, being a good partner will increase the odds that you will attract someone who enjoys sex. Being a good sex partner can work as a feedback loop. When you show up more enthusiastically and skillfully, your partner is more likely to become energized and excited. Their increased excitement, in turn, will make things more fun for you. That will make it easier for you to excite them even more, and so on.

In Part Four, I share with you activities and concepts that have helped me to develop a more enjoyable sex life, and to relate better outside the bedroom as well. The ideas are not entirely original, and I don't claim to be the world's greatest sex expert. However, I've adapted many concepts to the unique needs of people who have had asexual or low-interest partners. I have also been fortunate to have partners committed to personal development in different but equally important ways. I'm grateful for their roles in directly and indirectly co-creating some of the learning experiences and approaches ahead.

I'll reiterate a simple but important point: Sex never exists in a vacuum. I've found that even with a high-interest partner, our sex life temporarily wanes when we're having difficulties in other areas of our relationship. That is why suggestions in the following chapters cover several life areas, some outside the bedroom. The initial attraction and hormone boost will keep you going early in a relationship. After that, sexual satisfaction will probably dip if you don't put in the effort or aren't compatible in other ways.

11. Enhance Communication & Negotiation Skills

• • •

Learn to ask for what you want

As Katie's lack of enthusiasm for sex became more apparent, I became less confident about asking for what I wanted. I often feared that I would be rejected, and I worried that I was becoming a nuisance. I then carried this into my relationship with Sophia. I often hesitated to ask when I wanted sex if she didn't show obvious signs of readiness.

Ironically, the more I wanted it, the more I was afraid to ask. It felt easier to risk rejection when I didn't want it as badly. This, of course, reduced the quality and experience of sex from my end, because in many cases where I *really* wanted it, I didn't ask. Most of the times when I asked, I was only moderately horny, which meant the sex was often less intense on my end. I still got enjoyment from giving myself powerful orgasms, but I sometimes wanted to enjoy more of them in Sophia's presence.

If you wish to remain with a potentially asexual partner and find mutual happiness, you may need to develop better ways to express what you want. Amity Pierce Buxton has observed the importance of such expression in mixed heterosexual-homosexual couples, where both individuals need to assert their needs so that one isn't overly dependent on the other. This is important for any couple, but it may be especially difficult for mixed-orientation couples because their needs are often in direct conflict with one another.[107] Each partner may or may not be willing and able to flex enough to meet the other's needs while remaining happy.

One way to practice asking for what you want is to get involved with touch-positive groups as described under "Options for diversifying physical intimacy." For example, snuggle parties can help you to practice touch that's not as emotionally charged as sex. Other groups and books are listed under "Additional Resources."

When you open yourself up to new experiences, learning sometimes occurs in unexpected ways. More than two years after Sophia and I had gotten together, she facilitated a dance encouraging attendees to stretch their gender identity boundaries. I dressed in sexy women's attire and made a surprising discovery: I was more comfortable dancing in a sexy and provocative way, and even being lightly and playfully flirtatious with women. I realized that I had largely turned off my flirtatiousness for fear of seeming disrespectful toward women. The women's attire gave me a safer and more playful way to reawaken that part of myself. While my shyness might have been reinforced during my prior relationship, it was largely a habit I had developed long before that. The dance experience helped me to rediscover the fun of expressing my sexiness and desire.

Also realize that our culture often trains both women and men that it is impolite to ask for what you really want or need, even when it's appropriate or helpful. Martyrdom is often considered honorable, a sign of devotion and love. Asking, we are taught, may damage relationships. This spans many settings, and naturally extends to the bedroom. Sure, sometimes putting aside your needs or delaying gratification is important, and a part of real everyday life. But it's easy to go overboard. If you become unhappy and resentful, and aren't meeting basic needs, you may resort to passive aggressive means. That isn't nice, and it doesn't help anyone. *Not* asking can damage relationships.[108]

You don't need to read minds

People differ in terms of what gets them excited before sex, what turns them on the most during sex, and what they enjoy immediately after sex. While we'll talk about things that tend to help in most cases, there's no "one size fits all" formula for getting the mutual flames going. There are many books that talk about specific sexual techniques, some of which can be helpful to know, but you can't just whip them out at any time. During sexual interaction, the sensitivity of the body is constantly changing, and what feels amazing one moment may no longer feel good the next.

Let go of the myths that a good sexual partner can read your mind or know what you want most of the time, and that you need to be able to read their mind in order to be a good partner. Sure, as you get to know someone better, you will each learn more about what the other person wants, so you don't need to talk as much. However, you will never have it *all* figured out. Our bodies are not always predictable, and we can often surprise ourselves. Your wants will never be entirely in sync with any partner, regardless of how closely your sex drives match. You may need to stretch beyond your comfort zones to communicate what you want and to hear your partner do the same.

Several aspects of communication

Healthy communication starts outside the bedroom, but it impacts what goes on in the bedroom as well. It includes an ongoing commitment to the following:

➢ clarity and expression of your wants and needs, as discussed earlier

➢ listening to the wants and needs of your partner—sometimes even encouraging them to express themselves, and making it safe and exciting to do so in a candid way

➢ deep curiosity about how your partner is, emotionally and otherwise

➢ mindfulness of how you are feeling at any given moment, and a vulnerable and open willingness to express that

➢ owning your emotions and reactions rather than blaming your partner (for example, using *I* statements like "I feel tender" rather than *you* statements like "You make me angry")

> willingness to say "no" when you don't want something, and to encourage your partner to do the same, so that you are better able to trust each other's "yes"

> willingness to negotiate when something isn't working for you or your partner

> willingness to have conversations about emotional connection on a regular basis, so neither partner feels ignored or neglected, and so issues don't build up over time

Collaboratively expressing desires

A partner with little or no interest in sex may rarely initiate or help to co-create physically intimate activities. Consent may be a relatively simple exchange: You ask your partner for permission to engage in a sexual act, and they either say "yes" or "no." Just getting a "yes" and having sex at all may seem so amazing that asking for more may seem excessive. You may have developed the attitude that it's not okay to ask for what you want in the bedroom. Also, your partner may express very few requests or preferences, other than a desire for sex to be brief, or a desire for a position shift whenever something feels uncomfortable.

However, things don't have to be this way. Nor should they be, argues Thomas Macaulay Miller:[109]

> "Because it centers on collaboration, a performance model better fits the conventional feminist wisdom that consent is not the absence of "no," but affirmative participation. Who picks up a guitar and jams with a bassist who just stands there? Who dances with a partner who is just standing and staring? In the absence of affirmative participation, there is no collaboration . . . This process involves communication of likes and dislikes and preferences, not a series of proposals that meet with acceptance or rejection."

If your partner seems unable to enjoy sex and doesn't engage in consent beyond simply saying "yes" or "no" to your advances, consider asking them if they'd be willing to participate more actively. This can also lessen the perception that they are simply going along with things or making a sacrifice for you, which doesn't help anyone in the end. Continually sending the message that one is being a martyr is not an act of love.

Keep in mind that even if you are clear on what you want and good at communicating it, your partner won't always be willing or able to do things just how you like them. Or, there may be those times where everything is so right that the experience is impossible to duplicate.

Should you end up with a partner who desires and enjoys sex, they may have many more requests than you're accustomed to. In fact, the more they have learned to enjoy sex, the more specific their requests are likely to be. It's important to recognize that such requests are probably not an attempt to discourage you from having sex, and are probably not a criticism of your abilities or desirability. Rather, they're merely an indicator that your partner wants to enjoy sex with you. Their requests will more often be geared toward making the sex feel even better.

In your collaborative expression of desires, you probably don't want to compare your current partner to past partners. However, you can learn a lot about your partner and how to please them even more if you can comfortably ask questions like, "So was there anything that a past partner did that was really exciting for you? I probably can't do it exactly the same way, but I'd like to try it with you."

Practice the art of leveling

A good skill to know in any physical touch setting, including the bedroom, is *leveling*. Leveling is adjusting an interaction to a level that is comfortable for both people. It means proactively negotiating how you would like to interact before doing so. It is a way of getting to common ground and mutual respect.[110] Leveling can be especially useful if you've been interacting at one level of physical intimacy, and now wish to jump to a significantly greater level of intimacy. While leveling is not needed as often once you know someone well—it can interrupt spontaneity—it can be helpful if you are still getting to know someone and their preferences. It can also be helpful if you want to do something you know your partner is sometimes but not always willing to do.

For example, suppose that after spooning your partner naked for a short time, you decide that you would like to get more intimate. You ask your partner if you can give them oral sex. On one hand, they may say yes, in which case you could proceed. On the other hand, they may say, "I'm not ready for that just yet, but I'd love it if you kissed my neck." You can then agree to do that, or propose another type of interaction and wait for their response. This type of negotiation allows both people to be comfortable, and it opens up a broad range of possibilities beyond a simple yes/no.

To get more practice at negotiating touch, consider joining or forming a group that facilitates touch-positive events, as mentioned earlier. *The Snuggle Party Guidebook* also covers leveling.

Speak multiple sensual languages

We covered some of the styles of communicating affection under "Enhance Connection Beyond Physical Intimacy." In addition to those, many styles of verbal and non-verbal communication can accompany sex itself. Some people like a lot of verbal communication in the bedroom while others like very little talking. Some prefer gentle talk while others like it rough. Some like it sweet while others like it dirty. Some prefer a combination.

It can be helpful to learn what your partner likes, and to let them know what you like. Do they like you to talk about their *vagina, vulva, yoni,* or *pussy? Clitoris* or *clit? Breasts* or *tits? Penis, dick,* or *cock? Butt* or *ass? Balls* or *scrotum?* Do they enjoy using analogies to describe their body, like "soft, moist flower petals"? What other parts of the body do they love to talk about?

Do they prefer that you gently ask permission to engage in certain acts, or do they get more turned on when you tell them more assertively what you are going to do?

How about you? What kind of bedroom talk or non-talk gets you really hot?

Alongside words, there are many non-verbal ways to communicate in the bedroom. Your partner's other vocalizations, including their moans and groans, can let you know what they do and don't like. Paying attention to breathing, including gasps and panting, can be helpful. If you also allow yourself the freedom to express yourself in these ways, you can let your partner know when they are doing something you really like so that they can continue.

Pay attention to the nuances of how your partner's body, both their genitals and their body outside of that, respond as they are becoming more and less aroused. For example, how and when does the inside of their vagina swell up? Does their clitoris protrude more? Does the head of their penis swell a bit more? Does their scrotum pull up toward the body? Do they get little goosebumps on their legs or other parts of their body? Do they arch their back? Do they pull you toward them? What do they tend to prefer when these things happen? These are just a few examples.

Practice emotional honesty

If you are feeling negative emotions about something, particularly toward your partner, it can affect your ability to experience arousal and enjoy sex. This is true for both women and men. Poet and activist James Broughton wrote that the penis is the exposed tip of the heart. If you have any major issues to work out with your partner, you may need to address them before you can launch into bliss between the sheets.

If you currently struggle with communicating emotions effectively, explore the Nonviolent Communication (NVC) model, created by Marshall Rosenberg. Visit cnvc.org for a wealth of resources, including basic NVC concepts and lists of words for describing specific feelings and needs.

Reduce criticism & express more gratitude

When you are around someone frequently over time, it can become easy to take for granted the things they do that you appreciate and enjoy. Even when you are very grateful for your partner, you may forget to let them know, especially if "words of affirmation" isn't one of your primary Love Languages. (See the section "The Five Love Languages" for more details on this.) You may settle into a pattern of expressing your opinion of how your partner does things primarily when it *isn't* working for you. This is true not only in the bedroom but also in other aspects of the relationship.

In couples with highly incompatible sexual needs, both partners may feel cranky because neither can provide the other with what they want. This likely results in additional criticism going both ways. Once Katie became less willing to have sex regularly, I felt more irritable. I became more likely to criticize her for other things because I felt like she wasn't keeping up her end of the relationship deal. During those times, I often felt that she was overly critical of me, too. This is similar to observations that heterosexual partners often report frequent criticism from closeted gay partners.[111]

Criticism may also serve emotionally protective functions for one or both people. It can distract them from the bigger and scarier underlying sexual incompatibilities. It can also reduce the likelihood of physical intimacy. In reality, of course, such emotional defense mechanisms don't help either person. Criticism is one of the quickest ways to erode a relationship.[112]

It is also possible that in some couples, the asexual partner tolerates more undesirable behavior from the sexual partner largely out of guilt and shame. In other words, because they are unable to provide their partner with a "normal" sexual experience, they don't feel they have the right to expect as much love. It's hard to know how often this occurs, as there's presently little research on asexual-sexual couples. The behavior they endure could range from increased criticism to addiction and physical abuse.[113]

If your relationship is filled with any of the above behaviors, stop and consider how they affect you and your partner. Even if you are with a sexual partner, it will be harder for either of you to enjoy life amidst such behaviors. Determine what you have the power to shift within yourself. Consider when you would like to improve your life.

It is human nature to feel happier, more connected, and sexier after hearing authentic praise from a partner. So take note of a few things each day that you appreciate about your partner, and let them know it. You can do this verbally throughout the day, via written notes, or verbally just before bedtime. Expressing gratitude can yield broader benefits as well: Couples who have at least five positive interactions for every one negative interaction are much more likely to stay together.[114]

12. Tips for Being Fully Present & Aware

• • •

In this moment—just this moment

A big part of intimacy is being present in the moment. It's not just about *doing* things in a present and non-distracted fashion, but also about simply *being*. Unfortunately, the same amazingly complex human brains that make our lives so interesting also have a downside when it comes to this. Unlike most other animals who spend most or all of their time focused on the present moment, we have the ability— and tendency—to focus on various aspects of the past and future.

If you are thinking about what happened at work earlier today, or what you need to be doing tomorrow or even two hours from now, it's going to be hard to enjoy sex. Additionally, your partner will be able to tell that your energy and attention is somewhere else. I certainly noticed when Katie did that, and Sophia and I have sometimes caught each other doing it.

Eckhart Tolle's *The Power of Now* communicates this message in a number of ways: The only moment in which we ever live—the only time we ever have to be, do, or experience anything—is this instant. We can never do anything 5 or 10 minutes into the future, or 5 or 10 minutes into the past. There is only the never-ending, eternal present. A few years ago, inspired partially by Tolle's book, I wrote a song titled "In This Moment." It uses the example of a couple having sex to illustrate presence.

Being in the now can be challenging in today's busy world. Multitasking is encouraged, and various distractions such as electronic communication and entertainment devices require discipline to ignore. Additionally, if your partner often doesn't *want* to be in the present moment in the bedroom, you may be accustomed to patterns that make this even more difficult. You may need to practice. Should you end up with another partner who sometimes prefers to spend an hour or more having sex, you will want to be able to enjoy it.

Make a commitment to yourself to stay in the moment as much as possible during sex. If you feel too distracted to do that, it might be better to say "maybe later," or to take a few minutes to yourself to get in the moment. You might jot down any ideas or reminders to get them out of your head, take a short walk, mute your smartphone, or try some of the strategies in the following sections.[115]

Get out of your head & increase body awareness

When you are not in the present moment, it may be because your mind is busy, thinking about too many things. Those things are often outside of yourself, which makes it difficult to pay attention to yourself and your body. If you are not paying attention to your body, your partner can't do it for you. You might not even be able to notice the full extent of pleasure they are attempting to share with you.

Simply stopping to scan your body for a minute or two each day can be useful. Shortly before getting out of bed in the morning, or just before falling asleep at night, are two possible times. Start by wiggling your toes just a bit, and consider how they feel. Take a deep breath in and out, and envision oxygen flowing into your toes. Are they relaxed? Tight? Warm? Cool? Awake? Tired? Now slowly move up your body: feet, front and back of lower legs, knees, upper legs, groin, belly, and so on, up to the top of your head.

As you practice becoming more aware of your body, you will be even more open to physical sensations during activities like sex. This will not only help you to experience more pleasure, but also make it easier to communicate with your partner about what you are feeling and what you want in any given moment.

Other ways to get out of your head and into your body include physical activities like walking or dancing, focusing on breathing, or meditating. Let's talk about a few of these.

Focus on your breathing

Breathing is mentioned in so many different self-help books, and as a component of so many psychological and spiritual disciplines, that I have lost track. The bottom line is that conscious breathing is very important. It is a great tool for bringing yourself into the present moment and for keeping yourself there. But as simple as it sounds, it is easy to forget, and it takes practice.

Focusing on breathing is helpful for several reasons that relate to sex. When you become stressed, you are likely to breathe more shallowly. This deprives your brain and body of oxygen. This, in turn, can make you feel even worse. When you lose control of your emotions as well as your breath, it can create a self-perpetuating downward spiral.

Breathing deeply and rhythmically, on the other hand, gives both your body and mind more energy. You become more aware of your immediate surroundings and more receptive and sensitive to sensory stimuli. The parts of your brain responsible for higher-level cognition remain online, rather than just the more primitive parts responsible for things like the fight-or-flight stress response. You become more relaxed, which makes it easier to experience pleasure. Breathing deeply can also help you to sustain sexual energy for longer periods.

When you are in the bedroom, try just taking slow, deep breaths as you begin to interact with your partner. You might even try synchronizing your breathing for a minute or two as you look into each other's eyes. Outside of the bedroom, try setting aside a specific time each day to spend just a minute or two breathing slowly and deeply. If you can connect it with an existing habit, such as showering, waiting for your bread to toast, or watering the garden, you'll be more likely to remember to do it.

The idea is to start with very small steps to make it easy, and to gain practice over time so that you remember to do it when it's most important. You can also practice it as part of meditating.

Meditate

Meditation provides a way to practice some of the other concepts covered in this section, such as focusing on breathing and getting out of one's head. It has helped many people to reduce anxiety and stress, by giving them a bit more control over their minds and bodies. In the book *10% Happier*, news anchor Dan Harris chronicles his exploration of different self-help methods after having a panic attack on national television. Despite initial skepticism, the simple practice that made a significant difference for him was meditation.

Meditation can improve your sex life indirectly by making it easier to manage stress and potential conflict with others, including your partner. When you are less reactive and more loving, you will both be in the mood to connect more. When you are less emotionally spent, you will also have more energy for romps in the sack. Meditation can enhance your sex life directly by providing practice for getting into a more mindful and relaxed state. When you can let go of things that would otherwise distract and bother you, you will be more sexually available—for both giving and receiving. Research confirms that therapy emphasizing mindfulness—present-moment, non-judgmental awareness—improves sexual desire in women.[116]

While there are dozens of ways to meditate, they can be grouped into at least two broad categories. The first, *focused attention meditation*, involves focusing on one specific thing. This can be your breath, a mantra, a body part, or a specific visualization. The second, *open monitoring meditation*, involves recognizing whatever you happen to experience—thoughts, sounds, smells, and so on—simply accepting and allowing things to be without judgment. [117]

For example, focusing on your breathing might involve controlling it in certain ways, such as suspending it for a few seconds after your inhale or exhale, or simply paying close attention to it as you breathe naturally. This takes your mind off other things, because it is difficult to focus on more than one thing at once.

As an example of open monitoring, Buddhist teacher Pema Chödrön suggests acknowledging your thoughts with a simple, neutral phrase such as "thinking," whenever your notice your brain latching on to them.[118] Such practice provides a reminder that you can choose which thoughts to focus on. Rather than being caught up in the noise of your thoughts and feelings, you can step outside of them to observe them.

To meditate, you don't need to adopt the stereotypical posture of sitting cross-legged in the lotus position. You can sit in a comfortable chair, or even under a tree. If you are not used to meditating, don't try to start out with 30-or 60-minute sessions. Start with something like five minutes. You can even focus on your breath for just a few moments while sitting in the car at a red light, or while standing in line. One coach I worked with suggested that I begin with 10-minute meditations. When he first told me that, I thought, "Oh, that'll be so easy!" Quietly being with myself for 10 minutes ended up being more challenging than I had anticipated. However, I did experience additional peace of mind after trying it several times.

To some extent, meditation can also be incorporated into other activities, such as jogging or walking. I've found that jogging a few times per week clears my mind. Yoga often includes meditation alongside other exercises, and I've experienced benefits from attending yoga classes just once per week for a few months. Those who do it more frequently may experience even greater benefits. These activities also improve physical conditioning, which can further enhance sex.

Practice being less goal oriented with sex

As I have often discussed with life coaching clients, creating goals is helpful with many aspects of life. In the bedroom, however, too much goal focus can bust the party balloon like a porcelain piñata.

Don't get me wrong—I think orgasms are amazing. I believe we should all strive to have orgasms frequently, as long as it doesn't interfere with other aspects of living. However, with media like pornography being one of the primary ways we learn about sex, we are already programmed to focus on orgasm as the primary goal. Because the focus is often on male ejaculation, many men and women in heterosexual couples may overlook the importance of the woman's orgasm. Even if a man follows a "make sure she comes, too" philosophy, he may approach the woman's orgasm with the same intense goal focus with which he's learned to approach his own orgasm.

Regardless of your sex and orientation, these dynamics may be exacerbated with a partner who isn't enthusiastic about sex. If they have a "let's just hurry up and get it over with" attitude, you may have learned to be the same way, perhaps at the sacrifice of your pleasure. I know what it's like to have a partner who wants sex to be brief, and I know the frustration of feeling pressure to climax quickly. I also know what it's like to have a partner who enjoys longer sessions of lovemaking, and I know the pleasure of being able to relax while having sex.

When either partner feels performance pressure to have an orgasm or to make their partner have an orgasm, regardless of orientation, it can make things more difficult, and take even longer. Too much goal focus can add anxiety that decreases enjoyment for both partners. If your partner is open to it, try some of the following:

Agree upon a time at least once a week when you can have an extended lovemaking session, where you and your partner have sufficient time to enjoy yourselves. While the exact amount of time is up to you, it's important to agree upon a minimal amount of time in advance and to stick to that agreement. At least 45 minutes to an hour is probably a good start. Try to agree upon a time when neither of you will be overly tired, frazzled from stressful activities, or distracted. This might require arrangements such as a babysitter.

If your partner is up for it, practice stimulating them in pleasurable ways for a set period, between 10 and 20 minutes, without the goal of orgasm. You can then switch roles. They get to request what they want. It might include just parts of the body outside of the genitals, it might focus exclusively on the genitals, or it might include both. If they happen to orgasm, that's great, but that's not the goal. If they don't orgasm, that's great, too. Stimulation without goal focus is one of the ideas behind Orgasmic Meditation, which we'll describe briefly when we talk about masturbation.[119]

Focus on the full body & sensual touch spectrum

Earlier we covered the importance of diversifying your definition of physical intimacy, including other sensual but non-sexual activities like snuggling and massage. This is important both outside and inside the bedroom. Focusing on the body outside of the genitals can also help with reducing goal focus. This is one of the reasons that sensate focus, discussed in detail under "Possible things to expect in therapy," often helps couples experiencing sexual difficulties. The non-genital touch doesn't have to be totally platonic. It can also be quite sexy, and it can occur alongside genital touch.

We all have erogenous zones, or points on our bodies where touch is particularly arousing. Ask your partner where their erogenous zones are, and how they like to be touched there. Tell them where yours are, and don't be afraid to ask them to touch you there sometimes. Get specific about how to do it as well—for example, "I love it when you lightly drag your nails across the insides of my thighs, starting from just a few inches on either side of my yoni, and going down to my knees." Illustrate it to your partner by doing it yourself if needed. You could even add more specifics, like, "I especially love it when you sometimes do this while you are licking my clitoris and labia."

If you and your partner have difficulty coming up with ways you like to be touched, invite them to engage in exploration with you. Even if they experience such touch as enjoyable but not sexually arousing, it can provide an additional way for you to share pleasure.

Take time to turn a woman on

Each person experiences desire differently, and requires different things to turn them on, even when they experience sexual attraction and enjoy sex. Some people often experience desire relatively spontaneously, almost out of the blue. Others have more "responsive desire"—they may not realize they want sex until certain contextual factors are present to set the mood, or they're engaged in activities leading toward sex. This might include, for example, a candlelight dinner, a sexy text, or even snuggling on the couch. Women, on average, are more likely to require some contextual factors to trigger desire.[120] Because you probably won't often have time or energy to set an elaborate stage, get to know simple things that can help you and your partner get in the mood. And if you're the one who needs more context, you don't always need to rely on your partner to get the ball rolling—you might light a few candles yourself, or put on some sexy music.

You can't just insert a dildo, penis, or fingers into your partner's vagina prior to some warm-up and necessarily expect it to feel good. While this is particularly important for men in heterosexual relationships to know, it's also something that many women aren't taught. It goes hand-in-hand with several other good sex practices: not being overly goal-oriented, focusing on the full body, and letting go of the myth that sexual activities need to be equally enjoyable for both partners at all times.

I attended a wonderfully informative and entertaining presentation by Paul Joannides, author of *The Guide to Getting it On*. He showed photos of the outer labia of women who were fully aroused alongside photos of the outer labia of women who weren't fully aroused. The labia of the fully aroused women were visibly more swollen and lubricated, and they protruded outward. For the woman, this often accompanies greater exposure of the tip of the clitoris, which makes stimulation even easier. Alongside any store-bought lubricants, the greater natural lubrication means greater comfort during penetration. For her partner, it means a more energized, juicier vagina during penetration, whether with a penis, fingers, dildo, or other toys.

While I've heard some women claim that they can orgasm within a minute or two after stimulation begins, this is not true for most women. Women's sexuality expert Betty Dodson explains that on average, "a woman's erection needs 20-30 minutes of adequate clitoral stimulation" for her to become fully aroused. This, by the way, doesn't just include the outer exposed tip of the clitoris; it includes the whole clitoral body, which can also be stimulated indirectly via the G-spot and "deep spot" inside the vagina.[121]

Each woman differs in terms of how much stimulation of other areas she prefers before her clitoris or G-spot is stimulated directly, whether and how she likes to be penetrated while her clitoris and the surrounding areas are stimulated, what type of pressure and speed she likes, and so on. These preferences will also vary each time. So communication is always needed, especially as you are getting to know each other's bodies.

Ian Kerner's *She Comes First* provides detailed, creative ideas for approaching cunnilingus in an even more enjoyable way. (*Passionista* is his follow-up guide to great fellatio.) Good sex isn't just about technical skills; it's also about attitude, presence, and taking the time to help your partner feel desirable and at ease.[122]

Learn about Tantra

Tantra is a set of ancient spiritual lifestyle practices and concepts connected to traditions including Hinduism and Buddhism. While sacred sexuality is only a piece of the entire philosophy, some of its elements can enhance the depth and quality of connection between lovers. A few elements that connect to sexuality:

➤ The use of breath to increase energy, awareness, and sensation. This includes breathing that at times may be shallow and fast, and at other times slow and deep.

➤ The use of vocalization to heighten energy and sensation in both partners. This can include, for example, deep, guttural moans.

➤ Slower builds to orgasm, to prolong the experience, heighten energy, and increase the frequency of multiple orgasms. Through practice, some males develop the ability to have multiple "energy orgasms" without ejaculation at all.[123] Other elements of Tantra can still be beneficial regardless of whether one chooses to incorporate this practice.

➤ Connection through extended eye gazing. This may be done while engaging in non-sexual or sexual touch, and looking into each other's eyes during moments such as orgasm can make the experience even more powerful.[124]

➤ A belief that the "earthly" and "divine" elements of humanness cannot be separated—they are all part of a cohesive whole. Aspects of your being such as sexuality have both physical and spiritual components. The body itself is seen as part of the spiritual experience, rather than as something you should strive to transcend completely. Honoring your earthly desires does not need to be at odds with spiritual development. Pursuing pleasure can be a path to increasing awareness and enlightenment.

➤ Belief in a system of seven chakras, or energy centers in your body, each corresponding to a different aspect of being. As you increase your awareness of each, and learn to activate them through various means, you increase your level of spiritual development and fulfillment. The second or sacral chakra, for example, is tied to sexuality, abundance, and creativity. I've noticed that when I don't feel sexually fulfilled, I'm sometimes more likely to focus upon scarcity in general, and my creativity may wane. The fifth or throat chakra is tied to communication—if you are holding back on your verbal expressiveness, it will get in the way of your overall fulfillment. You may be unable to express your wants and needs constructively, and that will affect other areas of your life. I believe that regardless of how literally you take such metaphysical models, they can serve as useful guiding analogies.

These concepts are taken out of a much larger context, so I recommend further reading if you are truly interested. A number of authors have written books to make Tantra more accessible to westerners. I have listed several under "Additional Resources," alongside at least one work on Taoist approaches, which have some similarities.

13. Revisit Porn & Masturbation

• • •

From partnered sex replacement to complement

As Katie became clearer that she had little interest in sex, I came to rely upon porn and masturbation for the majority of my sexual needs. Then, in my new relationship with a woman who wanted sex, I became a bit overzealous in trying to ensure I was available any time the opportunity for sex arose. At the very same time, I had difficulty voicing my desires with enthusiasm when I had them, for fear I would be rejected. This created tension and required adjustments. It took me a while to get to a place where masturbation, and occasionally porn or erotica, complemented my partnered sex life rather than largely replacing it.

If you have had a partner who is not enthusiastic about sex, you might rely upon porn and masturbation more than the average person does. Many people report having stronger orgasms during masturbation than during partnered sex, so you even may have come to prefer solo sex if your partner hasn't been that enthusiastic. There has been a great deal in the media about the easy availability of internet porn, widespread porn addiction, and various hypotheses regarding how it may impact sex lives. How concerned should you be if you frequently masturbate to porn? If so, what can you do about it, whatever your partner's level of interest in sex?

Masturbation: Positives & Precautions

As for masturbation just by itself, there doesn't presently seem to be any hard evidence that it harms one's sexual performance. In fact, it may be beneficial in moderation. A few studies have linked frequent ejaculations for men with lower occurrences of prostate cancer.[125] Some sexual health professionals advocate a "use it or lose it approach," maintaining that frequent use of the sexual organs keeps them functioning better.[126]

What constitutes "frequent" varies by person, but I'll share a bit about myself: During periods when I have an orgasm at least once every other day, whether solo or with my partner, I also tend to crave more orgasms and have an easier time becoming aroused. My orgasms also seem to be more powerful. So, if I haven't had an orgasm in a day or two, and I have a bit of extra time, I'll sometimes engage in solo or partnered sex just to keep things functioning optimally, even if I'm initially not craving it that much.

Many experts also advocate frequent orgasms for women, including via self-stimulation and via stimulation by a partner, for emotional and physical health benefits.[127] Such experts believe that masturbation can help you to get to know your body better, by experimenting with different approaches to see what feels best to you. Only when you understand what feels good will you be able to communicate to a partner what you want. When you can communicate your preferences to others, partnered sex will also feel better.

Betty Dodson has hosted masturbation parties and workshops that allow women to become more familiar with their body and how it responds to stimuli. Nicole Daedone encourages Orgasmic Meditation, or OMing. In this practice, each woman works with a trained partner who strokes her clitoris for an extended period. Other forms of sex are not allowed during the OMing sessions. To reduce performance anxiety, orgasm is not viewed as a goal.[128]

There's no hard evidence that frequent use of intensely stimulating toys can threaten a person's ability to enjoy partnered sex—for example, women becoming "addicted" to vibrators and being unable to have partnered orgasms.[129]

There are exceptions to the above. If you masturbate so frequently that your recent orgasms reduce sexual desire and make it harder for you to become fully aroused, that could interfere with intimacy. If you happen to masturbate so often that it interferes with daily functioning, causes risk-taking behavior, creates pain, or makes you feel out of control, consider seeking the support of a therapist.[130]

Porn: Positives & precautions

You can relate to porn in many ways, and it exists in a variety of forms. You might sometimes use it on your own. You might sometimes watch it with your partner as an accompaniment to your sex life with them. Or, you might watch it almost every time you wish to experience sexual pleasure.

Much porn provides stimuli that are very different from real-life partners and scenarios. The actors often have "perfect" body proportions that few everyday people have, and they are often engaging in extreme acts that the average person may have neither the desire nor the stamina to try. Females may have unrealistically dramatic orgasms, and the goal of male ejaculation—the "money shot"—is often treated with utmost importance. While dominance and submission energy can be fun and playful, porn often excludes the softer emotional and relational connection that many people prefer to have alongside it in real life. Furthermore, porn provides incredibly easy access to novelty, with a range of virtual sex partners and scenes just a click away.[131]

For such reasons, some believe that if masturbating to porn makes up a significant part of your sex life, your brain and body may become trained to respond only to very specific visual and touch stimuli—that is, certain types of porn and a computer mouse. If you become habituated to this level of intensity and novelty, much as one develops a tolerance to alcohol or other substances, you may find it harder to become aroused by real-life partners.[132]

This all being said, the jury still appears to be out on the impacts of pornography. A few websites include testimonials from various individuals who explain that their sex lives have improved because of giving up masturbating to pornography.[133] One study found a relationship between greater porn use and less gray matter in one part of the brain, but it left open the question of whether watching porn causes brain changes or whether people born with certain brain types watch more porn.[134]

A recent review of studies suggests that many of the commonly cited pornography impact studies are flawed. The impacts of porn use are often not teased out from the impacts of internet use and sitting at the computer in general. Also, while there appear to be more reports of erectile dysfunction among younger men, it's difficult to know whether this actually represents an increase in the actual prevalence or simply a greater awareness and likelihood of reporting dysfunction. The role of factors such as age of first access are not yet fully understood—for example, if you started using online porn at age 10, you may or may not be at greater risk than someone who started using it at age 16.[135]

I can't say I've noticed any lasting impacts personally, having drastically reduced my use of porn after developing a relationship with a sexual partner. However, I believe it might have decreased my satisfaction while I was with an asexual partner, as the drama and novelty of porn likely made my sex life feel even less exciting in comparison.

Strategies for relating to masturbation & porn

Even if the jury still appears to be out on some aspects of masturbation and porn, what steps you can take if you believe they have affected your ability to enjoy partnered sex?

If you suspect that you suffer from an addiction—for example, your porn use or masturbation is so excessive that it's getting in your way of everyday functioning, you feel the need to masturbate to porn so frequently that it makes you unhappy, or you don't feel like you have any control over when you do it—then consider seeing a therapist. If you feel you have reasonable control, and you have mild or moderate concerns, you might find some of the following suggestions helpful.

As for masturbation, one key is to avoid masturbating shortly before having sex, especially if you are male. Depending on how long it takes you to become aroused again after ejaculating, this could range from only a few minutes to a few days. If you are concerned that you might be masturbating in a way that is desensitizing you to a partner, try varying your techniques. This could mean using a less intense vibrator or holding your penis less tightly.

As for porn, you might try lessening or stopping use if you feel it is causing you difficulties. As noted above, many people have had success with this; check some of the resources referenced in the endnotes. Another option is pornography that attempts to lessen the negative elements mentioned earlier. Some innovative people are creating pornography that treats the actors fairly, shows acts that would give both women and men pleasure in real life, and portrays a relatively gentle, loving, consensual relationship between them. It may be marketed under labels such as *ethical pornography* or *feminist pornography*.[136]

With both porn and masturbation, also consider how openly you communicate with your partner about these topics. I'm not suggesting that you share every detail or instance, but that you consider letting them know that you sometimes masturbate and use porn if that is the case. Do they have any questions or concerns about it? If you feel the need to hide your habits from your partner completely, your relationship might need some work in other areas.

You may also find it useful to discuss personal boundary preferences around self-pleasuring with your partner. Sometimes masturbating in the bed next to them, particularly if they are not in the mood for sex, might seem okay with you. However, could it come across to them as being passive aggressive? It might seem like you are trying to communicate, "Okay, since you are not going to help me out, which is what I really want, I'll just have to do it myself." This may not be the case at all, but assumptions often occur in the absence of clear communication. Also, do you have any questions or concerns about your partner self-stimulating without your involvement? Talking openly won't necessarily be comfortable at first, but it may help you to be more compassionate and understanding of one another.

When communicating with your partner about masturbation, dynamics around the balance between autonomy and intimacy may come into play. For example, each of you may have different preferences around how often you simply want an orgasm or physical release, versus how often you want physical and emotional intimacy with your partner.

In relating to a low-interest partner, you may have swung the pendulum too far in the direction of autonomy—that is, you may have developed a habit of doing your own thing nearly all the time. Perhaps you have even grown to prefer it somewhat, as it may have seemed like the best option available. You probably don't want to stay at that end of the spectrum, though; otherwise, you wouldn't be reading this book. Even when your partner isn't willing and available when you are horny, you may want to "save yourself" for when they are, at least some of the time.

Discuss at least some of your preferences around this with your partner, especially if you live together. This will help to minimize behaviors driven by unspoken expectations. If you desire a more physically intimate relationship, it may require some level of compromise, regardless of your partner's level of interest in sex. Even in couples with two sexually motivated partners, the timing of desire won't always align.

I have found a few different approaches helpful with Sophia, whose sex drive is currently pretty similar to mine. If I'm horny, would prefer to have an orgasm sometime within the next few hours, and know there's a chance she and I could both be available within that time frame, I'll often give her "first dibs." In other words, I'll let her know I'd love to have some sexy time with her within the next few hours, and if not, that's okay—I'll self-pleasure, and then hopefully connect with her at the next point in the near future when we're both available and willing.

If she asks if I'm willing to wait longer, I'll consider several things: whether I'll likely have energy and space to enjoy sex by the time she is available, whether it has been several days since we last connected, and whether having sex on my mind could feel distracting given my agenda for the day. If I'm simply in the mood for an orgasm or physical release, if we've very recently had sex, or if I know that one or both of us has a busy or stressful day ahead, I may simply choose to self-pleasure.

We've also worked on becoming more comfortable masturbating in front of each other. I still have difficulty with this sometimes, probably due to the societal shame factor around masturbation, but it has been worth the effort. The sense that it's slightly "taboo" also makes it more exciting because it feels like we're even more vulnerable to each other.

Masturbating in front of a partner who enjoys watching you may also be helpful if your previous partner accommodated sex but minimized how much you looked at each other. Perhaps they always wanted the lights out or rarely looked at you during sex. If you shared this preference, that's fine. But if you didn't share this preference, you might have internalized an attitude that you are not attractive during sex. Allowing yourself to see and be seen with a mutually appreciative partner may add some additional juice to your connection.

If one of us is very horny, but the other one is very tired, one will offer to hold the other one while they masturbate. Or if the tired person has enough energy, they might help—moving one's hand can take less energy than moving one's entire body or giving oral sex.

Sometimes if Sophia wants some orgasms and it is late at night, we've very recently had sex, or I've had a busy day, she'll tell me that she's planning to start masturbating. She usually adds that I'm welcome to watch or participate if I wish, but that it's not expected. I occasionally do that with her as well. This can be a fun way to initiate when you're horny but don't have a strong preference regarding whether your partner is involved, and when you want your partner to feel included without feeling pressured.

14. Enlist Creativity & Variety

• • •

Do sexy creative work

If you have any creative hobbies, consider trying them with a sexy edge. This will help to integrate your sexuality with other creative parts of your brain, and may help you to become even more expressive and energized in the bedroom. If you have a favorite hobby you haven't enjoyed in a while, all the better!

For example, as I was beginning to reclaim the sexual energy I had partially repressed, I wrote a small cookbook combining one of my favorite foods, chocolate, with a bit of sexiness. I also wrote a few sexy songs that I shared online. One song, mentioned earlier, expressed the importance of being present in the moment. Another accompanied a blog article about body image and sexuality. I submitted two poems for a collection of works blending sexuality and ecological sustainability, and I wrote a few short pieces of erotica. I found it very energizing to create these works, as I was validating an important part of myself.

If you enjoy baking, you might make some desserts with a sexually suggestive edge and host a dessert party with friends who would appreciate them. I recently met a woman whose hobby is baking sexy birthday cakes, sometimes in the shapes of breasts, penises, or vulvae. If you enjoy photography or video, there are obviously many possibilities for getting in touch with your sexy side.

It is up to you whether you share your work publicly, publish it anonymously, share with just a few close friends, or keep it all to yourself. It also doesn't have to be explicitly sexy—while you might want to stretch your boundaries a *little* bit, start with something that feels natural, safe, and relatively comfortable for you. You can gradually expand your comfort zone over time if you wish. The important part is that you have fun and practice expressing yourself. Once you get in touch with the activities you enjoy, you will likely find an abundance of possibilities.

You might also try to find a workshop that blends sexiness with creativity. I had a great time participating in a workshop facilitated by a friend who creates theatrical performances about sexuality, often with a humorous and playful edge. I enjoyed activities like creating humorous sexual scenarios (fully clothed) with others, often in an improvisational fashion.[137]

Try sexy dancing

Moving in an erotic way outside of the bedroom is another way to get more in touch with your body, and to get the energies flowing more openly. It exercises many of the same muscles that you use in the bedroom. Whether you choose to do it at home alone or with others, dance can allow you to experiment moving your body with less pressure than you might experience when you are fully naked in front of someone.

While Katie enjoyed dancing, she was often embarrassed when I danced with her in a sexy way. So when I later found myself around other people who were dancing in a sexy way, and I was able to do the same, I was very excited.

One problem is that you may simply wish to express yourself in a setting where there's little chance of being "hit on." Many bars and dance clubs can feel like meat markets, especially for heterosexual women. Fortunately, there are alternatives in some locations. Some dance instructors offer pole dancing classes geared toward women who have no intention of performing in a nightclub, but who simply want to feel sexier, get some exercise, and have fun with other women in a safe setting. An increasing number of cities and towns offer weekly ecstatic dance events, where participants dance very expressively.

People sometimes get sexy, but it's in an environment where dancers are usually sober and conscious connection is emphasized.

Play along entire spectra of sexual polarities

Sexual interaction and play are often dances of polarities—masculine and feminine, dominance and submission, mystery and familiarity, separation and closeness, roughness and gentleness, and giving and receiving.[138] It doesn't matter what your and your partner's physical sex and orientations happen to be. Your activities inside and outside the bedroom don't need to be limited by society's definitions of what's "normal" for someone of your physical sex, sexual orientation, or gender identity.

Femininity and masculinity are not mutually exclusive. Expressing more of one does not equate to less of the other. Additionally, "masculine" traits and styles of expression do not necessarily equate to to strength, and "feminine" traits and styles of expression do not equate to weakness. Nurturing, as just one example, is a very powerful act that sometimes requires considerable strength. Being able to embody the full spectrum can make a person seem both stronger *and* more attractive.[139]

Rather than thinking of themselves as fluid along a continuum with feminine at one end and masculine at the other, some people find it more helpful to disregard labels like *feminine, masculine, female*, and *male* altogether. Sex and relationship therapist Chris Donaghue suggests the following:

> "We should strive to have no identity, gender, or sexual orientation because a coherent identity is impossible . . . Labels around sex and identity are limiting and do not allow for the flexibility that sexual health and relational sustainability require."[140]

Even if you have no desire to overlook such labels altogether—I don't know if I'll ever get there myself—there are benefits to allowing yourself and others flexibility in sex and gender expression. You likely have certain ways you show up in your everyday life, out of habit.

These ways of interacting are currently the most comfortable for you. You may act in very similar ways in the bedroom. If that is the case, consider acting differently in the bedroom, to create some variety in your day-to-day life.

What happens when you switch things up a bit, even for a few moments here and there, as a fun experiment? For example:

➢ If you usually have a style of sweet, gentle lovemaking, what if you occasionally got just a bit rougher with your partner?

➢ If you usually have a style of just thrusting straight in and out of your partner, what if you occasionally allowed your entire body to writhe in a dancing, snakelike fashion while fucking?

➢ If you are usually quiet while pleasuring your partner to orgasm, what if you moaned, groaned, and breathed in a way that accompanied their sounds?

➢ If you usually don't use many "feeling" words, what if you occasionally described to your partner in detail what you are feeling as you are having sex?

Becoming more gender fluid in your expression will likely require practice and conscious attention to your thinking. Give your partner a heads-up that you would like to experiment with your expression. Ask if they support that, and ask if they'd like to join you. As you try out what feels good to you, your partner may embrace certain shifts and struggle with others. The more openly and honestly you can talk about it, the better.

Other ways to bring in creativity & variety

Here are a few additional ideas for bringing creativity into your sex life with your partner:

➢ Change the setting. If you normally do it in the bedroom, try it on the couch, on the floor (with sufficient padding), or in the woods.

➢ Incorporate sensual foods into your foreplay. Think strawberries, chocolate, maple syrup, or agave syrup. Playing with different temperatures, by chilling items or warming them, can also be fun.

➢ Read erotica to each other. Better yet, write some erotica to read to each other.

➢ Try role-playing. Talk in advance to make sure both of you are on board. Always have an agreed-upon "safe word" that either of you can say if you become uncomfortable with the role-playing and want it to stop immediately.

➢ If you usually have sex at a certain time of day, try having it at a different time.

➢ In cases where you have difficulty meeting some of each other's desires, consider whether a toy could help. For example, maybe you are male, and so the idea of wearing a strap-on dildo initially sounds ridiculous. However, maybe your partner sometimes likes to be penetrated with an aggressive style or angle that you worry could injure your penis. Strap-on to the rescue!

15. Care for & Explore the Body

• • •

Regularly engage in movement

This one might seem obvious, but because sex is a physical activity, you are more likely to enjoy it if you have a reasonable degree of physical fitness.

Your partner's lack of sexual interest in you may or may not have affected your motivation to stay in physical shape. You may have stopped caring about physical fitness partially because your partner doesn't seem to care how you look. You may already prioritize physical fitness for reasons beyond your partner. You may have increased your fitness efforts in a vain attempt to be more attractive to your partner, or to others who seem to show more interest.

Whatever the case, physical fitness can enhance your ability to enjoy sex. It doesn't need to be about having a specific body type. Our culture often idealizes body types that are incredibly difficult—sometimes even impossible—to obtain and maintain without measures such as plastic surgery. It is largely about having the energy and physical capabilities to enjoy the sexual activities you want to engage in. Improved blood circulation, increased stamina, and lower stress levels are just a few fitness-related factors that can improve sex.

You don't have to go to a gym or run several miles to incorporate movement into your daily and weekly routines unless you enjoy those activities. Consider the following possibilities:

➢ using the stairs instead of an elevator if you are only going up or down a few levels

➢ taking a short walk during lunch

➢ purposely parking a bit farther from the store when you go shopping, so you walk a bit more

➢ walking rather than sitting down while chatting with a friend on the phone

➢ riding a bicycle instead of taking a car when possible

➢ taking a fitness class you enjoy

➢ participating in a recreational sport you enjoy—it doesn't need to be competitive

To be safe, always consult with a medical or fitness professional before changing your physical activity levels significantly.

Eat well

There is a broad range of dietary approaches, and each body is different. While my experience and research have led me to a mostly plant-based diet with lots of fruits and vegetables, I leave it to you to consult with a nutrition expert to determine what works best for you. I include here just a few general food-related concepts pertinent to sex, to get you started.

First, when you become aroused, your sexual organs depend on a healthy heart and circulatory system to function at full capacity. So your diet needs to support that. If your arteries become filled with plaque and constricted due to a poor diet, it will reduce blood flow to your sex organs. This can contribute to conditions such as erectile dysfunction. On the other hand, a healthier circulatory system can result in firmer and longer-lasting erections, increased blood flow to the vaginal area, and so on.

Second, how you eat affects the health of your gut. The health of your gut, in turn, affects your ability to absorb nutrients from your food, and to create chemicals vital to physical and mental health. As just one example, the bacteria in your gut—known as the microbiome—apparently manufacture more than 90% of your body's supply of the neurotransmitter serotonin. This chemical plays a key role in mood regulation.[141] While there is still much research to be done in this area, we know that moods can impact sexual behavior. If you are anxious or in a bad mood, sex probably won't be as enjoyable for you.[142]

Alongside eating healthy, also eat sensually. Occasionally practice how you eat. For example, take time to focus on the textures of your food, chewing slowly and savoring the flavors. If you have learned to rush through activities such as sex with your asexual partner, this may have carried over into other areas of your life. Slowing down activities such as eating may expand to the bedroom, reminding you that it is okay to have slow, pleasurable sex.

Eating sensually also means including foods that may be natural aphrodisiacs. Such foods may have sexy textures, physiologically arousing qualities, or richness in vitamins and minerals important to sexual functioning. Plenty of resources exist on herbal aphrodisiacs; just be sure to read up on any potential side effects as well as benefits.

Learn the anatomy of pleasure

If you had sex education in school, it probably covered basic anatomy as it pertains to procreation. However, it may have neglected specifics about which parts of the sex organs tend to provide the most pleasure, different ways of stimulating them, how men and women differ on average with regard to arousal, and so on.

It is important to know about your partner's body so that you can navigate and appreciate it with more confidence. It is important to know about your body so that you are better able to describe to your partner what you want. The more you know, the more you will also be able to suggest and experiment with new techniques that may be pleasurable for both of you.

Did you know, for example, that the clitoris extends well beyond the exposed tip and can also be stimulated indirectly through points inside the vagina? That the perineum (taint) and anus are rich with nerve endings that can provide pleasure? That the prostate can be stimulated from either the perineum or the anus, increasing the intensity of pleasure for some men? That nipple play can increase arousal and pleasure for many women and for some men? Do you know how to flex your PC muscle? (If you don't know this one, you soon will.)

Learning about anatomy through books and websites is only the first step. As discussed under "Revisit Porn & Masturbation," hands-on solo and partnered practice is also important.

Practice for Pubococcygeal Power

Can you say "pubococcygeus muscle" three times quickly? This hammock-like muscle extends from the pubic bone to the tailbone in both sexes and supports the pelvic organs. To identify your PC muscle, attempt to stop urinating midstream—the muscle you are contracting is the PC muscle. The same contraction should cause a tightening in both your urethra and anus. For this last reason, you can also identify the PC muscle by imagining you are trying to keep from passing gas.

Voluntary contractions of this muscle, which should be done while not urinating, are often called Kegel exercises, or pumping the perineum. This activity is sometimes recommended to help prevent incontinence after events such as childbirth and prostate surgery, to strengthen the intensity of orgasms, to strengthen erections, to increase control over the tightness of the vagina, or to delay ejaculation when desired. In Tantric practices, pumping the perineum is suggested as a way to spread sexual energy throughout the body.

Experts vary on how much they recommend exercising the PC muscle, but for individuals with any of the above conditions, a few medical sites recommend a starting point of three sets of 10 contractions per day.[143] So healthier individuals can probably get away with fewer, with even a few sets per week helping a bit. The three sets should be spaced apart throughout the day, and each contraction can be held for anywhere between three and five seconds to begin with. Don't squeeze so hard that it hurts and don't overdo things by attempting to do more in the beginning. For women, some recommend inserting a spherical or oval object into the vagina to assist with the exercises. Jade eggs and ben wa balls are advertised for this purpose. Using items not intended for this purpose may carry additional risks.[144]

If at all in doubt, or if you have any of the above conditions, it's best to seek the advice of a qualified medical or health professional. Some people have PC muscles that are too tight, and doing too many Kegels can throw things further out of balance. For this reason, some experts recommend doing "reverse Kegels" or "pelvic floor drops" alongside or in lieu of regular Kegels. This exercise involves relaxing the same muscles in the way you would relax them right before going to the bathroom.[145]

16. Make Time for Connection

• • •

Prioritize bedtime & wake-up rituals

For many of us, few things are as important as getting a good night's sleep. Lack of rest can profoundly affect our functioning in many areas of life. Relationship satisfaction is much easier to maintain when both partners are well rested.

Bedtime and wake-up time also offer physical intimacy opportunities for many couples. This includes not only sex, but also other important regular bonding rituals such as conversation, snuggling, and prolonged eye contact.[146] Sexual mismatches can create tension that disrupts these important times of day, which affects a couple's ability to maintain secure attachment. Sexual mismatches might even provide unconscious motivations for creating conflict at these times:

➤ If one partner fears sexual intimacy—or another type of intimacy, for that matter—creating conflict is one way to prevent it.

➤ If either partner is feeling neglected in some way, they might provoke conflict in an attempt to get attention where other strategies have failed. (In some cases, negative attention can feel better than no attention.)

As mentioned earlier, Katie and I had altercations whenever our cat attacked my legs in the middle of the night, startling me awake. I wanted to place Fuzzles outside the bedroom at night.[147] Anticipating the next painful pounce, I often had difficulty falling asleep. Katie countered that making him sleep on his own would be unkind. I became increasingly upset that my partner seemed to place Fuzzles' sleep preferences above my need to get a good night's sleep.

After a few years of having these disagreements a few times each month, I took action. I trained Fuzzles to sleep outside the bedroom while Katie was gone for a week.

We later realized that our sexual differences may have fueled our debate, at least in part. When Fuzzles slept with us, I rarely attempted to initiate sex for fear that he would pounce. And any time that we had an argument, I lost most of my desire for intimacy with Katie, including sex. So it's possible that our ongoing disagreement had a benefit for Katie, even though she didn't consciously realize this at the time. Our disagreement may have had a benefit for me, too, giving me an excuse to express anger and frustration about other things, including our differences. Of course, crankily shouting at 2 am would never make any partner want to be more intimate with me, and it would never directly address the deeper disconnection I was experiencing.

Pet-related arguments are just one example. Bedtime and wake-up time, rather than being points of relaxation and connection, can become times of stress-inducing conversation around planning and to-do lists. (This can occur with sexually well-matched couples as well.)

If any of the dynamics above remind you of your relationship, take conscious action to avoid carrying the same patterns forward. Consider creating new behaviors that encourage intimate connection at bedtime and wake-up time. Set aside time earlier in the evening for discussing any stressful or administrative topics so they don't bleed into bedtime. Incorporate simple but meaningful rituals into your bedtime or wake-up routines, even if just a few times per week. Look into each other's eyes for five minutes, with each person giving the other several statements of appreciation. Light a candle or two after turning out the lights, creating a more romantic and relaxing atmosphere while signaling that you are not quite ready for sleep. Start small and simple, and use your imagination.

If you have been fighting about an issue over an extended period, there may be deeper underlying causes. Consider seeing a therapist.

Be ready to look at issues beneath the surface so you can let go, forgive, and focus on other things.

Prioritize date time

Sexual differences can impact how often you spend quality time alone with a partner. If you don't honor your needs for such time, by having regular date nights or otherwise, it can have unexpected consequences.

One weekend, my parents were visiting from out of town and offered to watch Charlie so that Katie and I could go out on a date. I eagerly accepted because we hadn't been out on a date together without child in tow for several months.

Before we even talked about where we might ago, Katie asked if we could use part of the time to visit Tom, a sick friend in the hospital. Tom suffered from a lifelong illness requiring frequent hospital stays. Because Katie and I had so little time alone, I felt torn and became defensive. I suggested that perhaps she could visit him on the way home from work sometime that week, as she had done during several of his prior hospital stays. Perhaps I would do the same. Following a brief argument, she hesitantly agreed to a "just the two of us" date.

We ended up not enjoying the date very much following our argument. To make matters worse, this turned out to be Tom's last hospital stay. He became incoherent and died before we had a chance to visit. We were both deeply upset. Katie was angry with me, and I felt incredibly guilty. My decision had kept us from paying our friend a final goodbye visit. It was a tough situation for both Katie and me.

After we later revisited some of this in the context of our asexual-sexual differences, the conflict made more sense. I felt it unfair that I usually had to play the role of safeguarding our alone time. If such time had not been so rare, I probably would have agreed to the visit. At the same time, Katie was being a very loving and giving person, just in a platonic way that didn't prioritize sexual partnership. For her, going out to dinner with an infant or spending date time visiting a friend wasn't competing with our intimacy. It *was* intimate—just not in the way that I sometimes needed.

Remember that everyone varies in their intimacy needs. Also, a lack of sexual attraction or libido doesn't always equate to a lack of desire for alone time or romance. We all differ in our preferred love languages and styles of intimacy, as described under "Enhance Connection Beyond Physical Intimacy." You'll need to communicate with your partner to determine what works for both of you.

Avoid the "task teeter-totter"

As I got to know Sophia, I observed within myself a residual thinking and behavior pattern that I had developed over some years. She and I had arranged to get together for "juicy time," and she was running 10 or 15 minutes late. Even though on a conscious level I knew she wasn't avoiding me, I still felt frustrated, knowing that our time was already limited due to a commitment later that morning.

However, I didn't want to waste time, either. So I decided to take my daily shower, even though Sophia was often perfectly fine with me waiting until after sex to shower. We had often told each other how we appreciated the other's natural body scent. Just after I jumped in the shower, Sophia returned. Upon seeing that I would be occupied for a few minutes, she decided to eat and do laundry. After I got out of the shower and saw that she would be busy for another 10 minutes or so, I then decided to gather my laundry as well.

By the time we finally climbed into bed together, I felt frustrated. I recalled a pattern that I had developed in my previous relationship. Often when we had prearranged time for physical intimacy, Katie would become engrossed in another task, take longer than anticipated to complete a prior commitment, or something similar. I would then sulk about not feeling desired, and busy myself with other things. Sometimes by the time we finally got together, I would be too tired and frustrated to enjoy intimacy. So here I was, now with a partner who clearly desired me, repeating the same pattern.

As Sophia and I brainstormed ways to avoid this back-and-forth pattern in the future, she noted that it felt like a "task teeter-totter." This analogy seemed to fit well. On a teeter-totter or seesaw, two people don't stay at the same level—whenever one goes up, the other goes down, and vice versa. Furthermore, if one person suddenly gets off the teeter-totter, the other drops to the ground and is left in the dirt. Both people are left unsatisfied.

Simple awareness is one way to avoid the task teeter-totter. If you have experienced such patterns in the past, just knowing that can help you to avoid repeating them in the future. As with other baggage, inform your future partner(s) of this tendency. This way you'll both recognize the importance of keeping date times when possible, and of providing each other with reassurances when keeping them is not possible. Also, don't make assumptions when your partner is running late for a date. Should you find yourself becoming busy and frustrated, take a step back to ask yourself what's going on internally.

Practice foreplay throughout the day

While mutual sexual arousal can sometimes occur quite suddenly, it never hurts to have some playful anticipation. Some people become much more aroused and receptive to sex when they have some to think about it and let the tension build. This can begin outside of the bedroom, hours or even days before you connect with your partner. It doesn't need to be complex or time-consuming, and it doesn't need to be overtly sexual. Brief written notes, verbal messages, acts, or mini-gifts that express love, appreciation, and admiration are all possibilities.

Below are a few ideas to try with your partner. If your partner isn't turned on by overtly sexy talk or behavior, consider expressions of affection without the sexual overtones. The chapter "Enhance Connection Beyond Physical Intimacy" may spark additional ideas corresponding to different love languages and intimacy types.

➢ Send a brief text message in the afternoon, letting your partner know you are thinking naughty thoughts about them and are very much looking forward to seeing them that evening.

➢ Leave a brief handwritten note on your partner's nightstand, expressing gratitude for recent lovemaking. A specific detail in a sexy note or phone message can make it even juicier: "I loved the way you [fill in act]; it made me feel [fill in emotion or sensation]."

➤ Slip a small chocolate heart in with your partner's lunch, perhaps with a note.

➤ Share with your partner a comment in person, or later by phone, about some specific way they looked sexy that morning.

➤ Give your partner a playfully sexy touch that you know they enjoy, such as a little pat or squeeze on the butt.

Reduce screen time

Non-essential *screen time* includes watching movies, viewing TV shows, playing video games, and scrolling through social network feeds on your smartphone.[148] There's now even a term for snubbing someone by choosing to look at your phone instead: *phubbing*. The more time you spend with electronic devices, the less time you have for lovemaking. Also, the less time you have for other activities that promote bonding and often help to set the stage for sex. This may include sharing about your days over dinner or taking a walk together. It may include talking about "chop wood carry water" issues earlier in the day, so that you have more mental and emotional space free for intimacy later.

I'm not suggesting that you cut out your on-screen leisure time altogether, as it can be enjoyable and relaxing. If you and your partner mutually enjoy a show, it can provide time for snuggling and bonding. Humor and romance can get you in the mood for deeper connection, and some people need time to unwind before they're ready for deeper connection. However, if you find that sex isn't happening as often as you would like, consider examining your screen habits. This is particularly the case if any of the following happen frequently:

➤ one of you wants sex before bed, but the other complains that it's too late and they're too tired—and one or both of you spent at least an hour on screen earlier that evening

➤ one of you wants sex in the morning, but the other complains that they haven't yet had enough sleep and they're too tired—and one or both of you spent at least an hour on screen the preceding evening

➤ one of you wants sex, but the other replies that they'd first like to talk about a few important things—and one or both of you spent at least an hour on screen very recently

A related tip: Unless you're expecting an important call or message, turn off your phone ringer—including the vibrate function if it's audible—before lovemaking. Even if you don't check it, knowing that someone is trying to get in touch may distract you and your partner.

17. Have Realistic Sexpectations

• • •

Relax your synchronized ecstasy expectations

Through watching television, movies, pornography, and other media, many people develop some unrealistic ideals of what sex between two sexual people looks like. If you have spent significant time with a partner who rarely or never seems to enjoy sex as much as you do, you may have an idealized image of what sex with a more sexual partner looks like.

One myth you may have internalized is that both people must be experiencing equal pleasure at any given moment. No two people are going to match up on what things turn them on the most. Mutual satisfaction will usually require some give and take.

For example, Pat knows that Kelly enjoys receiving oral sex, even though giving it is not Pat's favorite thing. Kelly knows that Pat enjoys intercourse in a position that doesn't excite her. So they usually do some of both whenever they have sex. Both people are happy giving generously, knowing that they will also receive what they want.

The catch here is knowing how much you are willing and able to give enthusiastically and asking your partner to do the same. If either of you is giving in a non-enthusiastic way, it could trigger "my partner doesn't really want to do this with me" feelings that you want to put behind you.

The next time you have sex, try setting aside some time for each person to focus totally and completely upon their own pleasure, without needing to have any concern about the other—unless, of course, stimulating the other person simultaneously is a turn-on for the receiver.

I didn't fully realize the importance of having "just focused on me" time until well over a year into my relationship with Sophia. Often, I would give her oral sex to bring her to climax a few times, sometimes interspersed with her giving me some oral sex to get me more aroused. We both enjoyed giving oral sex and did so generously and enthusiastically.

Most exciting for me, though, was having face-to-face intercourse, looking into each other's eyes. We'd often intersperse some of that with the oral sex, but would have the bulk of intercourse afterward, usually continuing until I climaxed. Sometimes she would also climax additional times during intercourse, even though helping her climax wasn't my primary focus at that point.

One day, Sophia wasn't as enthusiastic about receiving oral sex, and she wanted to move into intercourse sooner after giving me oral sex. After we had done so, I noticed that she was making a greater than usual number of requests about how I was moving. Could I thrust with longer strokes? Could I change the angle a bit? Could I thrust more deeply? Not so deeply?

Rather than attempt to negotiate when Sophia asked me to shift away from something that felt good to me, I simply accommodated her requests. I ended up, after nearly 45 minutes of intercourse, being unable to climax. While I sometimes enjoyed taking a long time, this was a case where I didn't want to take that long. I was frustrated because it felt like every time I got into a rhythm with something that felt really good, she would ask me to shift.

Reflecting upon the occurrence later, I had an important realization. While I had learned to accept requests while giving oral sex, I had come to view intercourse as the time where I could focus more on my pleasure. I wasn't accustomed to negotiating how to have intercourse. In my prior relationship, Katie had rarely offered input on how to make intercourse more pleasurable for her. She would usually chime in only when something felt uncomfortable. But Sophia was now beginning to express more preferences around this part of sex.

At the same time, I felt unjustified in expressing my own needs. The face-to-face and penetrative nature of intercourse seemed to suggest that it should be equally enjoyable for both people at all times. I felt that perhaps the person being penetrated should have even more say because they were making themselves more physically vulnerable.

I knew that Sophia wasn't trying to be difficult in any way. She was simply less shy about voicing her preferences than Katie or I were, and she had no way of knowing how her requests were affecting me. I also realized that expecting both people to be experiencing equal pleasure at all times was unrealistic.

I realized that if I weren't honest about my needs, my frustration would affect Sophia as well. I decided that in future instances, I would be more open about letting her know what I needed. I would also be open to discussing alternative ways to meet her needs. This seemed to help.

Related to the above, two people's timings with arousal and climax will rarely match up exactly. Heterosexual porn often shows the woman climaxing when the male does, even when she has received little stimulation that would get the average women fully aroused. (See the section "Take time to turn a woman on.") While such timing alignment sometimes happens in real life, having an expectation that it will always happen can lead to disappointment.

However, this doesn't rule out the fun practice of using language, sounds, breathing, and facial expressions that mirror your partner's energy as it builds, and as they approach climax. The point is not to be pretending to have an orgasm, but to feel and convey a strong sense of empathy for what your partner is feeling. My experience has been that this heightens both people's arousal and sensations tremendously. When I'm tuned into my partner as she's building and climaxing, I love imagining what it is like for her. I enjoy having a "conversation" using our moans, breathing, and other vocalizations. I also love when she does that with me.

One last point on this topic: While it may be ideal for each of you to climax at least once each time you have sex, there may be occasions where schedules just don't allow enough time for both of you to do so.

However, that doesn't need to rule out sex altogether. Your schedule might allow for a few "quickies" in one day where each of you gets to have your turn. For example, you might not have a full hour in the morning or evening, but maybe you have 20-30 minutes in the morning and another 20-30 minutes in the evening. If one of you prefers to have orgasms in the morning and the other in the evening, that's a bonus.

Find your body acceptance & hygiene balance

Do you find certain parts of the body or certain body functions gross? Sex involves various holes, fluids, scents, and sounds. Some of these things could be a challenge for you to appreciate. On one hand, it is important to know and communicate your hygiene and grooming needs. Most people have a basic level of cleanliness expectations for themselves and their partner. On the other hand, you and your partner need to honor and accept your bodies to enjoy sex. It's hard to relax and experience pleasure when you are worried about the way your and your partner's bodies look, sound, and smell.

We are often raised with many "eww, gross" messages about the body as it is; and a partner who is unenthusiastic about sex may have inadvertently reinforced such messages for you. Even if they don't find your body "gross," their lack of sexual interest may have led you to wonder whether it is unattractive. This could make it difficult to determine what minimum hygiene standards you require to find sex safe and enjoyable without going overboard. While you'll need to figure out much of this for yourself, I'll share a few opinions and suggestions.

I'll begin with the best-known bodily function that can threaten intimacy: flatulence. Sometimes you will need to fart during sex. When you allow your pelvic area to relax fully, this becomes even more likely. And as you may already know, "holding it in" can make it more difficult to enjoy sex. If you ever sleep or drive together, one of two things will happen: Your partner will hear and smell your farts, or sometimes you will be very physically uncomfortable.

It is possible to allow your body to do its thing while still respecting your partner, for example, by giving your partner notice if their nose happens to be near your hiney. If you have such a strong aversion to farts that you can't stand to be in the same bed or room after someone has farted, you might need to ask yourself how much you value being around your partner naked.

Also know that men aren't the only ones who are messy during sex. Some women lubricate quite a bit when they are aroused. It is also normal for some women to ejaculate or squirt when they are excited—it doesn't happen only in porn. Research shows that some women release a combination of urine and female "prostate" fluids from their urethra. (Male ejaculate can also contain small amounts of urine.) Because wonderful sensations often accompany its release, it is something to celebrate.[149]

However, due to its association with peeing, female squirting can cause self-consciousness and anxiety about dirtiness or loss of control. You may need to talk with your partner to get to a place of mutual comfort, so you can both relax and fully enjoy yourselves. If female or male ejaculate is something you don't wish to swallow, you can simply let it run out of your mouth while your partner orgasms and you give them loving attention. If you don't like it in your mouth at all, you can use your hands and fingers to help out as your partner approaches climax. If you are performing cunnilingus, you can just move your mouth up and back slightly. Putting a towel on the bed can eliminate the need for a sheet change.[150]

If either or both of you are female, you may need to negotiate around what you're each comfortable doing during menstruation. There are many options for getting sexy; don't just assume your partner is not in the mood for anything at certain times of the month. This may be irrelevant, due to birth control, menopause, or health-related factors.

Body hair may require negotiation. Some societal expectations of women and men regarding grooming, sometimes promoted by the mainstream porn industry and other media, are unrealistic. This includes the expectation that women's bodies—and often men's—be almost entirely free of hair. In a somewhat paradoxical way, we've come to promote a prepubescent look as being sexy. Many women already expend a significant amount of time and effort shaving their legs and armpits, and men shaving their faces and necks. Frequent waxing and shaving that completely removes hair can be rough on the skin.

I'm not saying that a completely or mostly shaved genital area can't be a treat for you and your partner sometimes. I happen to find both shaved and unshaved vulvae very beautiful. Having it totally shaved all the time is not something I would request of my partner unless she enjoyed it. This is also for selfish reasons, as super-short hair can feel prickly while it is growing back. Men also need to be conscious about this when shaving around their mouths.

That being said, there are times when neatly trimmed pubic hair can be helpful. Having shorter hair helps with oral sex, as it is less likely to get caught in the teeth or to stand between tongue and skin.

Anal play is another area where body acceptance and hygiene preferences both come into play. There are several books and resources that cover how to engage in anal play in a relatively safe, pain-free, and clean fashion, with either a female or male partner. The anus itself is surrounded by a large number of sensitive nerves, and it allows for stimulation of the prostate gland and clitoral complex from different angles. Take precautions to avoid moving bacteria from parts of the body where they are beneficial to parts of the body where they may be troublesome. For example, after having a body part or toy in an anus, never put it in a vagina without thoroughly washing it first.

Some people find long nails sexy, not just for looks, but for sensations like feeling nails in one's back during sex. However, if you're using your fingers for penetration, such as stimulating your partner's g-spot during cunnilingus or their prostate during fellatio, short nails are safer. An emery board is also handy, and latex gloves alongside generous lubrication can make things even smoother if your partner is sensitive. As some people are allergic to latex, synthetic alternatives are available.

If you and your partner are open-minded and comfortable with each other, consider experimenting with your natural body odor. When neither of you has to be at work or any important social engagements for a day or two, consider skipping a day of showering. This may not work if your partner is truly asexual, but the extra accumulation of pheromones (the chemicals that many animals' bodies use to communicate with each other, sexually and otherwise) could get you and your partner even more excited around each other. While it is important to exercise good hygiene, sometimes our society can be *too* concerned with cleanliness.

Regardless of whether you are on the giving or receiving end, you don't want to push your partner into doing something they are not comfortable with. Your partner may be willing to try new things on the giving end, but may want to ease into them. They may also be self-conscious about their bodily functions when they are on the receiving end. Even if you are perfectly comfortable with their bodily functions, they may need time to become more relaxed around you. They may worry that you will find them gross. People can vary greatly around this. There may be some things they will never be willing to do. You will need to talk openly about your preferences.

Do your best to avoid reactions that send an "Ooh, gross!" message to your partner. If your partner wants something that's likely to trigger such a reaction from you, it's probably better to negotiate an activity or approach that's more comfortable to you, or to warn them in advance that you could have such a reaction if you are stretching your boundaries. Ask them to do you the same favor, especially if you already feel self-conscious about your body. At the same time, if your partner is stretching their boundaries and trying something different for the first time, try to be forgiving if they have an unanticipated reaction. Try not to view such a reaction as an indicator of how desirable they find you.

Accepting the body doesn't mean making yourself unsafe. To keep yourself safe and free of disease, exercise some restraint with people you don't know very well. For example, you might agree to certain activities only after a partner has had STI testing and has refrained from unprotected sex (or possibly any sex) with others for a given period.

As you become closer to someone, know what types of safer sex precautions and hygiene you desire so that you can fully immerse yourself in increasingly intimate acts. As just one example, if you feel uncomfortable putting your mouth and tongue all over your partner's vulva or penis until they've freshened up with a few wet wipes, and they don't already do that, don't be afraid to ask. Then get in there enthusiastically!

Your partner is likely to appreciate an honest and enthusiastic approach more than one where a lack of excitement sends the message that you're not comfortable with their body. And after they experience how much you love to connect with them, they'll probably be happy to continue accommodating any reasonable hygiene requests you happen to have.

18. Know Thyself

• • •

Learn what other factors impact your desire

Regardless of how enthusiastic your partner is about sex, it is difficult to increase your sexual satisfaction without reasonable knowledge of what influences your sexual desire.

Even in relationships involving two sexual people, it takes conscious effort to determine what factors cause each person's attraction and desire to vary. In a relationship with a low-desire partner, you may have spent so much time thinking about how to turn your partner on, how to make things just right for them, and how to take advantage of opportunities when they arise, that you may have thought little about what turns *you* on. What gets *you* in the mood, and what stimulates *you* the most?

In a relationship with a low-desire partner, you may have fallen into a habit of simply taking it whenever you can get it, or possibly only after the need becomes so great that it feels desperate. Perhaps you can live with that. But if you want your partner to initiate on occasion, you'll need to give them some tips for turning you on. This requires self-awareness.

If your partner has rarely or never initiated sex, you may have little practice dealing with situations where you are not in the mood, and your partner is. Yes, you read that previous phrase correctly: You are *not* in the mood, and your partner *is*. If your low-desire partner does become more interested in sex, or if you eventually find yourself in a relationship with a more sexual partner, this could occur from time to time.

The first few times this happened to me, I wasn't quite sure how to deal with it. I did not want to turn down an amazing gift from the universe. At the same time, I needed some help to get turned on. Whether it was because I was tired, had experienced a stressful day, or was distracted by something else, I wanted to be able to communicate to my partner what she could do to help.

Many factors can influence romantic and sexual desire, including how your day went, how much physical energy you have, whether you currently feel emotionally close to your partner, and whether you feel safe and supported in the relationship. If you notice some of these factors affecting your current mood, you may need to talk with your partner before you can enjoy sex.

As mentioned earlier, we often expect women to be able to "turn on" rapidly as men are often able to do, even though women often need more time and have more complex arousal needs. It is important for women to talk about any such differences they have with their partner.

While many men may be able to "turn on" in a broader range of contexts, particularly at a younger age and in the earlier phases of a relationship, this is not always the case. It's a common myth that most men can rapidly rise to the occasion anytime an opportunity for sex arises. Therefore, a man may assume that if he *can't* get turned on quickly, something must be inherently wrong with him. Men, like women, can benefit from paying attention to the factors that impact their desire, and from making efforts to communicate with their partners about them.

If you don't feel safe exploring the real underlying factors impacting your desire, you might blame your partner whenever you have difficulty getting turned on—whether they are partially to blame or not. This may be especially tempting if your current or past partner has been unenthusiastic about sex previously. I've been in this rut before. But remaining in a blame rut won't make you a better sex partner, and it probably won't lead to better sex.

Honestly accept your dark side

Before you can improve yourself, you usually need to recognize and accept your unattractive parts that you wish to change. We all have a dark side or shadow side that sometimes comes out, often when we're interacting with the people we love most. Particularly when we're feeling threatened or insecure, we all have ways of pushing our partner's buttons, making them more likely to become upset or lose their cool.

Mean behavior toward your partner may have a short-term emotional payoff for you, such as enabling you to take the moral high ground or making you feel like you've regained power or control. As discussed under "Stop depriving yourself & others of pleasure," you might occasionally withhold affection in an attempt to get what you want. Of course, meanness ultimately doesn't help anyone—it erodes the goodwill in a relationship.

David Schnarch has witnessed such behavior so often, even among other marital and family therapists, that he has coined the phrase "normal marital sadism."[151] Our ability to be cruel to our loved ones is often compounded by mind mapping, mentioned earlier. Again, mind mapping is the ability to make a mental image of another person's mind. We can use knowledge of our partner's preferences, emotional triggers, desires, and past reactions to predict how they'll respond to future behaviors, statements, emotions, and situations. We can use this ability to help our partner feel good, or we can use it to be mean.[152] Hopefully this doesn't often occur in a cold, premeditated way in your relationship, but it may occur when you are feeling insecure or upset.

As an example of such meanness, suppose you feel jealous that your partner went out dancing without you tonight. You have observed in the past that dancing gets them in the mood to talk and cuddle with you after they get home. So shortly before it's time for them to get home, you text them to let them know you are feeling pretty low-energy and are going to bed early—even though you are not that tired. When they get home, you pretend to be asleep, and thus unavailable for cuddling or talking. Oh, and you also know how much they love to share fudge brownie ice cream with you. So you bought a pint and finished it off yourself, "accidentally" leaving the empty container on the counter where they would see it when they got home.

Schnarch has observed that withholding sex, sometimes for months or more, is a common form of mean behavior among couples. This isn't surprising in light of an observation mentioned earlier: Both children and adults sometimes purposefully withhold affection or attention to manipulate others.[153] He offers the following for consideration:

> "The path to good sex is not 'telling your partner what you want.' It involves dealing with what I call 'normal marital sadism': your partner probably already knows what you want, and the fact you are not getting it means he or she doesn't want to give it to you."[154]

I'm not suggesting that your partner has been doing this, or that the earlier suggestions on communication should be discounted in any way. In my case, I don't believe that Katie ever withheld sex to be mean or vengeful. However, depending on the dynamics of your relationship, this topic might be worth exploring with a therapist. It is possible for asexuality to be feigned as a cover for emotional manipulation or as a defense against your sadism. Just don't spend *too* long on this topic. Over several sessions, one therapist kept asking Katie whether she was harboring anger toward me. While it was an interesting and worthwhile question initially, it eventually frustrated both of us.

Whatever the case, keep in mind that you always have the potential to be mean and manipulative. I have done some snarky things myself when I was feeling especially vulnerable, upset, or angry with my partner. It is important to recognize the specific ways in which you are "sadistic" toward your partner, and under what circumstances you are most likely to behave in this way. Maintaining awareness helps to keep such tendencies in check.

Discover workshops & groups

While there are many books, videos, and online resources available for relationships and sexuality, stretching outside your comfort zones and putting concepts into practice may be difficult to do on your own. It often takes interaction with other people to discover your true blind spots and growth edges. If this is the case, consider offerings by some of the individuals and organizations listed under "Additional Resources."

PART FIVE:
Connect, Integrate, & Look Ahead

Part Five Overview

. . .

YOU HAVE TAKEN some important steps. You have gained a basic understanding of what asexuality is and is not, and you have gained some clarity about your wants and needs. You have courageously explored some of your attitudes about sex and the role you may be playing in your situation. You have considered your partner's point of view, laid the foundation for forgiveness and acceptance, and learned about outside-the-box options. You have learned a range of techniques for showing up more powerfully as a sex partner, regardless of whether you remain in your current relationship.

With Part Five, it is time to carry this inner work and self-reflection forward, and actively involve other people. The biggest next step is talking more with your partner if you are still committed to working things out. What are their wants and needs? Are they willing to explore these questions more deeply with you? Another piece is determining whether you wish to enlist the support of others, possibly including a therapist, support group, and friends or family, if you haven't already done so. The following chapters include considerations and strategies around enlisting such support.

In the process of exploring with your partner, one or both of you may bring up the option of ending your romantic relationship, if this hasn't already occurred. Because that is a risk, we'll cover considerations and options around that.

If our conversations lead you to explore an open relationship, or if you have already decided to leave your current relationship, you will probably find some pertinent tips under "Manage Baggage with Future Partners."

Finally, as you continue to move forward and involve others in your circle of support, it can be helpful to frame your struggles in a larger context. Part Five concludes with a reminder that you are far from alone and that your journey can inspire many others.

19. Talk with Your Partner

. . .

Seek to understand your partner's truth

Before you can determine which options are most likely to make both you and your partner happy, it is important to understand the following:

➢ What changes, if any, need to occur in your relationship for your partner to be happy? This includes all aspects of your relationship, not just sex and physical intimacy.

➢ How does your partner currently identify? For example, do they already identify with a label on the asexuality spectrum? Do they still consider themselves sexual, but just with low interest?

➢ How certain and comfortable are they with their current identity? How much exploration or research have they done in this area?

➢ Regardless of any label(s), and setting aside your needs for the moment, what types of physical intimacy would they prefer, and roughly how often? This may be more important than any labels, which can mean different things to each person.

➢ Without further self-exploration, such as working with a coach or therapist, could they be happy while meeting your minimum needs? This includes not only frequency but also quality. For example, can they be enthusiastic about sex if that's something you need? Or would it feel like too much of a compromise? Would it feel like tolerating rather than being content?

> ➢ If needed, how willing are they to do more exploration around your relationship, including sexual intimacy, perhaps with the support of a coach or therapist?

You may need the support of a coach or therapist before you are even able to discuss the questions above. Some of them may be very difficult to answer.

Mutual honesty and courage are necessary to move forward with your relationship. Some details or opinions may be uncomfortable to hear at first. When Katie revealed that being physically intimate with me, especially kissing, often felt to her like "making out with a sibling," that was tough to hear. And it's not that different from stories shared by some asexual individuals on the AVEN website. If you and your partner can communicate challenging emotions in a clear and civil way, that's great. If not, consider enlisting professional support.

The first question in the list, regarding changes your partner desires in any part of your relationship, is particularly important for a few reasons. First, if your partner isn't currently getting other needs met in the relationship, that alone may be reducing their level of interest in you, regardless of their orientation or natural libido level.

Second, including other needs and aspects of the relationship may give your partner more incentive to look at sex. If they think that sex is the only thing that may change, and they are not currently that interested in sex anyway, then they may have little motivation to engage in what may be a very challenging exploration. This is especially true if they are currently dissatisfied with other aspects of the relationship. Such dissatisfaction is likely. If you are not currently getting your needs met and have been feeling cranky, horny, and distant from your partner, there's a decent chance that you haven't been showing up in the way they'd like you to, either.

You may be caught in a self-feeding downward spiral. In my case, for example, Katie's lack of enthusiasm for sex contributed to one of my biggest fears about being a parent—that we would have very little time or energy for intimacy with each other once we had a child. I felt increasingly cranky as I sensed her lack of desire, and I resented that she seemed to want me as a co-parent but not as a sexual partner. My reservations about becoming a parent, alongside my increased moodiness, likely made me even less attractive to her as a partner— sexual or otherwise.

Finally, attention to your partner's needs on a broader level is a reminder that you are interested in more than just sex. While sex is important to you, and a continued lack of it could be a deal breaker, you also value other aspects of the relationship and want your partner to be happy.

It is possible, of course, that even after careful attention to your partner's needs, they still may not be willing to explore sexual aspects of your relationship any further. However, the odds of change are probably greater than they are without such attention.

Asexual blogger Coyote offers the following advice for broaching the topic of potential asexuality with your partner:[155]

➢ Before communicating with your partner, consult a number of sources to learn what asexuality is and is not, determine your needs, and put yourself in their shoes. This book has already gotten you started in each of these areas.

➢ Don't confront. Communicate. Share with them some resources that describe asexuality, and ask if they'd be willing to talk about their perceptions. I gave Katie information on a few websites including AVEN and told her I was curious to hear her reactions. See the "Understanding asexuality" section of "Additional Resources."

➢ Keep in mind that societal misunderstanding about asexuality, and about sexuality in general, may make it difficult for your partner to know if they are asexual.

➢ Know that your partner might react to asexuality in a cautious but supportive way, recognizing it as a valid orientation. Or, they might react in a critical or defensive way, wondering if it is a mental disorder or simply a label some people adopt to feel "special." If they form the latter opinion, they might worry that you view them as broken.

> If they react in a critical way, do your best to share with them accurate information, regardless of whether they identify with the label. This will help to ensure that they eventually recognize their identity if they are asexual. It will also help to prevent them from inadvertently harming others who are asexual by having misinformed attitudes about asexuality.

> Let them know that you are not planning to leave them automatically if they decide they may be asexual. Rather, their exploration will help to inform conversations about how you can both be happy. You still have a lot to talk about before making any big decisions.

The same article also advises remaining calm, so that your conversations can be civil and productive. As mentioned earlier, this may not be the easiest thing to do. Even if your partner doesn't experience sexual attraction, the two of you probably share a deep bond. A threat that such a bond could soon be severed can make anyone anxious. If needed, first seek the support of a friend, therapist, or others, so that you can then speak with your partner more calmly.

Create & compare Want/Will/Won't lists

Clinical sexologist Lindsey Doe outlines the idea of partners creating "'Want/Will/Won't" lists of romantic and sexual acts and comparing them.[156] While this can work for any couple, the *Asexual Advice* blog notes that it can be especially valuable for mixed-orientation couples. It can also help to integrate some of the questions from earlier sections.

The exercise entails each partner creating three columns, labeled W*ant*, W*ill*, and W*on't*, either by sketching on two large sheets of paper or by using sticky notes on flat surfaces. Each person then brainstorms and lists activities in each of their three columns as follows:

> **Want:** List activities that you would really like doing with your partner, your ideal ambitions. Examples might include having

orgasms, having intercourse with oil rubbed all over your bodies, and having sex in the middle of the woods.

➢ **Will:** List activities that you are willing to do with your partner, but that don't get you very charged up. These can be things that you are neutral about, or only moderately excited about. They represent additional "common ground" with your partner, outside of any wants that you share in common. Examples might include exchanging shoulder massages, kissing on the lips, performing fellatio, and moaning loudly.

➢ **Won't:** These are things that you are not comfortable doing and don't want your partner requesting of you; they represent hard limits. Examples might include kissing with tongues in mouths, doing a 69, and rimming.

It is up to you how many items to list in each column; you might come up with 10, 20, or even 30. After you have both come up with your lists, you can then compare notes to see how much your wants overlap with your partner's wants and wills. You can always add items as you are comparing notes. This exercise can help you to determine whether you share enough common ground for both of you to be happy.

You might wish to add some of your "must haves at a minimum" as well. This could be in the form of a fourth column. Or, you could add stars or asterisks to such items in your "want" column to indicate that they're especially important to you.

If you need to get more specific after you've compared notes the first time, you can add some details such as frequency. For example, you might put "intercourse three times per week" in your "Want" column. Your partner might put "intercourse two times per week" in their "Will" column. This will enable you to get an even clearer idea of how much you overlap. However, consider excluding this level of detail initially. Getting caught up in such details right off the bat could limit brainstorming and reduce possibilities for identifying common ground.

If you have trouble coming up with lists of activities, consider setting up an anonymous profile on a dating site that uses compatibility questionnaires to match people. To maintain anonymity, don't post your picture or enter any potentially identifying information. One such site is OkCupid. This will enable you to browse some of the questions about sex preferences that the site and its users have created, to get some ideas. One word of caution: Don't get too caught up in browsing profiles of "matches" unless you and your partner have agreed to an open relationship.

Determine whether you can accept your partner's truth

As mentioned earlier, emotional and psychological work, including that of a sexual nature, requires significant effort. The process can also bring up pain and discomfort. So someone needs to be fully willing to do it—not just for a partner, but for themselves.

It is up to your partner whether they join you in pursuing change, and whether this change involves recruiting professional support. It is also up to them whether the change includes further questioning and exploration of their sexual identity, versus operating from the assumption that they are—and likely always will be—asexual.

If your partner is happy and secure in their identity as an asexual (outside of wishing that you wouldn't request sex so frequently), and they don't wish to question this, that's their right. It doesn't matter whether you believe they are a "true" asexual or not. Trying to push them to continue exploration is no more ethical than attempting "conversion therapy" with someone who is lesbian or gay. It could cause harm.

In such a case, your discussions going forward should be based on the assumption that their level of sexual interest is not likely to change. If you are secretly harboring hope for such change as you discuss options, you may be setting both of you up for later disappointment and resentment. Your job is to decide whether you can happily accept the implications that your partner's truth has for your relationship. Can you be happy with the compromises that an asexual partner is willing to make for you? Or, will you still secretly want more, in a way that decreases how lovingly you're willing to show up for them?

Also, can you wholeheartedly believe that they are asexual? Can you trust that they are coming from a place of integrity, or will you continue to have doubts? Will you wonder whether they are making excuses, acting from a place fueled by emotional trauma, purposely being disagreeable or manipulative, or simply not trying hard enough to explore their sexuality? Be honest with yourself about how you perceive them. If you can't trust your partner, and if you are second-guessing their motives, it will profoundly impact your ability to relate. You could end up feeling deprived, unable to trust, and unsupported all at once.

If your partner is ambiguous about their sexual identity, find out if they are willing and able to engage in further exploration. If they are not, talk about whether you can meet each other's minimum requirements for happiness despite this uncertainty. If major ambiguity in your relationship continues for too long, both of you will remain unclear on the best actions to take, what expectations are fair to have, what types of requests are realistic, and so on.

After clarifying your needs and your willingness to engage in self-exploration and change, you and your partner will probably be in one of these situations:

➢ You agree that a mutually satisfying compromise may be possible without further intervention or support. One or both of you are willing to try some new strategies to save your relationship.

➢ You agree that additional support is required to come to a workable place, and you agree upon a plan for seeking additional support. This plan may involve both of you seeing a coach or therapist, or it may involve only one of you to begin with.

➢ You don't agree that a workable compromise is possible without additional support, but both of you are not willing to get support.

If you are in a relationship and desire to remain with your partner, then hopefully you will fall into one of the first two categories. But you might not.

Even if your partner is clear that they don't wish to explore their sexuality, you may still wish to enlist the support of a therapist or coach. However, you will likely be approaching them with a different set of initial goals. Rather than trying to figure out whether you and your partner can get your desire to align more closely, you may be trying to determine whether and how you can be happy with very different sex drives.

You don't have to be clear on all of your goals before visiting a good therapist or coach. Helping you to clarify what you want is part of their job. Nonetheless, wondering what to expect can feel overwhelming. In the next sections, I'll share a few thoughts on how you might approach therapy or coaching, and I'll describe some questions and techniques that a therapist might incorporate.

20. Come Out & Seek Support

. . .

There's no substitute for in-person support

While this book may provide you with valuable information, it is no replacement for the support of a therapist or coach. During or after reading this book, you may find such help useful. If you are already working with a professional who is helping you, you can skip or skim this chapter. If you are trying to go it alone or haven't gotten results with someone you have been working with for a while, read on.

Finding a coach or therapist who feels like a good fit can be challenging as it is, let alone finding one who has at least some training and experience relevant to asexual-sexual couples. While a face-to-face visit and your intuition are the best guides, I'll offer a few potentially helpful tips here.

Determine your goals

First, determine some of your major goals for seeing a coach or therapist, based upon your prior conversations with your partner. This may help to narrow things down. For example, if your partner is secure with their identity as an asexual, and you would like to make your relationship work in light of that, try to find someone who has worked with mixed-orientation couples. Even if you can't find someone who has worked with asexual-sexual couples, perhaps you can find someone who has worked with gay-heterosexual, lesbian-heterosexual, or bisexual-heterosexual couples, and who at least has an awareness of asexuality. Ask if they are fine operating under the assumption that your partner is asexual, if your partner is already certain about that.

If you and your partner have any interest in exploring alternative relationship options like an open relationship, you may want to find someone who has knowledge and experience with such topics. At the very least, ask them up front if they have any personal objections to working with clients exploring this area.

If your partner is unclear about their identity and is willing to explore this, then consider professionals who have dealt with sexual identity issues. If possible, find someone who has knowledge specifically about asexuality and low sexual interest issues. If your partner believes that their lack of interest could be tied to past trauma or other events, consider professionals whose expertise includes physical trauma, abuse, or body awareness.

Because shifting your relationship will also involve your behavior and the dynamics between the two of you, try to find someone with whom you are both comfortable working.

If you and your partner have already decided that you're incompatible, and a peaceful-as-possible separation seems like the only viable option, then consider coaches or counselors who specialize in separation and divorce.

Pitch the idea to your partner

If you are not comfortable suggesting professional support to your partner, or fear that it may come across as laying blame, you can initiate action by offering to see a relationship counselor yourself. This illustrates to your partner that you're willing to take on some of the efforts and explore your attitudes and behavior.

Because you're currently more interested in sex than your partner is, you may have more motivation to get the ball rolling. For your partner, talking or reading about sexual desire may seem as exciting as counting a box of toothpicks. Although Katie used to read dozens of novels each year, it took her a few months to get through half of a sex-related book our therapist assigned. Understandably, it wasn't the most stimulating topic for her. In the meantime, I continued to read on my own, and to be grateful for the efforts that she made.

Keep in mind that "What is my sexual orientation?" is a big and scary question for anyone to explore. If your partner seems unclear about their identity, you might ask if they're willing to explore broader topics without attachment to whether they uncover a "cause" of asexuality. This might include, for example, both of your feelings and preferences about sexuality, and sexual shame and guilt. This may be a less intimidating way to approach things. Also, these are topics that probably affect most couples, regardless of their orientations. This way, you and your partner are likely to get useful tools out of therapy regardless of the answer to the sexuality/asexuality question.[157]

Consider qualifications & credentials

Whatever the therapist's background, you will want to ask them what knowledge they have of asexuality, and whether they believe that a person can be asexual. If your partner is questioning their orientation, does the therapist have a particular process they follow or a set of topics they explore with potentially asexual clients?

Credentials vary by country, and a number of training paths qualify people to work on sexuality-related issues. In the U.S., sexuality professionals can have graduate degrees in Counseling, Social Work, Psychology, Marital and Family Therapy, or Human Sexuality. Some individuals receive most or all of their sexuality-specific training in courses or workshops following their traditional education.

Some sexuality practitioners belong to professional organizations with online directories. These include AASECT (American Association of Sexuality Educators, Counselors, and Therapists) and SSTAR (Society for Sex Therapy and Research). A few more are listed under "Additional Resources." Each organization has different membership requirements and membership levels. If a professional you're considering has a particular membership or credential, check the membership organization's site to learn more about what it means. Ask the professional you're considering for more specifics if needed.

At the same time, there are some professionals with relevant knowledge and experience who don't belong to a professional organization. They may prefer freedoms in their approaches and continuing education that aren't dictated by someone else. They could have training that's relevant but not specifically approved by these organizations. And because sexuality remains a taboo and highly charged topic in our culture, there are some approaches within the profession that the mainstream has been hesitant to endorse, even if they work for some people.

It is up to you whether to use someone with traditional credentials or someone outside the mainstream. If you're considering someone who doesn't have a few years of formal therapist-related training or the equivalent, try to get some recommendations or testimonials from trustworthy sources at the very least. An unskilled person could make matters worse.

If your partner has not yet investigated possible medical causes for their low interest, and may wish to do that, ask the practitioner you are considering whether they have specific medical doctors to whom they refer clients—an endocrinologist or a urologist, for example.

There are now many people who bill themselves as sex and relationship coaches. I believe that coaching-style approaches to human transformation have tremendous value. I obtained coach training after earning my graduate degree in counseling. My opinion is that if you prefer such an approach, utilize a coach who has a few years of formal training in a therapy-related field, in addition to any coach training. Talking about sexuality can bring up a lot of personal triggers and biases, and you want to be working with someone who has learned to be mindful about this. If they haven't worked on their issues around sex, they could feel uncomfortable discussing your issues at the necessary level of detail.

Talking about sex with a couple can also bring up many heated emotional dynamics, and you want a professional who has the tools, demeanor, and confidence to be comfortable with that. I'm sure there are some great sex coaches out there with relatively little conventional training, but they may be more difficult to find.

I'll also be one of the first to say that formal education and credentials don't mean everything. Katie and I worked with a therapist who had a doctorate, several decades of therapy experience, and credentials to train other sex therapists. She didn't seem to believe that asexuality existed. She questioned whether Katie was holding onto resentment toward me, which initially seemed reasonable to explore. However, she returned to this theory several times despite Katie's continued insistence that she was not. This frustrated Katie and contributed to her giving up on therapy after several sessions. To the therapist's credit, she provided some homework and techniques that have proven effective with many couples—but she seemed stumped when Katie didn't respond to any of them. Some of them have helped me to improve my sex life over time, but they didn't do much for Katie, or for our relationship.

A good friend is currently pursuing graduate studies in clinical psychology, with the goal of becoming a Marriage and Family Therapist. Partially because she is bisexual and polyamorous, she chose a program with one of the first LGBTQIA concentrations in the U.S. However, she has had to speak out about topics that aren't adequately covered in—or are excluded from—courses where they should be addressed. These topics include asexuality, mixed-orientation relationships, and polyamory. She has also observed that many of her fellow graduate students, and even some professors, seem shy about discussing sexuality topics in general.

The key point here: Don't assume that just because someone has an advanced degree in counseling, therapy, social work, clinical psychology, or something similar, they've learned about asexuality or are comfortable working with sexuality-related topics. It's best to ask.

Ask for word of mouth

Ask friends for recommendations for coaches or therapists who deal with relationship issues, and with sexuality issues if you are comfortable asking about that. You don't need to share many specifics, especially if your partner isn't "out." Then call the professionals on the phone to ask what experience and expertise they have that's relevant to your situation. Checking their website may also be helpful, but some great therapists have very little information online.

Determine a time frame

As mentioned earlier, it may take time to determine whether you and your partner can ultimately be happy together. If your exploration includes questioning your partner's sexuality, you may be in libidinal limbo for some time. A "cause" may surface within just a few weeks or months, or one may not, even after much exploration.

For this reason, you might wish to agree upon an initial exploration period that feels fair to you and your partner. At the end of that period —three months or six months, for example—you agree to discuss where you both are, and whether you wish to continue the exploration. In the case that your partner truly is asexual, you don't want it to start feeling like beating a dead horse for either of you.

Possible things to expect in therapy

Here I outline just a few elements of what you might experience, based upon some common models. I also explain why a few of the techniques and frameworks could have limited value for asexuals, even though they may work wonders if your partner isn't actually asexual. Your therapist may or may not use some of these approaches.

Know that you are on a journey that requires great courage from both of you. It is impossible to know what you will discover in therapy. You might come up with a solution for maintaining your relationship. You might not. You might discover that relationship dynamics involving your thinking and behavior are a partial cause. You might discover that your partner actually did suffer early abuse or trauma and repressed it. You may find that *both* of you are repressing some deeply buried energy. You might grow even more deeply attached and loving. Or, one of you might choose to end the relationship rather than continue to explore.

Whatever the case, if you are both willing to do some work with honesty and integrity, you will be more likely to end up in a place where you are both happier—whatever form your relationship ultimately takes.

A professional will likely ask for a detailed sexual history, covering your present relationship and earlier periods. They may explore major events like childbearing, menopause, loss of a family member, or other significant relationship stressors. Again, if your partner did at one time feel attracted to you or others, it is possible that they are not truly asexual—other dynamics could be at play.

The therapist may encourage both of you to examine your attitudes and behaviors toward one another. This can be a worthwhile learning experience, but it can also be challenging and uncomfortable at times.

A therapist might also suggest a medical doctor and tests for levels of hormones associated with sexual interest—thyroid gland excretions and testosterone are two possibilities. One person explained to me that they once had a sex drive, lost it, and then regained it after making some dietary shifts with the guidance of a homeopathic practitioner. I don't know if this has ever worked for individuals who have never experienced sexual attraction or interest. Keep in mind that while it's important to explore possibilities, it's also important to respect your partner's right to refuse further exploration.

Now, let's look at a few counseling strategies often employed with couples who have sexual differences. In addition to learning about these through books and training, I've experienced some of them firsthand as a client. Afterward, I briefly explain why the approaches may have limited impact if one partner turns out to be genuinely asexual.

Some therapists suggest that the higher-interest partner can kindle the flame by doing more outside the bedroom. For example, simply helping with the dishes and other household chores may leave your partner with more energy, gratitude, and desire for you. If one partner feels the other isn't contributing fairly to the relationship, whether it's money, childcare, or otherwise, a buildup of resentment and stress can decrease interest in sex.[158]

Others suggest that many people become overly familiar with and dependent upon their partners. This fusion and familiarity stifles eroticism, which thrives on a bit of mystique and the tension that accompanies separateness. To increase desire, you must first become more differentiated—that is, you must allow yourself and your partner more independence and space to be yourselves.[159]

Some therapists will explore the times of your relationship when you were both happiest, and ask you to be specific about what you were doing to make things work then. The idea is that if you were both sexually content at one point, then you already possess valuable knowledge of how you can create mutual happiness once again.[160]

Still others recommend that the lower-interest partner utilize fantasy—a person, place, or thing that turns them on sexually—as a way to get more turned on with their partner. This can be done entirely in one's head, through reading or viewing erotica, or through incorporating a particular setting or sex toys.

One popular method of improving sexual interaction is called sensate focus. This involves removing intercourse and other genital contact from the menu for a short time and focusing on foreplay-type activities of gradually increasing intensity. Beginning with sensual touch and massage, the idea is to broaden the range of interaction so that each partner finds at least some aspect that they enjoy. The theory is that by the time the couple has sex involving the genitals again, it will be mutually enjoyable within the context of a broader range of touch.[161]

Sensate focus can be helpful if one partner often has difficulty getting aroused, even though they may enjoy some aspects of sex once they are aroused. It can also be helpful if one partner tends to focus too exclusively on achieving a fast orgasm, depriving the other of the opportunity to become aroused at all. Some people simply require more foreplay before stimulation of their sex organs brings them pleasure. If a couple has other intimacy or trust issues that stand in the way of enjoyable sex, slowing things down may provide an opportunity for such issues to surface. The couple can then talk about them.

Some therapists may wish to delve more into the past. For example, they may wish to explore whether your partner was abused as a child, whether they received negative messages about sex from their family, or whether they're harboring anger or resentment that affects their ability to connect with you. The therapist may also want to explore similar questions with you.

Finally, some sex experts believe that the lower sex drive partner must take responsibility for initiating sex at least some of the time, regardless of whatever other steps are taken. Just this step alone, they argue, can have a big impact.[162] However, initiation may be especially challenging for asexual-sexual couples.

One or more of the above approaches might light a spark. Keep in mind that these are highly simplified descriptions and that approaches vary across professionals. However, if it turns out that your partner is asexual, the approaches could have limited value. Here's why:

Your partner may be highly grateful that you spent all day helping with household chores or decreasing their workload in other ways. They may have more energy and desire to spend quality time with you, and perhaps a greater *willingness* to have sex, but still no attraction. You'll probably still need to be the one who initiates things; and even then, your partner may not be that excited.

A similar thing holds true with increasing independence or differentiation—your partner may enjoy hanging out with you and talking with you more, but this doesn't mean they're going to want to have sex. In fact, fully allowing them more space to be their authentic self could mean requesting *less* sex from them. But that would compromise your basic needs.

If your partner has never experienced sexual attraction, they may spend little or no time fantasizing about sex with others. If that's the case, attempting to identify sexual fantasies to facilitate arousal will probably not work. However, if they still find certain situations, objects, or settings pleasurable, despite lack of attraction, that could provide material to work with.

Similarly, there may not be a past sexual spark for your partner to rekindle, because it may never have been there in the first place—neither with you, nor with anyone else. Revisiting happier times might hold value for other aspects of your relationship, but not for sexual intimacy.

As for sensate focus, you and your partner may both discover new ways to connect physically and emotionally. However, your partner may or may not be more willing to tolerate your preferred sexual activities, even when you regularly preface them with a range of other types of touch. And it may still always be up to you to initiate.

If deeply buried resentments or childhood trauma are indeed at play, they could take many months to identify and work through. No professional support will yield results overnight. But if you sense after several sessions that things aren't headed in at least one useful direction, try a second therapist before giving up. While therapists' competence levels can vary greatly, sometimes only a slight variation in approach or style can make a difference.

Find a support group

While not a substitute for therapy, peer support can also be helpful. The "Additional Resources" chapter includes some websites where you can connect with others sharing similar problems, as well as resources that may help you to locate in-person groups.

If you hope to remain in a mixed-orientation relationship, you may find some of the online support groups helpful. AVEN, already mentioned, features a discussion group for sexual partners of asexuals. A few other groups cater to the broader umbrella of mixed-orientation couples. Depending on your own orientation and identity, check the Straight Spouse Connection and Straight Spouse Network websites, or the LGBTQIA resource center for your local area. Keep in mind that these groups may have limited knowledge and resources regarding asexuality.

If you prefer a local in-person group, post an announcement in one or more online groups. See if there are others in your geographic area who wish to form a group. Or, start a group on Meetup, Facebook, or another social media site. Keep in mind that there's some risk involved in disclosing your identity and home address to people you don't know, especially if their online identities are anonymous. For this reason, take precautions such as using a venue other than your home for your meetings, and consider inviting a trusted friend or two to the first few meetings.

If you can locate a local therapist whose expertise includes mixed-orientation couples, ask if they'd be willing to facilitate a group. Let them know you would be willing to help get the word out if needed, to help generate enough interest. If they have access to a meeting location, that will save you some organizational work.

If you are seriously considering ending your relationship, you may want to explore a separation and divorce group. You may find that sexual issues in general are quite common among separating couples but are still taboo to discuss. Shortly after I joined a group and shared my story, both female and male members expressed gratitude that I reminded them of this topic and brought it out into the open. Two women's husbands had come out as gay, so we were able to empathize with each other, even though each situation is unique.

Just remember that sexuality is a highly charged topic for many people, and your story may trigger some strong and potentially judgmental opinions. You may want to get a sense of how well facilitated the group is before sharing in detail. Also, keep in mind that some of the members might have been the partner with the lower level of sexual interest. Some may even identify as asexual.

Here's another reason to explore general separation and divorce groups: When ending any long-term relationship, or when transitioning from a romantic/sexual partnership to a friendship, certain dynamics commonly occur, regardless of the partners' orientations. Sexuality is just one piece of the picture. My group used the book *Rebuilding: When Your Relationship Ends* by Bruce Fisher and Robert Alberti. I found it incredibly useful. Rebuilding.org lists locations and contact information for groups using this book.

Finally, joining a support group provides an opportunity to help others while helping yourself. Some of the things you share about your struggles will probably inspire someone else or help them feel less alone in their journey. This may have side benefits such as increasing your sense of power and adding meaning to your struggles.

Coming out to others

For people coming out as asexual and their sexual partners, there are even fewer established supports than there are for people coming out as gay, lesbian, or bisexual and their heterosexual partners. As of this writing, the Human Rights Campaign's informational page for National Coming Out Day does not mention asexuality. Nor do their informational page and brochure for coming out as a supporter or ally. I hope that changes soon.[163] If estimates that around 1% of the population is asexual are accurate, millions of people may still be in the closet.[164]

Asexuality makes some people even more uncomfortable than homosexuality does. For many of us, the thought of a sexless life evokes pity—we cannot imagine how an asexual person could possibly be happy, even though many of them describe themselves as perfectly content. Therefore, an asexual person may fear others' potential opinions that something is "wrong" with them. This can exacerbate another fear: Because they are such a minority, could publicizing their orientation limit their options for potential partners? In online discussion groups, some asexual individuals share dilemmas regarding when to come out to a new person they are dating: Should they mention their orientation in their online profile, as a heterosexual, gay, or lesbian person would likely do, or should they wait to share this detail after a second or third date?

Due to all of this, your partner may be hesitant to come out to friends and family. They may ask you to remain silent about it, too. While this is understandable, it also makes it more difficult for either of you to get social support beyond the confidential services of mental health professionals. Coming out is also a way to raise awareness and increase support for everyone, helping to limit potential misunderstandings among other couples.[165] If millions of people worldwide are asexual, and many of them and their partners are quietly suffering in incompatible relationships, breaking the silence may help countless people. Furthermore, as more asexual people are out, they'll be able to find one another more easily, increasing their options for potential—and compatible—partners.

Only you and your partner can decide whether, when, and how much you wish to come out. I hope this book helps you to make that decision in a more informed fashion.

Friends & family

You may want to seek support from a few friends and loved ones as well. With many life challenges, it's normal and important to share your situation with such people. Talking to others can help to build supportive connections, gather collective wisdom, generate solutions, and regain perspective that may have been lost in the context of your relationship. For example, you may have forgotten the ways in which you are attractive and want others to help you remember.

Talking openly and honestly about sexuality is still taboo, though. Most people usually keep hush-hush and suffer silently. Given that sex is such a strong mode of connecting for many people, this is particularly unfortunate. Just when you are already feeling disconnected in profound ways, it can be more difficult to connect with others in ways that help to compensate.

Alongside the already-taboo nature of sexuality in general, asexuality presents additional challenges. It's usually assumed that a person must be physically attracted to at least one sex. So if your partner claims that neither penises nor vulvae get their heart racing, it may raise many questions and doubts among family and friends. Just a few examples of misunderstandings:

"Maybe Marcus isn't really asexual; maybe it's just that Cindy lacks skills in the bedroom!"

"I'll bet Anaya was abused as a child—I knew her family seemed a bit odd."

"Maybe Lisa just isn't the right person for Tanisha."

"Maybe Brook simply lost interest in sex because Alex is so demanding."

"Perhaps you can make Isabella love sex by doing X, Y, and Z. Why can't you just hang around and stick it out a bit longer? I'm sure she'll change soon."

"Jeremy is just a sex addict who could never be happy with one partner. Anyone would seem 'asexual' to him."

Such misunderstandings may stem from a variety of underlying beliefs: You or your partner has the power to change their sexual orientation, your partner isn't even truly asexual, or someone is to "blame" for your partner's asexuality. Such beliefs can trigger defensiveness among family members and make it difficult to talk openly. Your partner's family may fear allegations of abusing or "breaking" your partner in some way. You and your partner may fear being judged as unloving, abusive, or neglectful.

Even if both of you decide to be open and out, you can't control what others will think or how they will react. Some may be deeply compassionate and understanding. Others may see your partner as being stingy with their body. Some may believe that you're shallow for expecting sex. Others may view your partner as not performing their marital duties. Some may believe that one or both of you aren't trying hard enough. Others may simply not care.

But the potential of misunderstanding from others may be highest if you choose to remain silent.

You may also have to deal with unanticipated sexual dynamics from friends after coming out, especially if you're still together with your asexual partner. For example, you may discover that some of your friends also feel undersexed in their relationships, and you could be tempted to "rescue" each other by becoming sexually involved. If you don't remain in open and honest communication with your partner(s), this could lead to destructive situations. Late in our relationship, after consulting with Katie, I spoke with a mutual friend about such a possibility. She was still interested in sex, but her partner had not been interested for a long time due to a chronic medical condition. We didn't become sexually involved, which was probably for the best because it could have complicated our friendships. However, I'm grateful that I had those conversations. They help me to appreciate the lengths to which we can go when we face challenges with physical and emotional intimacy.

Online group etiquette

A few things are important to consider if you choose to participate in online communities, particularly ones that serve both asexual individuals and allies.

First, keep in mind that some online communities were developed primarily to provide a safe space for individuals who are the minority in the rest of the world. As a sexual person, you are in the majority on such sites, so be aware of the need to respect this space. Even if you dialogue only in spaces reserved for partners and allies of asexuals, a broad range of people may read your posts. Many asexual individuals have been ostracized, have experienced challenging relationships with sexuals, and so on. We live in a very sex-oriented world. Therefore, some members may be on the alert for potentially offensive or misinformed statements. Do your best to respect others, and apologize if you make an honest error.

Second, remember that the community of people who identify with asexuality is diverse. As discussed previously, there are people who are genuine asexuals, and there are people who are questioning their identity because they have had traumatic experiences—or both. When someone has had deeply traumatic experiences, fear and other troubling energy may fuel interactions in unpredictable ways. This is especially true in online situations, where the absence of body language and vocal intonation increases the likelihood of misunderstandings. Be careful not to take too many things personally, especially when talking about highly charged relationship topics. There may be many other factors impacting someone's response. This is also true for sexual people.

Third, as you view conversations in online groups, you may be overwhelmed by the number of labels that people use to describe their sexuality. Some individuals see the labels they have adopted merely as tools, and will be more relaxed about terminology. Others view labels as an important part of their identity, and will request greater specificity and accuracy. In some cases, this may seem a bit "picky." For many people, however, requesting accurate language is a strategy for educating others, and for shifting incorrect perceptions. You may not agree with or even understand every viewpoint, and that's okay. Just be willing to examine your perceptions and occasionally question their validity.

Books

Beyond the discussions on AVEN, there is limited information available on coming out as an asexual, let alone as a sexual partner of an asexual. However, several self-help books do exist for heterosexuals whose partners have come out as gay, lesbian, or bisexual; a few are listed in the "Additional Resources" section. If you attempt to apply some of this information to your situation, keep in mind that there are some differences between a partner coming out as asexual versus another orientation.

If you're seeking additional ideas on finding a therapist, see *How to Find a Good Therapist*, by Ben Butina. It covers therapy in general, not just sex and relationship support, but much of the knowledge may still be useful.

A few words on sex differences

As you consider whether and how to seek support, it is important to be aware of some sex differences that may affect both women and men. Research suggests that men are less likely to seek help for mental health issues in general, and that they tend to experience more emotional difficulty following separation and divorce. Some believe that men tend to put more of their emotional eggs into the one basket of their romantic relationship, discussing few topics of heavy emotional content with other friends.

Women, on the other hand, often maintain a broader web of social support. However, because their income and professional opportunities remain lower than those of men on average, they may have greater concerns about rocking the boat due to greater financial dependence upon their partners. This is one reason a woman might hesitate to acknowledge that there is a major problem by seeking help.

These considerations are based upon average differences by sex; individuals may vary greatly. Regardless, if any of the above sound like you, it's especially important to extend your emotional support web beyond your romantic relationship, even if it feels challenging. Without such support, things won't necessarily get any smoother as time passes.

21. If You Can't Work Things Out

• • •

Letting go—the nagging "what if?"

While we covered this briefly earlier, I will go into a bit more depth here because it is important and potentially very challenging.

What if your partner is unwilling or unable to meet your bare minimum sexual intimacy preferences and has no desire to explore whether there are underlying issues? What if you have already tried at least a few months of therapy, medical tests, and different relationship strategies, and nothing points toward changing your partner's level of sexual attraction or desire? But despite this, you still hold onto hope that something will eventually change? As you probably recall, I did this for a while. Katie was willing to attend a handful of therapy sessions but soon became convinced that further efforts probably wouldn't change anything.

If this is the case, and if you wish to remain with your partner and be happy, you will need to accept that they may never desire sex with you—not just tolerate, but fully *accept*. If you continue to hope that your partner will change, even when it is highly unlikely, it can lead to a "witch hunt." For example, you might find yourself wondering whether your partner experienced abuse in their past. If not from a parent, perhaps from someone else: another close relative, a neighbor, a babysitter, or maybe a summer camp counselor? But even if such a person or incident does exist in your partner's past, they may have no desire to uncover it.

You might find yourself browsing online asexuality discussions, as I did, wondering whether some of the people who claim to be asexual are truly asexual. After all, some of them seem to express such levels of disgust with sex, and such anger, that perhaps something else is going on. Maybe they were traumatized or abused in some way. Maybe your partner was, too. It's easy to launch down thought paths of hypothetical explanations, especially if you're feeling confused, frustrated, and disconnected. It's normal to desire answers and clarity.

As mentioned earlier, there are likely some people who identify as asexual who are actually sexual, whose sexuality is repressed or dormant for some reason. At the same time, there are likely some people who have suffered trauma or abuse *and* who are genuinely asexual. While such abuse may influence their behavior and thinking, their asexuality doesn't necessarily stem from it.[166]

Consider this: Does it really matter whether nature or nurture caused your partner's asexuality? Even if there is some underlying cause, there's little you can do if your partner doesn't want to explore it—particularly if it is something that occurred at a very young age or that they deeply repressed. Also, it is hard for anyone to hear a suggestion that they might be "broken," especially from someone very close to them. Furthermore, if they do uncover something incredibly painful, are you willing to support them in that journey?

A therapist friend reminded me of an old joke while we were talking about asexuality:

Q: How many therapists does it take to change a light bulb?

A: Just one. But only if the light bulb *wants* to change.

Even experienced therapists acknowledge that each person has limited power over others. Furthermore, if you develop a habit of trying to change those closest to you, it may not only frustrate them, but also distract you from your own growth and development. If you are too focused on trying to control or change someone else, it can be a sign of codependency. In such cases, you may not be giving yourself the love and attention you deserve. Also, you may not be giving your partner sufficient space to be themselves.

Having a breakup conversation

If you decide that you and your partner are unable to relate in a mutually satisfying way, at some point you will face the difficult task of ending your romantic relationship. There's no easy way to have a breakup conversation with someone you love, especially if you've been together for a long time. Because each relationship is unique and precious in its own way, your own heart is the best guide for most of your words. However, it is possible to have such a conversation in a relatively gentle and non-blaming way. Here are a few suggestions that may be helpful, drawing upon what we've already covered.

First, remind yourself that you are not to blame and that it's okay for you and your partner to be different. The more you can forgive yourself, the less you will be tempted to blame your partner to make yourself feel better.

If you still desire to tell your partner why it is their fault, consider what you hope to obtain by doing so. For example, do you still have a need to prove to yourself that you are not a shallow or selfish person for choosing to leave the relationship? Are you hoping an apology or admission of guilt from your partner will make this opinion of yourself go away? If so, ask yourself if your partner really has the power to provide this for you. Because society provides confusing messages around sex and relationship expectations, you probably have personal homework to do in this area. We all do.

Second, keep in mind that your primary purpose for the conversation is to end your romantic relationship, not to manipulate your partner into meeting more of your sexual needs. You have recognized that it's not meeting your needs, and you are giving up on relating in that way. Trying in vain to "get more" as the relationship ends sends mixed messages. Easier said than done, I know.

Third, remember that this probably hasn't been easy for your partner either, and let them know that you are not blaming them. Try to put yourself in their shoes. Even if they don't have an interest in sex, they probably still love you a great deal. Ending the relationship is going to be very painful for them, too. As discussed earlier, they may be experiencing many strong emotions such as guilt and inadequacy. They may fear that they'll have difficulty finding another partner. Understandably, they may also feel defensiveness and anger. During the conversation, they may not have the bandwidth to provide a caring presence for you. Take care of yourself by making sure you have some other social supports in place—a friend, family member, or group who can provide you with a listening ear and a shoulder to cry on after you've had the difficult conversation.

Fourth, remind your partner that you love them and that you ultimately want them to be happy, too. Let them know that you are sorry for any sexual pressure that they've experienced from you.[167] If this feels like you are taking on too much of the responsibility, keep in mind your purpose for the conversation—to end the romantic relationship while minimizing any additional harm to either of you. You have both been through a lot already, and you both deserve to be happy.

If you must separate, consider a party

If you and your partner decide that separation is the best option, consider easing the blow with a celebration of your relationship and transition. Some people host individual, separate breakup or divorce parties just with their friends as a way of moving on. Others host events together with their soon-to-be ex-partners.

While it can be emotionally challenging, hosting an event together can offer several benefits:

➢ It can provide an opportunity to reflect upon the many positives of your relationship, which you may have forgotten while focusing on unfulfilled expectations.

➢ It can encourage you to honor the challenges you've overcome together, the important things you've learned, and the fun times you've had.

➢ The above may promote forgiveness and consideration about how you can continue to serve as friends and supports to one another.

➢ It can lessen mutual friends' and relatives' tendencies to take sides.

➢ It can communicate to loved ones that you would like their support.

➢ It may help to provide closure on one chapter of your relationship, and mark the beginning of relating to each other in a new way.

One topic to discuss before such an event is how public you wish to be about your differences. While honesty may help your friends and family to be supportive of each of you, your partner may have concerns about being outed.

Additionally, you'll want to establish expectations that discourage conversation involving blaming or taking sides. Some of your friends and family could have strong emotions about your separation, so make it clear in your invitations that you and your partner intend for the event to be amicable. As grief and feelings of loss are normal, consider devoting a specific portion of the event to the expression of these emotions. Alongside you and your partner sharing what you've appreciated and what you will miss about each other, other guests can share what they've appreciated and what they'll miss about relating to you as a couple. If you are not comfortable doing this verbally, you can encourage people to do it in writing. You can provide small sheets of decorative paper, a guestbook, or a large card. Just be sure to agree in advance how you'll share any memorabilia after separating.

22. Manage Baggage with Future Partners

• • •

Let go of what no longer serves you

In any long-term relationship, people develop patterns of thinking, feeling, and behavior. Many of these are adaptive, and help them to maintain harmony and personal well-being. However, some of the patterns you developed to cope in an asexual-sexual relationship may not serve you in a relationship with a more sexual partner. Additionally, if you have been in a relationship with an asexual person for a lengthy period, relating to a sexual partner may trigger dormant insecurities and behaviors.

It's important to remain mindful of your patterns and tendencies as you move forward, so you don't unintentionally sabotage current or future relationships. However, don't expect to have everything fully in place when your next relationship begins, as life is a continual learning experience. Things will never be perfect, and simply having a greater self-awareness is a major first step. The most active learning about relationships usually occurs while you are in a relationship.

Choose someone you desire, & vice versa

As mentioned earlier, you might have chosen someone you didn't strongly desire, or who didn't strongly desire you, without consciously realizing it. This may be due to any number of reasons—for example, as a way to reduce the chance of losing control or becoming emotionally overwhelmed. If you believe this was the case, do your best to ensure it doesn't occur in your next relationship or doesn't continue in your current one. Before jumping into another relationship, take time for self-reflection, and consider seeing a therapist if you believe that certain patterns may be at play. Each person and relationship are unique, so your set of baggage will also be unique.

Honestly discuss preferences early

In finding a partner with whom you share a mutual attraction, there will probably be some physical, hormonal, and biochemical factors over which you have little control. Additionally, sexual preferences can change significantly over time, influenced by variables including maturity of the relationship, age, life circumstances, trust, and compatibility in other areas of your relationship. Regardless, candid conversation up front will at least lessen the odds of discovering potential deal breakers later. It is important to find out what your partner's sexual preferences are, and to talk very openly about your own, prior to making any serious commitments.

You can proactively ask questions to see if your potential partner is generally on the same page as you are. If you've used an online dating site, you might have answered some sex-related questions even before meeting. However, you will still have to do your homework. You might open with something like, "I value open communication about all types of intimacy when I'm dating someone. That includes taking the time to understand each other's sexual preferences. Would you mind talking about this?"

Here are some specific questions you might want to cover. Of course, if you're asking them, you should also be willing to answer them.

➤ After you're intimately involved with someone, how many times a week would you ideally prefer to have sex with them?

➤ If your partner wants to have sex more frequently than you do, how would you deal with this?

➤ If your partner wants to have sex less frequently than you do, how would you deal with this?

➢ If your partner masturbates—either in your presence or not—does that ever bother you? When and how do you consider masturbation okay?

➢ What is your opinion of a partner viewing pornography while they're in a relationship with you? When and how do you consider viewing porn okay?

Keep in mind that just because your potential partner answers a question a certain way doesn't mean it is set in stone. You may need to talk about which items are negotiable and which are not. Doing the exercises described under "Create & compare Want/Will/Won't lists" may also be helpful at this stage.

If you and your partner are comfortable with it, you can get more accurate answers by asking how above questions have played out in past relationships. For example, "In past relationships, how often per week did you want sex during your first year together?" Or, "How often did you want sex after you were together for more than a year?" You could also ask how happy they were with the overall quality of the relationship(s), as that probably had a large impact.

It is up to you how many such questions you ask and how deep you go with them. The more honest you can be with each other, the more likely you will avoid a situation of significant incompatibility. Because sexuality is still considered taboo to discuss, it's normal to have some discomfort around this, especially if you don't know each other that well yet. However, if your partner seems *too* uncomfortable talking about sexuality, or seems offended that sexual compatibility is important to you, it might indicate that they have significant self-growth work to do in this area. It could also mean that their priorities aren't aligned with yours. You'll need to decide how comfortable you need your next partner to be when it comes to talking about sex.

Don't assume a new partner has the same preferences

Any two partners are going to have very different preferences and needs, including those around sex and romance. This is particularly true if you enter a relationship with a new partner who is more sexual than your previous one. Such differences are another reason it's important to talk openly and honestly about preferences, rather than making too many assumptions.

For example, as I've entered middle age, it often takes me longer to achieve orgasm than it did in my twenties. This doesn't decrease my enthusiasm or enjoyment of sex at all; in fact, it has some benefits. However, Katie was understandably not enthusiastic about extended sex sessions. With a new partner who enjoyed sex much more, I still found myself becoming concerned when it took me a while, mainly because I was afraid that she would become frustrated as well. I shared this openly with Sophia, and it felt wonderful when she explained that she enjoyed extended lovemaking sessions.

Another example: A few times when Sophia was not feeling well or was upset, she communicated that she wasn't comfortable with me kissing or even hugging her—sometimes she didn't want to be touched at all. This would have been difficult enough for me to adjust to as it is, because my natural tendency is to offer physical touch for soothing. However, Sophia's requests also reminded me of the point at which Katie refused to engage in any more extended or open-lipped kissing with me—not just in that instance, but ever again. I was still healing from feelings of rejection around that, and I probably still am. Over time, I realized that when I gave Sophia a bit of space to herself, she was usually soon enthusiastic about physical intimacy again. I had to remind myself that each person is different.

Don't assume requests for change are rejections

Your low-interest partner might have had various prerequisites for sex. For example, maybe the room had to be a certain temperature, the lights had to be a certain way, you both had to brush your teeth immediately beforehand, you'd better not have consumed anything with onion or garlic within the last several hours, socks had better be on your feet if they're going to take too long to warm up, certain body part(s) had better be shaved a certain way, and so on.

You may laugh as you read some of these. If you've had a partner who frequently had such requests, and who wasn't that interested in sex regardless, the requests might have been challenging for you. They might have seemed like conscious or unconscious attempts to avoid or postpone sex. While that is possible, they might have been perfectly legitimate requests. As discussed earlier, most of us have certain minimal standards for hygiene when it comes to sex. The same is true for our environments, our partner's behavior, and other comfort factors. For example, I don't like the room to be too chilly during sex, and I prefer having a radiant heater next to the bed if it is. If you've just eaten anchovies, I'd probably welcome a tooth brushing.

If you find yourself with a new partner, keep in mind that they'll have a unique set of preferences around comfort and pleasure during sex. Some might seem odd to you, but they're probably not attempts to avoid sex. Some of your requests may seem odd to them, too. Be careful not to fall back into the "Oh, here we go again" mindset and assume that a request for a change means rejection. If in doubt, ask. Trust that both of you want the same thing, and that both people being comfortable will help to create fireworks.

With Sophia, I was hypervigilant for signs of rejection for a long time. For example, one morning I asked her to feel into whether she'd be in the mood for sex as she began to feel more awake and alert. She said, "I'm not really awake yet. Can you just hold me a bit? That'll make it more likely that I'll get into the mood." At the same time, her face appeared to have a slightly annoyed look as she adjusted the covers. Almost instantly, I felt a strong fear of rejection, and my sexual energy dissipated. I thought, "She doesn't really want it, and I don't want to be pushing her into something she's not going to be that enthusiastic about."

Rather than keeping my emotions to myself, I asked if we could talk when Sophia was more awake. I decided that being open and honest, so that we could have a deeper emotional connection, was more important than whether we actually had sex that morning or not. Besides, I knew that if I held back anything emotionally, the sex wouldn't feel as good anyway.

I did my best to use "I" statements to describe what I was feeling and experiencing, including my fear that she wasn't interested in sex. I shared my desire to know what she was feeling and my awareness that my assumptions could be incorrect. I learned that she did often enjoy sex in the morning. Easing into it through physical touch could be very pleasurable for her, but too much verbal interaction as she awakened sometimes turned her off. I felt like we both understood each other better after talking. Partially as a result of that, we had wonderful sex later that morning.

Prepare for the return of flirtation insecurity

"Nothing ever goes away until it has taught us what we need to know. If we run a hundred miles an hour to the other end of the continent in order to get away from the obstacle, we find the very same problem waiting for us when we arrive. It just keeps returning with new names, forms, manifestations until we learn whatever it has to teach us."[168]

Pema Chödrön

Even before I consciously realized that Katie was asexual, I rarely felt sexual jealousy or even the slightest concern about her flirting with other people. In retrospect, this makes complete sense, given that she has never experienced sexual attraction. She didn't flirt, at least not in a sexually charged way. While I found her beautiful and sexy, she rarely dressed in a manner that others would consider sexually provocative. I'm not saying that I was entirely free of jealousy during my time with Katie. I sometimes fretted that other commitments and activities seemed to get in the way of intimacy—I just never feared that I was going to lose any affection due to Katie being *sexually* interested in someone else.

My relative lack of sexual jealousy didn't mean that I was free of unresolved issues in this arena. My issues had merely remained largely dormant, waiting for a future learning opportunity on the other side of the continent. After I met Sophia, my sexual jealousy levels increased significantly for a while. As is often the case when a long-term relationship is ending, I had chosen someone with a great abundance of what I felt was most lacking in my prior relationship—in this case, sexual energy.

My new girlfriend was much more in touch with her sexuality than the average person. She had been with several more partners than I had, and she had formally studied sexuality and sensuality at least as much as I had. She was sexually attracted to others, and others to her. In fact, she was dating several people when we met. That was a huge shift for me. I had to recognize that the same sexual energy I appreciated receiving from her would also lead her to find other people attractive. Furthermore, her energy would make others more likely to express sexual interest in her, especially in a community with many polyamorous people. I found myself wrestling with more jealousy than I had ever encountered in my prior relationship, and various insecurities were triggered. This presented opportunities for self-reflection and growth, but it was challenging.

First, I compared myself to people with whom Sophia shared mutual sexual interest and romantic history, in a way in which I had never compared myself to Katie's platonic friends. Even when Sophia reassured me that her other current and recent lovers weren't "replacement threats," I would engage in self-comparison driven by my insecurities. One person was significantly older, but I felt insecure that he had much more money than I did. Two others were significantly younger, and I allowed that to trigger my insecurities around aging. One composed dance music as I do, and I became jealous when Sophia gave him an opportunity to showcase his music at an event she facilitated, without extending such an offer to me. I initially blamed her for being insensitive, when it would have been more productive to look at my insecurities.

Secondly, I rediscovered some control issues remaining from my childhood. My father had been an active alcoholic for some years, during which time I took on the role of the "hero child." I overachieved in a vain attempt to make my family look good, to control my environment including my dad's drinking, and to compete with drinking to earn his increasingly scarce attention and love.

Many years later, with Sophia, I perceived her desire for other lovers as interfering with her love and attention for me, just as I had perceived my dad's desire for alcohol as interfering with his love and attention for me. This translated into a desire to control Sophia's interactions with other lovers. While many people would struggle with insecurities around their partner having other lovers, in my case such insecurities were likely even stronger, due to both my upbringing and my prior relationship with an asexual partner.

Should you end up with a partner who has significantly more sexual energy, be aware that you may discover new insecurities, too. This is possible even if you are not initially experimenting with polyamory. Self-development is an ongoing process.

Be grateful & giving but not codependent

The acronym GGG, coined by sex advice columnist Dan Savage, stands for "Good, Giving, and Game." It means that as sex partners, we should strive to be "good in bed, giving equal time and equal pleasure [to our partners], and game for anything—within reason."[169] I try to follow this as much as I can, and I greatly appreciate a partner who places a mutual priority on physical intimacy and connection.

However, as with anything, balance is healthy. If you find yourself with a sexual partner following a long-term relationship with an asexual partner, you will likely be incredibly grateful. Gratitude is usually a great thing. However, this fourth *G* could be so powerful that it temporarily throws the other three out of balance.

You might be *so* grateful that you are willing to compromise a lot just to ensure you keep this new person, particularly if your sexual self-esteem is still in a low place. You could become so giving for a while, so focused on making your partner happy, that you neglect yourself. That's where it can border on codependency, which includes excessive reliance on another person's approval.[170] Furthermore, even if it's not a good mutual match, you might forget there are many other possibilities for non-asexual partners out there.

It is not just about saying "yes," but also about compromise and saying "no" sometimes. It may be difficult to imagine or remember what it is like to have the roles reversed—where your partner wants sex, and you are the one who is not in the mood or who has other priorities at that moment. At first, you may have difficulty managing such situations so that both of you get your needs met.

Because I've experienced these things, I offer a few thoughts and tips in case you find yourself in such a position.

When I first met Sophia, I enjoyed having someone who appreciated my sexual energy and my romantic energy with sexual overtones. I fire hosed her with various types of flirtation. I dedicated to her a few romantic songs I had composed, I wrote nature-inspired poetry with erotic overtones, and I sent her sexy messages. I had fun doing these things, and the energy helped my creativity and boosted my spirits. These activities are not so different from what many people likely do in the throes of fresh attraction. However, the extent to which I was channeling my time and energy toward Sophia was not sustainable. I soon realized that if she and I developed a longer-term relationship, we'd both need to get used to lower levels of such energy.

As I got to know Sophia, I continued to be incredibly grateful for her mutual sexual attraction and higher libido. She was also grateful for mine, and this felt wonderful. Because I knew what it was like to experience unrequited sexual desire for someone I loved, I promised myself that I would do everything in my power to keep my new girlfriend from ever experiencing the same. Partially because of this, early in our relationship I temporarily agreed to some things that I wasn't fully comfortable with. My decisions ended up haunting us later.

One of these things was polyamory. I had read many good things about it but had never tried it. Having more than one sexual partner (just one common aspect of polyamory) seemed like a good insurance policy, in case my new girlfriend ended up being less enthusiastic about sex than I had hoped. But at the same time, there was a big part of me that wasn't prepared for it. Trying to get to know Sophia while she also dated other people often knotted my stomach—scheduling, jealousy, concerns about safer sex, and feeling that my needs and desires were being weighed against those of three other people. I couldn't bring myself to date anyone else, because with all the emotional processing and arguing we were already doing around polyamory, I had little time and energy left.

We worked through these things, with her ultimately being the one to say, "Hey, why don't we just be monogamous?" After that, things got calmer, but I then wrestled with jealousy and insecurity around her desire to hang out with her ex-lovers just as friends. Because they were members of several social circles to which we belonged, it took me at least a year and a lot of internal work to get over being emotionally triggered by them.

In retrospect, had I been in a place of greater self-confidence, I probably wouldn't have agreed to polyamory in the way that we attempted it, because I wasn't fully on board with it—even though I had told Sophia I was, and I had tried my best to accept it. And if that hadn't been okay with her, I wouldn't have pursued the relationship any further. That would have been the most honest thing to do at that point.

That being said, I'm grateful for the experience, because I learned a lot. I'm glad that I've gotten to know her much more deeply, and that I've had the opportunity to share many more intimate experiences. I haven't entirely ruled out the possibility of trying polyamory again someday, but it would have to be under very different circumstances. We've had better success with polysensuality, where we allow each other to engage in activities like snuggling and massage trading with other people, without sexual or romantic involvement.

Polyamory wasn't the only place where I compromised. Even if I was really tired, or it was the middle of the night, and Sophia wanted sex, I'd do my best to make myself available. In the middle of a day that I had set aside for creative work, I'd usually take time out. On a morning where I was still feeling tired, and she was awake before I was, I'd find a way to get myself awake.

This worked for the first several months of our relationship. However, I eventually realized that I was becoming somewhat of a sexual martyr and overachiever, and it was adversely impacting other parts of my life. I wasn't spending as much weekday time on work as I wanted to be, and I was working more evenings and weekends, partially due to flexing with Sophia's schedule. I often went to sleep later or got up earlier than I wanted and had difficulty concentrating the next day.

I didn't mind these things occasionally, as that's part of life. No relationship is perfect, and any couple will need to compromise on their schedules, especially in today's busy world. But it was happening more frequently than I wanted. And as my progress on projects stalled and other parts of life started to creep in, I started to experience more stress and didn't enjoy the sex as much anyway.

The tricky part about all of this is that it had a benefit or payoff for me, too. Or least that's what I thought, according to an internal subconscious agreement I had made with Sophia, without speaking it to her. That agreement was simply, "If I never say 'no' to you, then you will never say 'no' to me."

This agreement was bound to fail for at least three reasons: First and most obviously, it was unspoken. Second, it's not realistic or fair to expect anyone—neither oneself nor others—to be available all the time. Third, it wasn't being honest and honoring my needs.

Over time, Sophia began to say "not now" sometimes. Eventually, I also developed the courage to say "not now" sometimes. We initially had some uncomfortable conflict around this. But by talking through it openly, we were able to generate helpful strategies.

One strategy we came up with is to view sex in a less dichotomous fashion. In other words, it didn't have to be an all-or-nothing thing where only one of two outcomes were assumed possible:

➢ We both had amazingly energetic sex where we both received pleasure for an extended period and had mind-blowing orgasms.

➢ We didn't have sex at all.

We gave ourselves permission to stop being sexual perfectionists and realized there were many in-between possibilities for mutually pleasurable and connective sex.

We also generated several possibilities for compromises, with the choice being up to the partner who has less energy:

➢ We agree just to cuddle naked and engage in erotic touch, with no expectations. If it ends up leading somewhere more sexual, great. If not, no worries. We'll have sex again soon.

➢ We have "quickie sex" for an agreed upon time, where the horniest person can have an orgasm, and the other is fine with not having one.

➢ We set a time to connect later in the day.

➢ The less energetic person simply holds the other while they masturbate.

➢ The less energetic person pleasures the other with their hand or mouth, depending on what they have the energy for. Should the less energetic person happen to develop energy for intercourse, then that option can be negotiated; but the receiver should not pressure them for intercourse.

The last two options may require additional dialogue and exploration for you to become comfortable practicing them with your partner. I provide additional context under "Revisit Porn & Masturbation."

As for bringing the initial "fire hosing" of sexual energy back to a sustainable level, I found it helpful to channel some of my energy into other endeavors. Through physical exercise like jogging, cycling, and ecstatic dance, I have invested time and energy in my health and vitality. Writing two self-help books inspired by my relationship journeys, including this one, has deepened my sense of purpose and increased my sense of connection to others.

Additionally, I've shared some of the creative works I had already produced—including music and poetry—with a broader audience. These works now have potential that spans beyond building my relationship with Sophia; they may also inspire other people and broaden my connections.

If you find yourself fire hosing a partner with your sexual energy and attention over a long period, consider the examples above. What are some ways that you can channel your energy into your health, well-being, and other areas of your life, beyond your partner? In the end, this will likely give you more energy for your partner as well—and you may both have an easier time recovering if you eventually break up.

Revisit your intimacy & autonomy needs

This topic is related to avoiding codependency. I would sometimes become cranky on the weekends when Katie went to bed late in the evening and then got up early the next morning to enjoy activities with other people. These were all wonderful and healthy activities, such as athletic practices, social events, church, and volunteering. However, I was often disappointed when she lacked time or energy for physical intimacy, either in the evenings or the mornings. When I felt neglected in this way, I often lacked the desire to go out and do other things with her and her friends. From her perspective, I seemed controlling and self-isolating.

After we had brought the possibility of asexuality out into the open, we were able to explore causes of our head-butting in more depth. I acknowledged that I was sometimes controlling, and I agreed that it was healthy for each of us to have our own time and separate activities. I explained that the main thing I wanted was just a few hours of alone time that included physical intimacy each weekend. Of course, I hadn't previously understood why this often seemed like a low priority for her. And until I gave her a clear explanation about how my needs were often unmet, she was naturally unable to understand why I often got so cranky on the weekends. I had assumed that she'd get my hints, incorrectly believing that she understood what it felt like to want sex.

When I became involved with Sophia, whose sexual needs were more similar to mine, she and I made an interesting discovery. We both initially feared that the other person might not want as much physical intimacy because we had both been in relationships where we had felt sexually rejected. That wasn't very surprising. More surprising was that we initially shared another mutual fear: The other person might be too "clingy" and encroach upon our desired autonomy time. This fear was new for me, as Katie had rarely requested my time and energy for physical intimacy. It has taken time for me to learn how to express my autonomy needs alongside my intimacy needs. It is an ongoing process. Also, I've learned that just because a person has more sexual intimacy needs, it doesn't mean that they have fewer autonomy needs. Balancing these two areas is a constant dance, a dance that will be different with each partner.

Easing back into sex with a partner

Many people can bounce fluidly between non-partnered activities and partnered sex, without the former affecting their ability to show up powerfully for a real-life partner and enjoy the latter. But if you've learned to be almost entirely self-reliant for sexual needs with an asexual partner, it may initially feel difficult to relate to another person in a sexual way again.

With another person, you also need to cater to their sexual needs while expressing your needs clearly. You are no longer totally in control. In addition, some sex toys or even one's own hand can provide stimulation that another person's penis, tongue, vagina, hand, mouth, or finger cannot.

You may have learned to rely heavily on porn in the absence of a regular sex partner. As discussed under "Revisit Porn & Masturbation," the unrealistic body types and acts often represented in porn may make some people initially less responsive to real-life partners. It might take some time and patience to get used to the real thing again. Everyone differs on this. Whatever the case, open, honest discussion and time to develop (or redevelop) trust with your partner may be needed.

Also, if you haven't had much sex with another person for a while, you might experience performance anxiety. You may need to rebuild your confidence, and your partner may feel pressure for "everything to be just right" to compensate for your past sexual frustrations—whether those occurred with them, or with your prior partner.

It is also possible that you have gone elsewhere for sex without your asexual partner's knowledge and consent. If this is the case, then you need to get on a more honest path if you wish to develop a more intimate relationship. If you are planning to start over with a new partner, make sure you're not acting out ingrained patterns that are no longer necessary. Dishonesty and lack of trust can derail intimacy, regardless of how sexually attracted you and your partner are.

Be mindful of future partners' potential concerns

If you were with an asexual or potentially asexual partner for a long time, the topic of that relationship may come up with a future long-term partner. How much information you choose to share probably depends on many factors, including how much emotional baggage and healing you still have from your last relationship.

A future partner may have questions or concerns regarding your past. They might wonder whether your sex drive is exceptionally low, given that you were with someone who experiences little or no attraction or interest in sex. They might wonder whether your sex drive is exceptionally high, given that you left a previous partner partially because they weren't as interested in sex. Or, they might not understand asexuality at all, and worry that your prior partner's lack of interest was due to some fault of yours—a fault that could impact your ability to satisfy them, too. They could feel pressure to be exceptionally sexually available to you, for fear that you might also leave them for not being sexual enough.

The above are just a few possibilities; they may or may not match your partner's actual concerns, if they have any. The only way to know is through open and honest conversation.

23. The Bigger Picture: Catalyze Cultural Shift

• • •

Remember that you're not alone

You have suffered significant pain and discomfort in one of your closest and most important relationships. Being in love with someone who has little or no interest in sex, and who may be asexual, can be incredibly difficult for a sexual person.

It is important to focus on your personal healing. At the same time, remembering that many others are also suffering can ease your sense of loneliness. You are far from alone. Millions of people worldwide may be asexual, and a large portion of them may be in relationships with sexual partners.[171] Considering ways to help them while helping yourself can provide a greater sense of connection and power.

Pema Chödrön describes *bodhichitta*, a Sanskrit term meaning "noble or awakened heart." When your suffering leads to a feeling of kinship with all others, you may discover this aspect of yourself. One way to awaken bodhichitta is through a practice called *tonglen*, which involves two simple parts. First, when you encounter the pain of others, accept it and breathe it in, with the wish that nobody has to experience pain. Second, whenever you encounter any form of happiness, breathe it out into the world, with the wish that everyone may feel joy.[172]

In writing this book, I have attempted to imagine and breathe in some of the pain you have experienced. I've also attempted to share some of the joy and learning I've encountered alongside my suffering. I wish that you and your loved ones experience more joy and fulfillment, whatever form your relationships take. You and your partner deserve lives aligned with your authentic styles of loving and connecting. The world desperately needs more vibrant, fully alive, powerfully loving people.

We need to talk about sex

We've talked a lot about how asexuality is still largely misunderstood and hidden from view. Large numbers of asexual-sexual couples probably remain closeted or unaware of the nature of their underlying differences. Your struggles stem partially from a broader social shortcoming: Our culture doesn't talk enough about sexuality in general in a deep and candid fashion, starting at a relatively young age. Because of this, many people are left to figure out their sexual identities on their own. If someone's sexual orientation is relatively uncommon, it may be even more challenging to figure things out. By the time they do, a long-term partner and children may be involved. Then things get more complicated, and people suffer. Continued silence creates further disconnection. This is the last thing that anyone who is already feeling lonely and disconnected needs.

Sex is everywhere in our culture. We are inundated with sexy images and sound bites every day, through advertising, television shows, movies, music, and other media. Porn is easily accessible. However, most of these messages do little more than reinforce stereotypes and keep us thinking about sex. They don't challenge young people to take an honest look at their sexual identities. They don't encourage people to share and seek support for the confusing mix of emotions that often accompanies sexual development.

As a culture, we need to create environments where young people can feel comfortable and safe asking about sex in a vulnerable fashion. The conversations need to go far beyond just the mechanics and biology of heterosexual, procreational intercourse.

When people feel safer and more encouraged to talk about their sexual identities, regardless of how different from the norm they seem, we'll face fewer situations where people unknowingly enter relationships that aren't a mutual fit.

In a blog post titled "Why Openness is Awesome," my colleague Pace Smith makes three points that apply to talking about sex:[173]

➤ Sharing our sensitive stories can help other people.

➤ People with little to hide are less vulnerable to fear and shame.

➤ It's better for everyone to be more open about themselves so that a lack of privacy is shared by all, to decrease the frequency of situations where the powerful spy on the powerless.

This makes a lot of sense to me. What do you think? Each of these points will resurface in our remaining conversation.

The broad impacts of sexual silence

Our inability to talk openly and candidly about sex impacts everyone, not just asexual-sexual couples. It affects everything from mental health to democracy. As I share a few examples, it may remind you of someone in your life.

I often think about the world in which little Charlie is growing up. What types of societal messages will he receive about sexuality? What attitudes will he internalize? What if his identity turns out to be outside the norm in some way? Will he feel free to explore it, or will he repress it in ways that somehow make his life more challenging than it needs to be?

As mentioned earlier, I was frequently taunted and called "fag" and "queer" in elementary school, due to the way I spoke. That bullying hurt a lot. However, my life got easier as I got older and ended up being predominantly heterosexual—even though "queer" could be accurate today because my thinking on sensuality, sexuality, and gender is outside the current mainstream. Life didn't get any easier for my friends and family who are other orientations. I know grown adults with same-sex, long-term partners who have not yet come out to their parents. In China, even though homosexuality has been legalized since 1997, there's still a lot of pressure to form a "traditional" family. Millions of non-heterosexual people still engage in opposite-sex "fake marriages" to appease family and friends.[174]

If we discussed sexuality more openly and regularly, would children commit less violence against one another due to perceived sexuality or gender identity differences? Would children be more comfortable with their differences and grow up to lead even happier lives? Would parents and families be more supportive? Consider these questions for a child you care about.

The U.S. Supreme Court's 2015 decision that states may not prohibit same-sex marriage was a big step. It put America ahead of some other parts of the world, where some types of sexual expression are punishable by death. However, much work remains. It has only been a few years since two of my friends, the Rainbow Grannies, received death threats while campaigning for same-sex relationship equality. That hatred is not gone, as many people have expressed anger and frustration about the Supreme Court's decision. Also, there is no formal recognition of family units with more than two adults. This limits options for mixed-orientation couples who wish to remain in a committed relationship while including one or more additional partners. Such arrangements can help everyone meet their needs.

If we discussed sexuality more openly and regularly, would people feel less hatred toward others, including two grandmothers, just because their orientation is different? Would we have more socially accepted options for families for whom life partnership and sexual attraction don't fit into a neat box?

Other people I love have also suffered due to current societal attitudes about sexuality. One suffered depression during her senior years, even undergoing electroshock therapy at one point. A key cause of her depression: She feared she would burn in hell for having had premarital sex many years earlier.

If we discussed sexuality more openly and regularly, would this woman have sought more social support around these concerns, rather than suffering largely on her own for many years?

Through touch-positive events like snuggle parties, I've discovered how many people are deprived of all types of physical affection. I've learned how this deprivation is often tied to misunderstandings about sexual versus non-sexual touch. This includes a belief that activities like simply holding or being held by someone must be a sign of romantic and sexual attraction.

If we discussed sexuality more openly and regularly, would we erode many of these misunderstandings about touch? How many fewer people would experience touch deprivation in general?

Consider Tim, an acquaintance born with neurological conditions that profoundly impact his ability to communicate, socialize, and form intimate relationships. Tim's conditions, which include autism, are fairly common. However, their effects upon sexual development and expression are not yet well understood. After violating online pornography laws, Tim was almost imprisoned. Family and friends battled for several years to persuade courts that blanket sex offender policies didn't make sense for such cases. While Tim narrowly avoided federal prison, he must bear a sex offender label for the rest of his life. This is despite lack of evidence suggesting that he had ever, or would ever, approach someone in a sexually inappropriate manner. Tim's label will forever affect his employment prospects and living situation.

If we discussed sexuality more openly and regularly, would we view sex-related offenses—and the people who commit them—on a diverse continuum? Would the legal system have recommended actions more appropriate to Tim's unique circumstances in the first place?

Consider some of the publicized victimizations tied to sex. Numerous accusations of child molestation were leveled against the Catholic Church and its clergy members over several decades. The #MeToo movement broke the silence surrounding sexual victimization in other institutions and industries. Recall the 2014 mass shooting near the University of California, Santa Barbara campus. The killer's final video revealed one of his primary motives: anger that women didn't seem attracted to him. He was frustrated about being a virgin, and about never having kissed a girl.[175] He drew attention to scores of sexually frustrated and often misogynistic men in online communities.

If we discussed sexuality more openly and regularly, would some of these cases have been avoided altogether? Might the perpetrators have felt more comfortable seeking social and professional support for their sexual attractions or impulses? Would they have found harmless and consensual ways to meet their sexual needs? Would others have acted to halt further victimization sooner?

Escape the sexual control matrix

Remaining quiet about sexuality has another negative impact: It enables powerful social control that is potentially harmful and subject to abuse.

Sex lives and technology are becoming increasingly intertwined, at the same time many people conduct much of their sex lives in "secret anonymity"—or so they believe. Computing devices track large amounts of data on all of us. A few recent events serve as reminders of this and of the damage that can be done. Between 2012 and 2015, hackers made publicly available millions of user records from several sex-related websites, including Ashley Madison, YouPorn, and Adult Friend Finder. Many extortion attempts followed the release of the Ashley Madison database, capitalizing on users' fears of judgment and repercussions. Some exposed users, including a pastor, committed suicide.[176]

In response to these events, Dan Savage noted that public judgment about sexuality often ignores the complex nature of individual circumstances.[177] Some high-profile individuals were quickly branded as evil for appearing on the user lists. While I don't endorse cheating on one's partner, I was troubled that there seemed to be little discussion of complicating factors—for example, what if some of the users had asexual partners? This is similar to the black-and-white judgment that almost landed Tim in prison. His disabilities were initially ignored as he was lumped into a much larger category of sexual offenders. But that's what often happens when a topic is taboo: Because people are afraid to talk about issues in detail, they skim over important aspects. The nuances and variations are lost, and opinions become "either/or." Consequently, based solely upon their sexual behavior, people are judged as either:

➢ right or wrong

➢ moral or immoral

➢ good citizens or bad citizens

➢ totally under control or completely wild

➢ trustworthy or nefarious

➢ Madonna/nice guy or whore/bad boy

Granted, in some cases, sexual behavior is unacceptable and unethical to the point where it may actually render a person not trustworthy in other ways. But we often overgeneralize.

Perhaps you, like me, have signed up for free accounts and browsed adult sites at some time in your life, even if you've never cheated on a partner. Many people have—Ashley Madison alone claims to have over 30 million users, and pornography sites may account for more than 25% of all internet traffic bandwidth.[178]

That's just the beginning. The Sexual Control Matrix is about much more than adult websites. It is about large proportions of minors engaging in sexting—more than 50% according to one study, with nearly 30% sending nude photos of themselves. Many are unaware of potential consequences: being tried under child pornography laws, getting permanent sex offender records, and never being able to qualify for certain leadership positions or jobs.[179]

The Sexual Control Matrix is about a teenager or adult posting a racy photo or comment on a social networking site, and never being able to fully erase evidence of an impulsive moment. It is about you or a loved one being caught with a camera phone or drone, doing something considered even slightly "deviant," even if harmless. It is about public leaders or candidates being blackmailed or controlled with their sexual histories.

I don't endorse sexual behavior that may harm or harass others, and opinions will vary on what responses or punishments fit particular acts. Regardless, it's safe to say that in many instances, the potential impact on a person's life shouldn't be permanent. The above occurrences and possibilities serve as a warning to all of us. They illustrate some of the powerful dynamics of sexual behavior and social control that exist.

The following four factors combine to create significant social control, via potential for shaming, blackmailing, and similar methods. In this way, the taboo nature of sex can threaten our freedom and even our democracy:

➤ For most people, sex is a basic need.

➤ Social norms and institutions are often at odds with sexual needs.

➤ We have restrictively high ideals and social judgment for sexual behavior.

➤ Our technology increasingly expands possibilities for sexual interaction, while simultaneously allowing for increased surveillance.

Modern information technology and data tracking aren't going away, as they also have many benefits. Human nature isn't going away. And asking Big Brother for tighter data security will never protect it from everyone. Even where data are supposedly secure, someone with influence will always have access if they really want it. This can create a major imbalance of power.

Fortunately, we can influence norms, institutions, ideals, and judgment by striving to make discussion about sexuality less taboo. Imagine a day where talking openly about sex is not that big a deal! This, in turn, can lessen the extent to which sexuality may be abused to control others.

If we discussed sexuality more openly in our culture, we could reduce potentially harmful black-and-white thinking about it. People could be themselves more freely, because they could worry less about being judged harshly. Many asexual individuals would clarify their identities sooner. Asexual-sexual couples could explore alternative relationship arrangements more freely. By creating a culture that talks about sexuality more openly, we can help everyone.

What you can do

Fortunately, many people are speaking out and taking action to promote dialogue about asexuality and sexuality in general. This includes the creative people listed under "Additional Resources." However, there's still plenty of work to do.

Here are some ways that you can help, regardless of how much time and energy you have:

➢ Commit to continuous self-improvement. Working on yourself will also make you a better resource for others.

➢ Talk more openly with your partner about sexuality.

➢ If you discover that your partner is indeed asexual, come out of the closet as a sexual partner of an asexual. Start with a few close friends and family. If your partner isn't out, you can use pseudonyms or usernames that don't reveal your real identity in online public groups.

➢ Share thoughtful articles on sexuality topics via social networking sites. As people see such topics discussed more frequently, they lose some of their taboo energy.

➢ Donate money or time to organizations that support freedom of sexual expression, comprehensive sexuality education, and more open and honest communication about sexuality.

➢ Start conversations online, or host in-person discussion groups.

➢ Tell others about this book.

24. Pay It Forward with a Review

. . .

If this book has been helpful to you or others, please look it up on the website where you purchased it, and take a few moments to share your opinion through a review.

Just five minutes and a few sentences can help a book like this to reach dozens more people. That not only helps them directly, but also supports continued creation of materials like this, which take hundreds of hours to produce. That's a significant "return of good" on your investment, and a great way to help pay it forward. Many thanks in advance!

Comments on social networking sites are also greatly appreciated. You're welcome to share feedback with me directly through the contact page at asexualbook.com.

END MATTER

25. About the Authors

• • •

Evan Ocean's partner revealed her asexuality to him following many years together. Evan granted his friend Dave permission to publish many aspects of his personal story. However, he asked to be credited anonymously under a pen name, without further biographical details.

Dave Wheitner authored most of the book. One of his partners also realized she was asexual, and his story has many overlaps with Evan's. Dave blended details of their stories into a single narrative, changed certain elements to honor others' privacy wishes, and added the various levels of interpretation and self-help information.

Dave has long been intrigued by sexuality and human behavior. As a teenager, he enjoyed browsing sexuality research books at the public library—and not just for the pictures.

Raised in a blue-collar neighborhood by a financially limited but loving family, Dave earned a B.A. in Psychology from Yale (Psi Chi Psychology Honor Society), an M.A. in Community Counseling from Indiana University of Pennsylvania (Phi Kappa Phi Honor Society), an M.S. in Public Policy and Management from Carnegie Mellon (Phi Kappa Phi Honor Society), and life coaching certification. He has participated in various workshops and trainings on awareness, authenticity, sensuality, sexuality, personal growth, and leadership. He has created and facilitated touch-positive events.

Dave is an award-winning author of several books. *The Snuggle Party Guidebook*, a guide to obtaining more physical affection, also touches upon many aspects of sexuality. Formerly vegan but still mostly plant-based, he pairs sensual desserts with romantic activities for couples in *The Vegan Chocolate Seduction Cookbook*. His sensual poetry appears in *Ecosexuality: When Nature Inspires the Arts of Love*. He has written music with sexuality-inspired themes.

You can contact Dave regarding interviews, speaking engagements, feedback on the book, or other inquiries via the contact form at asexualbook.com.

26. Additional Resources

• • •

This section lists resources that I've discovered or that have been suggested to me. It is not intended to be exhaustive. I make no claims, guarantees, or endorsements regarding the efficacy or validity of any specific resources. Some of the books and sites may lead to other helpful resources.

Locating professionals

Note that having a sexuality-related certification, membership, or directory listing doesn't necessarily mean a professional is familiar with asexuality—it is always best to ask.

American Association of Sexuality Educators, Counselors, and Therapists (AASECT), https://www.aasect.org/

Butina, Ben. *How to Find a Good Therapist*. CreateSpace, 2008.

The Open List, http://openingup.net/open-list/

Poly-Friendly Professionals, http://polyfriendly.org/

Society for Sex Therapy and Research (SSTAR), http://www.sstar.org/

Understanding asexuality

Asexual Awareness Week, http://www.asexualawarenessweek.com/

Asexual Visibility and Education Network (AVEN), http://www.asexuality.org/

Asexuality Archive, http://www.sexualityarchive.com/

Asexual Explorations, http://asexystuff.blogspot.com/

Asexuality Archive. *Asexuality: A Brief Introduction.* http://www.asexualityarchive.com/, 2012.

Asexuality Facebook group (closed), https://www.facebook.com /groups/2204641049/

Asexual Visibility and Education Network (AVEN) Facebook group (public), https://www.facebook.com/groups/aven.network/

AVENwiki, http://wiki.asexuality.org/

Bogaert, Anthony. *Understanding Asexuality.* Lanham, MD: Rowman and Littlefield, 2012.

Coyote. "Am I Asexual?" *The Ace Theist.*

Decker, Julie Sondra. *The Invisible Orientation: An Introduction to Asexuality.* New York: Carrel Books, 2014.

Killermann, Sam. "The Genderbread Person v3." *It's Pronounced Metrosexual.* March 2012. http://itspronouncedmetrosexual.com /2015/03/the-genderbread-person-v3/

Tate Sprite. "Touch Made Simple." *What If This Is It.* https://cliffnotestolife.wordpress.com/2014/01/12/touch-made-simple/.

Coping with change & rebuilding yourself

If you have recently ended a relationship with a long-term partner, or believe you will soon be doing so, these books may provide additional support.

Chödrön, Pema. *When Things Fall Apart: Heart Advice for Difficult Times.* Boston, MA: Shambhala Publications, 1997.

Fisher, Bruce and Robert Alberi. *Rebuilding: When Your Relationship Ends.* Atascadero, CA: Impact Publishers, 2006.

Wheitner, Dave. *The Snuggle Party Guidebook: Create Deeper Friendships, Decrease Loneliness, & Enjoy Nurturing Touch*

Community. Portland, OR: Divergent Drummer Publications, 2014.

Increasing connection, touch, & physical pleasure

These resources cover a broad spectrum of connection. Some focus largely upon verbal interaction with minimal touch, some focus on platonic touch, and some include erotic and sexual touch. It's important to do your own research before attending any event, and to use your own judgment. Consider taking a trusted friend with you if you have any doubts about the reputation or safety of a specific facilitator or group.

Conscious Touch NW, https://www.meetup.com /ConsciousTouchNW/ (Example of a Meetup-based snuggle group.)

Cuddle Party, http://www.cuddleparty.com

Cuddle Up to Me, http://cuddleuptome.com

Czimbal, Bob and Maggie Zadikov. *A Guide to Healthy Touch: Vitamin T*. Portland, OR: The Abundance Company, 1991.

Grader, Rob. *The Cuddle Sutra: An Unabashed Celebration of the Ultimate Intimacy*. Sourcebook Casablanca, 2007.

Hess, Samantha. *Touch: The Power of Human Connection*. Fulcrum Solutions, LLC, 2014.

Human Awareness Institute (HAI Global), http://www.hai.org

Martin, Betty. *Learning to Touch: Receiving, Giving, Taking, and Allowing*. Forthcoming.

Network for a New Culture, http://www.nfnc.org

OneTaste (Orgasmic Meditation), http://onetaste.us

Resnick, Stella. *The Pleasure Zone: Why We Resist Good Feelings and How to Let Go and Be Happy*. Berkeley, CA: Conari Press, 1997.

SexPositive World, http://www.sexpositiveworld.org

Snuggle Central Facebook group, https://www.facebook.com/groups /161897667302168/

SnuggleHQ, http://snugglehq.com

Snuggle Party, http://www.snuggleparty.org

Tribal Love Network, http://www.triballove.net

Wheitner, Dave. *The Snuggle Party Guidebook: Create Deeper Friendships, Decrease Loneliness, & Enjoy Nurturing Touch Community.* Portland, OR: Divergent Drummer Publications, 2014.

Tantric & Taoist approaches to sex

Chia, Mantak, Maneewan Chia, Douglas Abrams, and Rachel Carlton Abrams. *The Multi-Orgasmic Couple: Sexual Secrets Every Couple Should Know.* New York: HarperCollins, 2000.

Odier, Daniel. *Desire: The Tantric Path to Awakening.* Rochester, VT: Inner Traditions, 2001.

Yeshe, Lama Thubten. *Introduction to Tantra: The Transformation of Desire.* Boston, MA: Wisdom Publications, 2005.

Alternatives to monogamous relationships

These resources provide a range of perspectives and guidelines on ethical non-monogamy approaches such as polyfidelity and swinging.

Anapol, Deborah Taj. *Polyamory in the 21st Century: Love and Intimacy with Multiple Partners.* Plymouth, United Kingdom: Rowman and Littlefield Publishers, 2012.

Block, Jenny. *Open: Love, Sex, and Life in an Open Marriage.* Berkeley, CA: Seal Press, 2009.

Easton, Dossie and Janet Hardy. *The Ethical Slut: A Practical Guide to Polyamory, Open Relationships, and Other Adventures.* Berkeley, CA: Celestial Arts, 2009.

Labriola, Kathy. *Love in Abundance: A Counselor's Advice on Open Relationships*. Eugene, OR: Greenery Press, 2010.

Ryan, Christopher and Cacilda Jetha. *Sex at Dawn: How We Mate, Why We Stray, and What It Means for Modern Relationships*. New York: HarperCollins, 2011.

Taormino, Tristan. *Opening Up: A Guide to Creating and Sustaining Open Relationships*. Berkeley, CA: Cleis Press, 2008.

Veaux, Franklin and Eve Rickert. *More Than Two: A Practical Guide to Ethical Polyamory*. Portland, OR: Thorntree Press, 2014.

General relationship & sexuality resources

A great number of relationship resources are out there. These are just a few that I've read or browsed, or that others have recommended. Some are intended to encourage exploration outside the norm.

Beattie, Melody. *Codependent No More*. New York: Harper and Row, 1987.

Chapman, Gary. *The 5 Love Languages*. Chicago, IL: Northfield Publishing, 2010.

Betty Dodson with Carlin Ross website, dodsonandross.com

Crooks, Robert and Karla Baur. *Our Sexuality*. Belmont, CA: Wadsworth, Cengage Learning, 2014.

Désilets, Saida. *Emergence of the Sensual Woman: Awakening Our Erotic Innocence*. Kihei, HI: Jade Goddess Publishing, 2012.

Friedman, Jaclyn and Jessica Valenti. *Yes Means Yes! Visions of Female Sexual Power and a World Without Rape*. Berkeley, CA: Seal Press, 2008.

Glickman, Charlie and Aislann Emirzian. *The Ultimate Guide to Prostate Pleasure: Erotic Exploration for Men and Their Partners*. Berkeley, CA: Cleis Press, 2013.

Glover, Robert. *No More Mr. Nice Guy: A Proven Plan for Getting What You Want in Love, Sex, and Life.* Barnes and Noble Digital, 2000.

Hendricks, Gay and Kathlyn Hendricks. *Conscious Loving: The Journey to Co-Commitment.* New York: Bantam Books, 2009.

Joannides, Paul. *Guide to Getting it On! A Book About the Wonders of Sex.* Oregon: Goofy Foot Press, 2012.

Kerner, Ian. *She Comes First: The Thinking Man's Guide to Pleasuring a Woman.* New York: HarperCollins, 2004.

Klein, Marty. *Sexual Intelligence: What We Really Want from Sex— and How to Get It.* New York, NY: HarperCollins, 2012.

Nagoski, Emily. *Come as You Are: The Surprising New Science that Will Transform Your Sex Life.* New York: Simon and Schuster, 2015.

Newman, Felice. *The Whole Lesbian Sex Book: A Passionate Guide for All of Us.* San Francisco: Cleis Press, 2004.

Perel, Esther. *Mating in Captivity: Unlocking Erotic Intelligence.* New York: HarperCollins Publishers, 2006.

Post, Stephen and Jill Neimark. *Why Good Things Happen to Good People: How to Live a Longer, Healthier, Happier Life by the Simple Act of Giving.* New York: Broadway Books, 2007.

Psaris, Jett and Marlena Lyons. *Undefended Love.* Oakland, CA: New Harbinger Publications, 2000.

Schnarch, David. *Intimacy and Desire: Awaken the Passion in Your Relationship.* New York: Beaufort Books, 2011.

Steele, David. *Conscious Dating: Finding the Love of Your Life and the Life That You Love.* Campbell, CA: RCN Press, 2008.

Taormino, Tristan. *The Ultimate Guide to Anal Sex for Women.* Berkeley, CA: Cleis Press, 2006.

Tatkin, Stan. *Wired for Love: How Understanding Your Partner's Brain and Attachment Style Can Help You Defuse Conflict and*

Build a Secure Relationship. Oakland, CA: New Harbinger Publications, 2011.

Weiner-Davis, Michele. *The Sex-Starved Marriage: Boosting Your Marriage Libido*. New York: Simon and Schuster, 2003.

Partner coming out & mixed-orientation relationships

Some of these resources are geared toward couples with two sexual partners, one who is heterosexual and one who is lesbian, gay, or bisexual. However, some of the same dynamics apply to asexual-sexual relationships. The discussion forums for partners and friends of asexuals on AVEN are more specifically focused on asexual-sexual couples. The Straight Spouse Network's "resources" page also lists some resources for children of mixed-orientation couples.

Buxton, Amity Pierce. *The Other Side of the Closet: The Coming-Out Crisis for Straight Spouses*. IBS Press, Inc., 1991.

Grever, Carol and Deborah Bowman. *When Your Spouse Comes Out: A Straight Mate's Recovery Manual*. New York: Haworth Press, 2007.

HUGS (Hope-Understanding-Growth-Support) Yahoo group for couples, https://groups.yahoo.com/neo/groups/HUGS_Couples2/

MMOMW (Making Mixed Orientation Marriages Work) Yahoo group, https://groups.yahoo.com/neo/groups/MMOMW/

Straight Spouse Connection, http://www.straightspouseconnection .com

Straight Spouse Network, http://www.straightspouse.org (also on Facebook at https://facebook.com/pages/Straight-Spouse-Network/1801244843710)

Coping with past trauma or abuse

Many people report that their lack of sexual attraction or interest in sex has no connection to past trauma or abuse. For some, however, there might be a connection. Should you or your partner suspect the latter, working with a qualified professional can help. That being said, here are a few books in this area.

Kepner, James. *Healing Tasks: Psychotherapy with Adult Survivors of Sexual Abuse*. Hillsdale, NJ: The Analytic Press, 2003. (This one is geared mainly toward practitioners.)

Levine, Peter. *Waking the Tiger: Healing Trauma*. Berkeley, CA: North Atlantic Books, 1997.

van der Kolk, Bessel. *The Body Keeps the Score: Brain, Mind, and Body in the Healing of Trauma*. New York: Penguin Books, 2014.

Sexual toy stores

"Just for me" toys can be useful for meeting some of your needs while you're trying to figure things out with your partner. Also, couples' toys can spice things up if you are transitioning into having a partner who enjoys sex more. These vendors also emphasize environmental sustainability and healthiness.

As You Like It, http://asyoulikeitshop.com

Good Clean Love, http://goodcleanlove.com

Good Vibrations, http://goodvibes.com

Ethical pornography

These sites focus on sexual entertainment that seeks to avoid exploitation of performers. They emphasize realism, consensual interactions, and fair compensation of performers. Given the various fetishes and niches, these are just the tip of the iceberg. Some advocates recommend practices such as subscribing or purchasing products through performers' websites, as this increases the odds that they are receiving a fair share of the revenue.

Bright Desire: Smart Porn for Men and Women, http://brightdesire.com

Make Love, Not Porn, http://makelovenotporn.tv

Feminist & women's erotica

Given that porn and erotica frequently exploit women, it is good to have other options.

Bitch Community Lending Library, librarything.com/catalog/bitchlibrary (Browse under the "erotica" tag.)

Blue, Violet. *Best Women's Erotica 2015*. New York, NY: Cleis Press, 2014. (This editor has also produced compilations for prior years under the same title.)

How to Make Me Come: Anonymous Essays on Female Orgasm, http://howtomakemecome.tumblr.com/

27. Works Cited

• • •

Some entries also appear under "Additional Resources."

"Am I Still Asexual If...?" Asexual Education. Accessed March 27, 2015. http://asexualeducation.tumblr.com/asexualif.

Anagnori. "What's the Difference Between Sex Drive, Sexual Attraction, Sexual Arousal, Sexual Desire, and Sexual Consent?" Anagnori. Accessed March 11, 2015. http://anagnori.tumblr.com /post/69803256941/whats-the-difference-between-sex-drive-sexual.

Angyal, Chloe. "The Performance Model of Sex, Now in Video Form!" Feministing, February 5, 2013. http://feministing.com/2013/02 /05/the-performance-model-of-sex-now-in-video-form/.

Anthony, Sebastian. "Just How Big Are Porn Sites?" ExtremeTech, April 4, 2012. https://www.extremetech.com/computing/123929-just-how-big-are-porn-sites.

"Attraction." AVENwiki, January 7, 2015. http://wiki.asexuality.org /Attraction.

"Attraction and Vocabulary." Asexual Education. Accessed March 10, 2015. http://asexualeducation.tumblr.com/attraction.

Austin Institute for the Study of Family and Culture. "Too Busy to Get Busy: Is Sexless Marriage on the Rise?" *Austin Institute for the Study of Family and Culture* (blog), December 22, 2014. http://www.austin-institute.org/research/1526/.

Babcock, Linda, and Sara Laschever. *Women Don't Ask: Negotiation and the Gender Divide*. Princeton, N.J: Princeton University Press, 2003.

Barry, Doug. "Study Finds That Playfulness Is the Most Attractive Quality Ever." Jezebel, August 5, 2012. http://jezebel.com /5931979/study-finds-that-playfulness-is-the-most-attractive-quality-ever.

Bauer, C., T. Miller, M. Ginoza, A. Chiang, K. Youngblom, A. Baba, J. Pinnell, P. Penton, M. Meinhold, and V. Ramaraj. "The 2015 Asexual Census Summary Report," October 25, 2017. https://asexualcensus.files.wordpress.com/2017/10/2015_ace_cen sus_summary_report.pdf.

Beattie, Melody. *Codependent No More: How to Stop Controlling Others and Start Caring for Yourself*. 1st edition. Center City, MN: Hazelden, 1986.

"Ben Wa Balls and Vaginal Tone." The Sex MD, July 26, 2011. http://www.thesexmd.com/ben-wa-balls-and-vaginal-tone/.

Bogaert, Anthony F. "Asexuality and Autochorissexualism (Identity-Less Sexuality)." *Archives of Sexual Behavior* 41, no. 6 (December 2012): 1513–14. https://doi.org/10.1007/s10508-012-9963-1.

Brotto, Lori A. "Asexuality Myths Debunked by Psychologist Lori Brotto on HuffPost Live (Video)." *Huffington Post*, June 28, 2013, sec. Queer Voices. http://www.huffingtonpost.com/2013/06/28 /asexuality-myths_n_3517368.html.

———. "Evidence-Based Treatments for Low Sexual Desire in Women." *Frontiers in Neuroendocrinology* 45 (April 2017): 11–17. https://doi.org/10.1016/j.yfrne.2017.02.001.

———. "Understanding What It Means to Be Asexual," March 15, 2015, sec. blog. https://www.theglobeandmail.com/life/health-and-fitness/health-advisor/understanding-what-it-means-to-be-asexual/article23454312/.

Brotto, Lori A., and David Goldmeier. "Mindfulness Interventions for Treating Sexual Dysfunctions: The Gentle Science of Finding Focus in a Multitask World." *The Journal of Sexual Medicine* 12, no. 8 (August 2015): 1687–89. https://doi.org/10.1111/jsm.12941.

Brown, Vanessa. "Why Sham Marriages Between Gay Men and Women Are on the Rise." News.com.au, March 14, 2016. http://www.news.com.au/lifestyle/gay-marriage/why-sham-marriages-between-gay-men-and-women-are-on-the-rise/news-story/34d22903f07e4bcbcb88124d757786dc.

Burgo, Joseph. "The Difference Between Guilt and Shame." Psychology Today, May 30, 2013. http://www.psychologytoday.com/blog/shame/201305/the-difference-between-guilt-and-shame.

Buxton, Amity Pierce. *The Other Side of the Closet: The Coming-Out Crisis for Straight Spouses and Families*. 1 edition. New York: Wiley, 1994.

Carpenter, Siri. "That Gut Feeling." American Psychological Association Monitor on Psychology, September 1, 2012. http://www.apa.org/monitor/2012/09/gut-feeling.aspx.

Castleman, Michael. "Vibrators: Myths vs. Truth." Psychology Today, February 15, 2011. http://www.psychologytoday.com/blog/all-about-sex/201102/vibrators-myths-vs-truth.

Chödrön, Pema. *When Things Fall Apart: Heart Advice for Difficult Times*. 20th Anniversary ed. edition. Shambhala, 2000.

Church, Noah B. E. *Wack: Addicted to Internet Porn*. 2 edition. Portland, OR: Bvrning Qvestions LLC, 2014.

"Codependency." *Wikipedia*, July 19, 2015. https://en.wikipedia.org/w/index.php?title=Codependency&oldid=781718566.

Cooper-White, Macrina. "Watching Porn Linked to Less Gray Matter in the Brain." *Huffington Post*, June 2, 2014, sec. Science. http://www.huffingtonpost.com/2014/06/02/porn-less-gray-matter-brain_n_5418607.html.

Coyote. "Differentiating Sexual Attraction and Sexual Desire." *The Ace Theist* (blog), December 13, 2013. https://theacetheist.wordpress.com/2013/12/13/differentiating-sexual-attraction-and-sexual-desire/.

———. "What to Do If You Think Your Partner Might Be Asexual." *The Ace Theist* (blog), March 24, 2014. https://theacetheist.wordpress.com/2014/03/24/what-to-do-if-you-think-your-partner-might-be-asexual/.

Czimbal, Bob, and Maggie Zadikov. *A Guide to Healthy Touch: Vitamin T.* Portland, OR: The Abundance Company, 1991.

Dahl, Melissa. "5 Ways to Better Understand Asexuality." Science of Us, August 10, 2015. http://nymag.com/scienceofus/2015/08/5-ways-to-better-understand-asexuality.html.

Daly, Annie. "Female Ejaculation: Is It Pee or Not?" Women's Health, January 15, 2015. http://www.womenshealthmag.com/sex-and-love/female-ejaculation.

Decker, Julie S. "Asexual, Aromantic, Partnerless, Child-Free . . . And (Yes!) Happy." Everyday Feminism, April 6, 2015. http://everydayfeminism.com/2015/04/asexual-aromantic-happy/.

Desilets, Saida. *Emergence of the Sensual Woman: Awakening Our Erotic Innocence.* Jade Goddess Publishing, 2006.

Dienstmann, Giovanni. "Types of Meditation: An Overview of 23 Meditation Techniques." Live and Dare. Accessed April 9, 2015. http://liveanddare.com/types-of-meditation/.

Dodson, Betty. "A Woman's Erection Needs 20-30 Minutes of Adequate Clitoral Stimulation." Betty Dodson with Carlin Ross, October 16, 2014. http://dodsonandross.com/blogs/betty-dodson/2014/10/womans-erection-needs-20-30-minutes-adequate-clitoral-stimulation.

Dodson, Betty, and Carlin Ross. "Masturbation." Betty Dodson with Carlin Ross. Accessed July 20, 2017. http://dodsonandross.com/topic/masturbation.

Doe, Lindsey. *How to Get the Sex You Want - 14,* 2013. https://www.youtube.com/watch?v=xoYxd3E3UXU.

Dolan, Yvonne, Terry Trepper, and Jennifer Yalowitz. "Sex, Love, and Videotape: SFBT with Couples." presented at the Conference on Solution-Focused Practice, Albany, NY, November 5, 2009.

Donaghue, Chris. *Sex Outside the Lines: Authentic Sexuality in a Sexually Dysfunctional Culture*. BenBella Books, 2015.

Feltman, Rachel. "Is Urine Actually Sterile?" Popular Science, January 11, 2017. http://www.popsci.com/urine-sterile-drinking-pee.

Fisher, Bruce, and Robert Alberti. *Rebuilding: When Your Relationship Ends*. 3 edition. Impact, 2006.

Ford, Tyler. "How Do You Know You're Asexual If You've Never Had Sex?" MTV News, June 22, 2015. http://www.mtv.com/news /2193237/tyler-ford-advice-column-asexual-pronouns/.

Garnick, Marc. "Does Frequent Ejaculation Help Ward Off Prostate Cancer?" Harvard Prostate Knowledge, April 2009. http://www.harvardprostateknowledge.org/does-frequent-ejaculation-help-ward-off-prostate-cancer.

Gates, Gary J. "How Many People Are Lesbian, Gay, Bisexual and Transgender?" The Williams Institute, April 2011. http:// williamsinstitute.law.ucla.edu/wp-content/uploads/Gates-How-Many-People-LGBT-Apr-2011.pdf.

Glover, Robert. *No More Mr. Nice Guy: A Proven Plan for Getting What You Want in Love, Sex, and Life*. Kindle edition. Barnes and Noble Digital, 2001.

Gordon, David, Austin Porter, Mark Regnerus, Jane Ryngaert, and Larissa Sarangaya. "Relationships in America 2014 Survey." Austin Institute for the Study of American Culture, December 2, 2014. http://relationshipsinamerica.com/.

Greengross, Gil. "Laughing All the Way to the Bedroom: The Importance of Humor in Mating." Psychology Today, May 1, 2011. http://www.psychologytoday.com/blog/humor-sapiens/201105/laughing-all-the-way-the-bedroom.

Hardy, Janet W., and Dossie Easton. *The Ethical Slut: A Practical Guide to Polyamory, Open Relationships & Other Adventures*. 2nd edition. Berkeley, Calif: Celestial Arts, 2009.

"Health Benefits of Masturbation." Women's Health Network. Accessed July 20, 2017. https://www.womenshealthnetwork.com /sexandfertility/health-benefits-of-masturbation.aspx.

Healthwise Staff. "Kegel Exercises-Topic Overview." WebMD, November 20, 2015. http://www.webmd.com/women/tc/kegel-exercises-topic-overview.

Heid, Markham. "Can You Masturbate Too Much?" Men's Health, January 28, 2016. http://www.menshealth.com/sex-women/masturbate-too-much.

———. "Could Porn Cause ED?" Men's Health, March 3, 2014. http://www.menshealth.com/sex-women/porn-erectile-dysfunction.

Heitz, David. "There's No Such Thing As Porn Addiction, Says New Research." Healthline, February 22, 2014. http://www.healthline.com/health-news/researchers-say-porn-addiction-not-real-022214.

Honan, Edith. "A Straight Support Group Fortifies the Former Spouses of Gays." *Reuters*, March 13, 2013. http://www.reuters.com/article/us-usa-court-gaymarriage-straightspouse-idUSBRE92C1F520130313.

HRC Foundation and PFLAG National. "Coming Out as a Supporter." Human Rights Campaign, 4/14. http://www.hrc.org/resources/straight-guide-to-lgbt-americans/.

Human Rights Campaign (HRC). "National Coming Out Day." Human Rights Campaign. Accessed March 28, 2015. http://www.hrc.org/resources/national-coming-out-day/.

"Hypoactive Sexual Desire Disorder." *Wikipedia*, February 16, 2015. https://en.wikipedia.org/w/index.php?title=Hypoactive_sexual_desire_disorder&oldid=785773690.

"Hypoactive Sexual Desire Disorder and the Asexual Community: A History." *Asexual Explorations Blog* (blog), March 28, 2009. http://asexystuff.blogspot.com/2009/03/hypoactive-sexual-desire-disorder-and.html.

Isay, Dave. "In a StoryCorps Booth, Love Is 'All There Is.'" NPR.org, February 11, 2011. http://www.npr.org/2012/02/11/146592554/in-a-storycorps-booth-love-is-all-there-is.

"I've Seen It Mentioned a Few Times That..." Asexual Advice, October 26, 2014. http://asexualadvice.tumblr.com/post/101044373784/ive-seen-it-mentioned-a-few-times-that.

Kaletsky, Kim. "Asexual and Happy." *The New York Times*, July 2, 2015, sec. Fashion & Style. https://www.nytimes.com/2015/07/05/fashion/asexual-and-happy.html.

Kerner, Ian. *She Comes First: The Thinking Man's Guide to Pleasuring a Woman*. New York: HarperCollins, 2004.

Khazan, Olga. "The Forgiveness Boost." *The Atlantic*, January 28, 2015. https://www.theatlantic.com/health/archive/2015/01/the-forgiveness-boost/384796/.

Kubler-Ross, Elisabeth. *On Death and Dying: What the Dying Have to Teach Doctors, Nurses, Clergy and Their Own Families*. 1st MacMillan Ppbk Ed 3rd Printing. Collier Books/ The Macmillan Company, 1971.

Labriola, Kathy. *Love in Abundance : A Counselor's Advice on Open Relationships*. Kindle edition. Eugene, OR: Greenery Press, 2010.

"Leaving a Sexless Relationship (Tactfully)." *Critique of Popular Reason* (blog), May 11, 2013. https://pianycist.wordpress.com/2013/05/11/leaving-a-sexless-relationship-tactfully/.

Leider, Richard J. *The Power of Purpose: Creating Meaning in Your Life and Work*. Oakland, CA: Berrett-Koehler Publishers, 1991.

Ley, David J. "An Erectile Dysfunction Myth." Psychology Today, August 29, 2013. http://www.psychologytoday.com/blog/women-who-stray/201308/erectile-dysfunction-myth.

Lindsay, Emma. "Squirting Is Peeing." *Emma Lindsay* (blog), February 15, 2017. https://medium.com/@emmalindsay/squirting-is-peeing-bbfd04aa2e88#.4ef06diz7.

Lisitsa, Ellie. "The Positive Perspective: Dr. Gottman's Magic Ratio!" The Gottman Institute, December 5, 2012. https://www.gottman.com/blog/the-positive-perspective-dr-gottmans-magic-ratio/.

Loewenstein, George, Tamar Krishnamurti, Jessica Kopsic, and Daniel McDonald. "Does Increased Sexual Frequency Enhance Happiness?" *Journal of Economic Behavior & Organization* 116

(August 1, 2015): 206–18. https://doi.org/10.1016/j.jebo.2015.04 .021.

Matousek, Mark. "What to Do With the Animal Self?" *Huffington Post* (blog), May 11, 2012. http://www.huffingtonpost.com/mark-matousek/what-to-do-with-the-anima_b_1475930.html.

Mayo Clinic Staff. "Kegel Exercises: A How-to Guide for Women." Mayo Clinic, September 25, 2015. http://www.mayoclinic.org /healthy-lifestyle/womens-health/in-depth/kegel-exercises/art-20045283.

McGowan, Kat. "Young, Attractive, and Totally Not Into Having Sex." Wired, February 18, 2015. https://www.wired.com/2015/02 /demisexuality/.

McKechnie, Alex. "Majority of Minors Engage in Sexting, Unaware of Harsh Legal Consequences." DrexelNow, June 18, 2014. http://drexel.edu/now/archive/2014/June/Sexting-Study/.

"Misconceptions About the Five Stages of Grief." Grief.com. Accessed August 1, 2015. https://grief.com/misconceptions/.

Morber, Jenny. "What Science Says About Arousal During Rape." Popular Science, May 30, 2013. http://www.popsci.com/science /article/2013-05/science-arousal-during-rape.

Mosbergen, Dominique. "Battling Asexual Discrimination, Sexual Violence And 'Corrective' Rape." *Huffington Post*, June 20, 2013, sec. Queer Voices. http://www.huffingtonpost.com/2013/06/20 /asexual-discrimination_n_3380551.html.

Nagoski, Emily. *Come as You Are: The Surprising New Science That Will Transform Your Sex Life*. 1 edition. Simon & Schuster, 2015.

Newman, Lily Hay. "Fallout From Ashley Madison Breach Includes Extortion and Possible Suicides." *Slate*, August 24, 2015. http://www.slate.com/blogs/future_tense/2015/08/24/police_rep ort_unconfirmed_but_concerning_suicides_among_those_outed _ashley.html.

nleseul (AVEN user). "The Five Love Languages." Asexual Visibility and Education Network, January 5, 2011. http://www.asexuality .org/en/topic/57853-the-five-love-languages/.

O'Neill, Nena, and George O'Neill. *Open Marriage: A New Life Style for Couples*. New York: M. Evans & Company, 1972.

Perel, Esther. *Mating in Captivity: Unlocking Erotic Intelligence*. Reprint edition. New York: Harper Paperbacks, 2007.

"Physiological Responses to Lust: How a Body Responds to Desire." *Love Is in the Air: The Neu.Com Blog* (blog), October 31, 2011. http://blog.neu.com/2011/10/31/physiological-responses-to-lust-how-a-body-responds-to-desire/.

Platt, Gareth. "Your Brain On Porn: How XHamster and PornHub Are Rotting Your Mind." International Business Times, March 6, 2015. http://www.ibtimes.co.uk/your-brain-porn-how-xhamster-pornhub-are-rotting-your-mind-1490804.

Post, Stephen, and Jill Neimark. *Why Good Things Happen to Good People: The Exciting New Research That Proves the Link Between Doing Good and Living a Longer, Healthier, Happier Life*. New York: Broadway Books, 2007.

Poston, Dudley L., Jr., and Amanda K. Baumle. "Patterns of Asexuality in the United States." *Demographic Research* 23, no. 18 (September 3, 2010): 509–30. https://doi.org/10.4054/DemRes .2010.23.18.

Rea, Shilo. "Carnegie Mellon Researchers Find More Sex Doesn't Lead To Increased Happiness." Carnegie Mellon University News, May 8, 2015. https://www.cmu.edu/news/stories/archives/2015/may /more-sex-does-not-lead-to-happiness.html.

Reddy, Sumathi. "Little Children and Already Acting Mean." *Wall Street Journal*, May 26, 2014, sec. Health and Wellness. https://www.wsj.com/articles/little-children-and-already-acting-mean-1401140267.

Reeves, Bryan. "The Biggest Fear Women Have When It Comes To Men: It's Not What You Think." *SEXY. CONSCIOUS. AWAKE.* (blog), March 5, 2015. https://www.sexyconsciousawake.com/the-biggest-fear-women-have-when-it-comes-to-men-its-not-what-you-think/.

Resnick, Stella. *The Pleasure Zone: Why We Resist Good Feelings and How to Let Go and Be Happy.* Conari Press, 1998.

"Reverse Kegels / Pelvic Floor Drops." *Pelvic Health Solutions* (blog). Accessed March 27, 2015. http://pelvichealthsolutions.ca/for-the-patient/what-is-pelvic-floor-muscle-tightness/reverse-kegels/.

Rider, Jennifer R., Kathryn M. Wilson, Jennifer A. Sinnott, Rachel S. Kelly, Lorelei A. Mucci, and Edward L. Giovannucci. "Ejaculation Frequency and Risk of Prostate Cancer: Updated Results with an Additional Decade of Follow-Up." *European Urology* 70, no. 6 (December 1, 2016): 974–82. https://doi.org/10.1016/j.eururo.2016.03.027.

Robinson, Lawrence, Jeanne Segal, and Melinda Smith. "Managing Conflicts with Humor: Using Laughter to Strengthen Your Relationships and Resolve Disagreements." Helpguide.org, April 2015. https://www.helpguide.org/articles/relationships-communication/managing-conflicts-with-humor.htm.

Rodger, Elliot. *Elliot Rodger's Retribution,* 2014. https://www.youtube.com/watch?v=zExDivIW4FM.

Savage, Dan. "Ashley Madison Hack: All Fun and Puritanical Games Until Somebody Gets Dead." The Stranger, August 24, 2015. http://www.thestranger.com/blogs/slog/2015/08/24/22750487/ashley-madison-hack-all-fun-and-puritanical-games-until-somebody-gets-dead.

———. "Savage Love: Aced Out." The Stranger, May 27, 2015. http://www.thestranger.com/columns/savage-love/2015/05/27/22283509/savage-love.

———. "Savage Love: Wrong and Right." The Stranger, March 1, 2007. http://www.thestranger.com/seattle/SavageLove?oid=167448.

Schnarch, David. "Charles Manson, Please Save Marriage & Family Therapy." Psychology Today, November 16, 2010. http://www.psychologytoday.com/blog/intimacy-and-desire/201011/charles-manson-please-save-marriage-family-therapy.

———. *Intimacy & Desire: Awaken the Passion in Your Relationship.* 1 edition. New York, N.Y.: Beaufort Books, 2011.

———. "Normal Marital Sadism." Psychology Today, May 25, 2012. https://www.psychologytoday.com/blog/intimacy-and-desire/201205/normal-marital-sadism.

Schnarch, David, and SheKnows. "An Interview with Dr. David Schnarch - The Sex Therapist." SheKnows, September 28, 2007. http://www.sheknows.com/love-and-sex/articles/1423/an-interview-with-dr-david-schnarch-the-sex-therapist.

SciCurious. "Serotonin and Sexual Preference: Is It Really That Simple?" Scientific American Blog Network, March 28, 2011. https://blogs.scientificamerican.com/guest-blog/serotonin-and-sexual-preference-is-it-really-that-simple/.

Segall, Laurie. "Pastor Outed on Ashley Madison Commits Suicide." CNN, September 8, 2015. http://money.cnn.com/2015/09/08/technology/ashley-madison-suicide/index.html.

"Sex Education." Last Week Tonight with John Oliver. HBO, August 9, 2015.

Siggy. "Why I Use 'Allosexual.'" The Asexual Agenda (blog), September 12, 2012. https://asexualagenda.wordpress.com/2012/09/12/why-i-use-allosexual/.

Smith, Benedict. "I Grew Up in a Polyamorous Household." Vice, June 2, 2015. https://www.vice.com/en_us/article/i-grew-up-in-a-polyamorous-household-528.

Smith, Pace. "Why Openness Is Awesome." Pace Smith (blog), December 13, 2011. http://pacesmith.com/why-openness-is-awesome/.

Srinivas, Vinod. "12 Types of Humor and How It Affects Relationships." LovePanky - Your Guide to Better Love and Relationships (blog), June 30, 2015. http://www.lovepanky.com/flirting-flings/get-flirty/types-of-humor.

Taormino, Tristan. Opening Up: A Guide to Creating and Sustaining Open Relationships. First Edition edition. San Francisco, Calif: Cleis Press, 2008.

Tatkin, Stan. Wired for Love: How Understanding Your Partner's Brain and Attachment Style Can Help You Defuse Conflict and

Build a Secure Relationship. 1 edition. Oakland, CA: New Harbinger Publications, 2012.

Taylor, Paul, Cary Funk, and April Clark. "As Marriage and Parenthood Drift Apart, Public Is Concerned about Social Impact." Pew Research Center, July 1, 2007. http://www.pewsocialtrends .org/2007/07/01/as-marriage-and-parenthood-drift-apart-public-is-concerned-about-social-impact/.

The Asexual Visibility and Education Network. "General FAQ." The Asexual Visibility and Education Network. Accessed November 10, 2014. http://www.asexuality.org/?q=general.html.

"The Five Stages of Grief." Grief.com. Accessed August 1, 2015. https://grief.com/the-five-stages-of-grief/.

Thomas, Anna. "Divorcing Differently: End a Marriage, Save the Relationship." Psychology Today, October 27, 2015. https://www.psychologytoday.com/blog/unseen-and-unheard/201510/divorcing-differently-end-marriage-save-the-relationship.

Thomson, Helen. "Female Ejaculation Comes in Two Forms, Scientists Find." New Scientist, January 9, 2015. https://www.newscientist .com/article/dn26772-female-ejaculation-comes-in-two-forms-scientists-find/.

Tobias, Keira. "No Sex, Please—I'm Asexual." Bust, June 20, 2015. http://bust.com/sex/14324-no-sex-please-i-m-asexual.html.

Trost, Matthew. "Cindy Gallop: Make Love, Not Porn." *TEDBlog* (blog), December 2, 2009. http://blog.ted.com/cindy_gallop_ma/.

University of California, Santa Barbara. "Aging and the Sexual Response Cycle." SexInfo Online. Accessed June 11, 2015. http://www.soc.ucsb.edu/sexinfo/article/aging-and-sexual-response-cycle-0.

U.S. Census Bureau. "U.S. and World Population Clock." U.S. Census Bureau. Accessed July 15, 2015. https://www.census.gov /popclock/.

Vann, Madeline R., and Pat F. Bass III. "7 Healthy Reasons to Have Sex (Right Now!)." EverydayHealth.com, June 12, 2014. http://

www.everydayhealth.com/sexual-health/seven-healthy-reasons-to-have-sex-right-now.aspx.

Veaux, Franklin. "Glossary of Polyamory Terms." More Than Two. Accessed March 19, 2015. https://www.morethantwo.com/polyglossary.html.

Weiner-Davis, Michele. *The Sex-Starved Marriage: Boosting Your Marriage Libido: A Couple's Guide*. Reprint edition. New York: Simon & Schuster, 2004.

Weintraub, Pam. "How To Grow Up." Psychology Today, May 1, 2012. http://www.psychologytoday.com/articles/201205/how-grow.

Wheitner, Dave. *Naked Idealism: Expose Your Authentic Self and Create a Sustainable Life and World*. Pittsburgh, PA: Divergent Drummer Publications, 2011.

———. *The Snuggle Party Guidebook: Create Deeper Friendships, Decrease Loneliness, & Enjoy Nurturing Touch Community*. 1 edition. Portland, OR: Divergent Drummer Publications, 2014.

Widdoes, James. "The Duchess of Dull-in-Sack." *Two and a Half Men*. CBS, 2012.

Yule, Morag A., Lori A. Brotto, and Boris B. Gorzalka. "A Validated Measure of No Sexual Attraction: The Asexuality Identification Scale." *Psychological Assessment* 27, no. 1 (2015): 148–60. https://doi.org/10.1037/a0038196.

28. Acknowledgments

• • •

I'm deeply grateful for my partners, for the various ways in which they influenced and supported the creation of this resource. I'm equally grateful for Evan and his willingness to share some of his experiences, which have many overlaps with my own.

Many thanks to Maren Souders and Marisa Black for generously providing valuable proofreading and content feedback. I'm also grateful for the sexuality experts who expressed confidence and interest in this project, and who provided testimonials.

Thanks to everyone in my life who has shown me various types of love: romantic love, sexual love, spiritual love, friendship, parental love, child's love, conditional and unconditional love, and so on. The interactions and conversations that influenced this book are too numerous to recount.

I appreciate the founders and members of the Portland Salon Group, SexPositive Portland, Network for a New Culture, and Conscious Touch NW for pointing out some of the resources in this book. Thanks to the creators of the various resources I have cited.

Thanks to Mrs. Seibert, my high school health teacher, for requiring each student to speak to the class about a sexuality topic. Mine was masturbation. Even though it was embarrassing at the time, it planted a seed of courage that helps me to talk about sexuality today. Various psychology and counseling teachers and mentors have helped me to build upon that. They include Bob Witchel, who passed on shortly before I completed this book.

Finally, I'm grateful to the higher power that connects all of us on this journey, however you may perceive it.

29. Endnotes

• • •

1 The Asexual Visibility and Education Network, https://www.asexuality.org/.

2 Bauer et al., "The 2015 Asexual Census Summary Report."

3 While some sexuality books use the term *low-desire partner*, I use *low-interest partner* to maintain the distinction between attraction and desire and to include different possibilities for lack of interest in sex. As discussed later in the book, someone may not want to have sex because they don't experience sexual attraction, because they don't experience sexual desire, or both. *Low-interest* is intended to encompass all of these possibilities, given that you may not currently know which describes your partner.

4 Siggy, "Why I Use 'Allosexual.'"

5 I use "predominantly heterosexual" because while I'm attracted almost exclusively to women, on occasion I also find non-female individuals attractive.

6 Bauer et al., "The 2015 Asexual Census Summary Report."

7 Bauer et al.; Dahl, "5 Ways to Better Understand Asexuality." The one percent estimate is from a 2004 study by Anthony Bogaert, examining a sample of more than 18,000 British adults, with asexuality defined as individuals who reported no attraction to partners of either sex.

8 Schnarch, *Intimacy & Desire*.

9 This, as with some other conversations in the text, is an abbreviated recollection, but it includes some of the key points.

10 Thanks to Laura Lavigne for creating the Happiness Sprinkling project.

11 Brotto, "Evidence-Based Treatments for Low Sexual Desire in Women."

12 Schnarch, *Intimacy & Desire*.

13 Thanks to Karla Baur and Sophia for a reminder of this concept.

14 Nagoski, *Come as You Are*.

15 Perel, *Mating in Captivity*; Schnarch, *Intimacy & Desire*; Weintraub, "How To Grow Up."

16 Nagoski, *Come as You Are*; Perel, *Mating in Captivity*; Schnarch, *Intimacy & Desire*.

17 Savage, "Savage Love: Aced Out."

18 The tendency to adhere to the ideals of a label spans well beyond the context of sexual orientation. Political labels and ethical/lifestyle labels (Republican, Democrat, vegan, environmentalist, feminist, liberal, conservative) are just a few other examples.

19 While I found variations of this joke on several websites, I was unable to identify the original source.

20 Schnarch, *Intimacy & Desire*.

21 Several resources informed this section: Anagnori, "What's the Difference Between Sex Drive, Sexual Attraction, Sexual Arousal, Sexual Desire, and Sexual Consent?"; "Attraction"; "Attraction and Vocabulary"; Coyote, "Differentiating Sexual Attraction and Sexual Desire"; Coyote, "What to Do If You Think Your Partner Might Be Asexual"; "Physiological Responses to Lust: How a Body Responds to Desire"; "Hypoactive Sexual Desire Disorder." While the "Physiological Responses to Lust" article utilizes the term *desire*, it discusses what some of the other articles refer to as *attraction*.

22 "Attraction"; Coyote, "Differentiating Sexual Attraction and Sexual Desire." Again, there is some inconsistency in the use of the word *desire* among authors. For example, *AVENWiki* uses the word desire in its definition of libido, which is defined as not necessarily being directed at a specific person, whereas Coyote defines desire as generally being directed at a specific person. For this reason I've used the term *crave* in my definition to minimize confusion. These definitions are relatively new and evolving.

23 Morber, "What Science Says About Arousal During Rape."

24 "Am I Still Asexual If...?"

25 Of course, if I found myself thinking very frequently about someone in this way, I might eventually want to talk with them about it, or talk with my partner if I weren't single.

26 Bauer et al., "The 2015 Asexual Census Summary Report."

27 "I've Seen It Mentioned a Few Times That..."

28 The Asexual Visibility and Education Network, "General FAQ."

29 McGowan, "Young, Attractive, and Totally Not Into Having Sex."

30 Bogaert, "Asexuality and Autochorissexualism (Identity-Less Sexuality)." Anthony Bogaert, who has done considerable academic work on the topic of asexuality, coined the term *autochorissexualism*

to describe the disconnect that some people experience between themselves and the target or object of arousal. However, Bogaert defines it as a paraphilia or unusual behavior rather than as a sexual orientation.

31 McGowan, "Young, Attractive, and Totally Not Into Having Sex."

32 Perel, *Mating in Captivity*; Schnarch and SheKnows, "An Interview with Dr. David Schnarch - The Sex Therapist"; Weiner-Davis, *The Sex-Starved Marriage*.

33 Kaletsky, "Asexual and Happy."

34 Decker, "Asexual, Aromantic, Partnerless, Child-Free . . . And (Yes!) Happy."

35 Mosbergen, "Battling Asexual Discrimination, Sexual Violence And 'Corrective' Rape."

36 Ford, "How Do You Know You're Asexual If You've Never Had Sex?"

37 Honan, "A Straight Support Group Fortifies the Former Spouses of Gays."

38 Buxton, *The Other Side of the Closet*.

39 Gates, "How Many People Are Lesbian, Gay, Bisexual and Transgender?"

40 Dahl, "5 Ways to Better Understand Asexuality"; Poston and Baumle, "Patterns of Asexuality in the United States."

41 U.S. Census Bureau, "U.S. and World Population Clock."

42 In *The Other Side of the Closet*, Buxton noted differences between women and men in coming out as gay, bisexual, or lesbian in the 1980s: "Only a small minority of gay or bisexual men come out before they marry or immediately after they realize their sexual orientation, unlike lesbians who tend to leave the marriage once they discover it."

43 "Hypoactive Sexual Desire Disorder."

44 For more information on some of the criticisms, see "Hypoactive Sexual Desire Disorder and the Asexual Community."

45 Thanks to Karla Baur for initially inspiring these thoughts. Also see Brotto, "Asexuality Myths Debunked by Psychologist Lori Brotto on HuffPost Live (Video)"; Brotto, "Understanding What It Means to Be Asexual."

46 Yule, Brotto, and Gorzalka, "A Validated Measure of No Sexual Attraction."

47 Much of the research on asexuality that's been done to date can be seen at the Asexual Explorations Blog, http://asexystuff .blogspot.com.

48   Some personal growth professionals have referred to the concept of an "easy problem," a problem that serves the function of distracting us from even more difficult problems, and that we may therefore actually hesitate to resolve. I was unable to locate the source of this concept.

49   Buxton, *The Other Side of the Closet*.

50   To be clear, I'm not proposing doing sexually suggestive things in front of children, but showing some level of physical and emotional affection regularly. If, for example, you and your partner have difficulty even hugging or snuggling without it causing tension about your sexual differences, you may inadvertently deliver a message to your kids that grownups aren't physically affectionate with each other. The importance and relevance of this will vary by culture.

51   Burgo, "The Difference Between Guilt and Shame."

52   "Leaving a Sexless Relationship (Tactfully)."

53   Sophia, Funk, and Clark, "As Marriage and Parenthood Drift Apart, Public Is Concerned about Social Impact."

54   Matousek, "What to Do With the Animal Self?"

55   "Sex Education."

56   Resnick, *The Pleasure Zone*.

57   Reddy, "Little Children and Already Acting Mean."

58   Reeves, "The Biggest Fear Women Have When It Comes To Men."

59   Buxton, *The Other Side of the Closet*.

60   Widdoes, "The Duchess of Dull-in-Sack."

61   Perel, *Mating in Captivity*; Schnarch, *Intimacy & Desire*.

62   Schnarch, *Intimacy & Desire*. Unfortunately, mind mapping can also be used in a not-feel-good, manipulative way as well, especially during arguments. This type of mind mapping should not be confused with the visual mapping out of ideas and goals often employed by life coaches and planners.

63   Conversations in public Facebook Asexuality Group.

64   This is likely to be more productive than trying to picture yourself in their pants. It has taken a while to get to where I can make jokes and laugh about these things—it is fine if you are nowhere near that point yet.

65   For some of these sentiments expressed firsthand by an asexual person, see Tobias, "No Sex, Please—I'm Asexual."

66   I recognize that some couples follow marriage guidelines outlined in religious doctrine in a more detailed or literal fashion than others. Even in such cases, partners will be at odds if they disagree over

interpretation and prioritization of such rules.

67 Gordon et al., "Relationships in America 2014 Survey."

68 Austin Institute for the Study of Family and Culture, "Too Busy to Get Busy."

69 Loewenstein et al., "Does Increased Sexual Frequency Enhance Happiness?"; Rea, "Carnegie Mellon Researchers Find More Sex Doesn't Lead To Increased Happiness."

70 Schnarch, *Intimacy & Desire*.

71 Kubler-Ross, *On Death and Dying*; "The Five Stages of Grief"; "Misconceptions About the Five Stages of Grief."

72 In *The Other Side of the Closet*, Buxton describes how heterosexual partners of closeted gay individuals feel intense anger for many of these reasons when their partners come out.

73 Vann and Bass, "7 Healthy Reasons to Have Sex (Right Now!)."

74 Khazan, "The Forgiveness Boost."

75 Khazan.

76 For examples of helpful and potentially harmful humor, see Robinson, Segal, and Smith, "Managing Conflicts with Humor"; Srinivas, "12 Types of Humor and How It Affects Relationships."

77 Heid, "Could Porn Cause ED?" It is not yet known to what extent laughter itself is the cause of these benefits, as laughter is often accompanied by other factors that may yield positive impacts, such as the presence of other people.

78 Barry, "Study Finds That Playfulness Is the Most Attractive Quality Ever"; Greengross, "Laughing All the Way to the Bedroom: The Importance of Humor in Mating."

79 Barry, "Study Finds That Playfulness Is the Most Attractive Quality Ever"; Greengross, "Laughing All the Way to the Bedroom: The Importance of Humor in Mating."

80 Buxton, *The Other Side of the Closet*.

81 Schnarch, *Intimacy & Desire*.

82 Tatkin, *Wired for Love*.

83 Also see Leider, *The Power of Purpose: Creating Meaning in Your Life and Work*; Wheitner, *Naked Idealism*.

84 Buxton provides similar advice for heterosexual partners of formerly closeted gay spouses, that is, limiting family and community obligations to work on oneself.

85 Wheitner, *Naked Idealism*.

86 Thanks to Leah Jackman-Wheitner for this idea.

87 Buxton, *The Other Side of the Closet*.

88 Some would argue that we could be taught more critical thinking even in these areas.

89 O'Neill and O'Neill, *Open Marriage*.

90 Fisher and Alberti, *Rebuilding*.

91 Wheitner, *The Snuggle Party Guidebook*.

92 Wheitner. Adapted from a definition provided by Kristen Reynolds and comments from Jas Davis.

93 We also explored whether I was engaging in a form of slut shaming, or judging Sophia as bad or inferior for having had a larger number of sexual partners. While I have been guilty of this, I don't believe I was doing that in this case. I had come to appreciate the ways in which I benefited from her prior sexual experience, and I appreciated how honest she was about her sexual history. Alongside judging myself, I was specifically curious about the meaning she attached to sex.

94 The site seems to be biased toward traditional marital partnerships. While I wish it were more inclusive, I still find the information and concepts valuable.

95 nleseul (AVEN user), "The Five Love Languages."

96 Post and Neimark, *Why Good Things Happen to Good People*.

97 A number of writers have discussed this theory; I was unable to determine the primary source(s).

98 Isay, "In a StoryCorps Booth, Love Is 'All There Is.'"

99 Perel, *Mating in Captivity*. This isn't true for all people, though; as Nagoski observes in *Come as You Are*, some people are more likely to want sex when they're stressed, and some are more likely to want sex when they're calm.

100 Weiner-Davis, *The Sex-Starved Marriage*.

101 Thomas, "Divorcing Differently."

102 Smith, "I Grew Up in a Polyamorous Household."

103 Veaux, "Glossary of Polyamory Terms."

104 See, for example, Taormino, *Opening Up: A Guide to Creating and Sustaining Open Relationships*.

105 Hardy and Easton, *The Ethical Slut*; Taormino, *Opening Up*.

106 Labriola, *Love in Abundance : A Counselor's Advice on Open Relationships*.

107 Buxton, *The Other Side of the Closet*; Schnarch, *Intimacy & Desire*.

108 Two good starting points for understanding how to become better at asking for what you want in general: Glover, *No More Mr. Nice Guy:*

A Proven Plan for Getting What You Want in Love, Sex, and Life; Babcock and Laschever, *Women Don't Ask*.

109 Angyal, "The Performance Model of Sex, Now in Video Form!" Thanks also to Kristen Reynolds for making me aware of this resource.

110 Czimbal and Zadikov, *A Guide to Healthy Touch*. LoveTribe has also helped to spread awareness of this concept.

111 Buxton, *The Other Side of the Closet*.

112 See the work of the Gottman Institute for evidence on this.

113 Thanks to Sophia for thoughts on this.

114 Lisitsa, "The Positive Perspective."

115 Because foreplay and sex sometimes inspire my creativity, I keep a small notebook or notepad on the nightstand, as it is quicker and easier to put notes into that than into my smartphone. If an idea pops into my head as we're getting warmed up, I'll pause for a moment to jot it down. This helps me to clear my mind and ensure I'm then giving Sophia my undivided-as-possible attention. I rarely do this once we're fully having sex, not just to be polite to Sophia, but because that's generally where my attention fully is.

116 Brotto and Goldmeier, "Mindfulness Interventions for Treating Sexual Dysfunctions."

117 Dienstmann, "Types of Meditation: An Overview of 23 Meditation Techniques." Dienstmann also proposes a third category of meditation, effortless presence: "the state where the attention is not focused on anything in particular, but reposes on itself—quiet, empty, steady, and introverted."

118 Chödrön, *When Things Fall Apart*.

119 See http://onetaste.us for more information on Orgasmic Meditation.

120 Nagoski, *Come as You Are*.

121 Dodson, "A Woman's Erection Needs 20-30 Minutes of Adequate Clitoral Stimulation."

122 Kerner, *She Comes First*.

123 As such experiences are highly subjective, this likely varies dramatically across individuals.

124 Schnarch, *Intimacy & Desire*.

125 Garnick, "Does Frequent Ejaculation Help Ward Off Prostate Cancer?"; Rider et al., "Ejaculation Frequency and Risk of Prostate Cancer."

126 University of California, Santa Barbara, "Aging and the Sexual Response Cycle."

127 "Health Benefits of Masturbation"; Dodson and Ross, "Masturbation."

128 See http://dodsonandross.com, http://onetaste.us.

129 Castleman, "Vibrators"; Ley, "An Erectile Dysfunction Myth."

130 Heid, "Could Porn Cause ED?"; Heid, "Can You Masturbate Too Much?"

131 Platt, "Your Brain On Porn: How XHamster and PornHub Are Rotting Your Mind"; Trost, "Cindy Gallop."

132 Heid, "Could Porn Cause ED?" See also https://www .yourbrainonporn.com.

133 Church, *Wack.* See also https://www.yourbrainonporn.com, https://www.nofap.com.

134 Cooper-White, "Watching Porn Linked to Less Gray Matter in the Brain."

135 Heitz, "There's No Such Thing As Porn Addiction, Says New Research"; Ley, "An Erectile Dysfunction Myth."

136 See, for example, http://www.makelovenotporn.com and https://brightdesire.com.

137 You can look Eleanor up at http://dancenakedproductions.com.

138 Perel, *Mating in Captivity.*

139 Wheitner, *The Snuggle Party Guidebook.* A visual resource that may help with this type of discussion is "The Genderbread Person," viewable online at http://itspronouncedmetrosexual.com. It illustrates how *feminine* and *masculine* are not mutually exclusive, and how the ways we choose to express ourselves can be independent of our sexual orientation and physical sex.

140 Donaghue, *Sex Outside the Lines.* Thanks also to Buster Ross and Jed Ward for their thoughts on this.

141 Carpenter, "That Gut Feeling."

142 The relationship between serotonin and sex drive, however, is somewhat complex. See, for example, SciCurious, "Serotonin and Sexual Preference."

143 Mayo Clinic Staff, "Kegel Exercises"; Healthwise Staff, "Kegel Exercises-Topic Overview."

144 "Ben Wa Balls and Vaginal Tone"; Desilets, *Emergence of the Sensual Woman.*

145 "Reverse Kegels / Pelvic Floor Drops."

146 Tatkin, *Wired for Love.*

147 Fuzzles is a pseudonym.

148 Thanks to Sophia for helping me to clarify my thoughts on this topic.

149 Daly, "Female Ejaculation"; Lindsay, "Squirting Is Peeing"; Thomson, "Female Ejaculation Comes in Two Forms, Scientists Find."

150 Contrary to a common opinion, urine is not entirely sterile. At the same time, neither are other body parts or fluids, many of which come into play during physical intimacy. See Feltman, "Is Urine Actually Sterile?" Given these facts, each person's comfort with this body fluid will vary, and each couple may need to negotiate.

151 Schnarch, "Normal Marital Sadism."

152 Schnarch, "Charles Manson, Please Save Marriage & Family Therapy"; Schnarch, *Intimacy & Desire*.

153 Reddy, "Little Children and Already Acting Mean"; Resnick, *The Pleasure Zone*.

154 Schnarch and SheKnows, "An Interview with Dr. David Schnarch - The Sex Therapist."

155 Coyote, "What to Do If You Think Your Partner Might Be Asexual." This is a very summarized version of the major points in the original article, and I've added some of my own interpretation.

156 Doe, *How to Get the Sex You Want - 14*.

157 Thanks to Gabriella Cordova for inspiring additional thinking about sexual guilt and shame.

158 Dolan, Trepper, and Yalowitz, "Sex, Love, and Videotape: SFBT with Couples"; Weiner-Davis, *The Sex-Starved Marriage*.

159 Perel, *Mating in Captivity*; Schnarch, *Intimacy & Desire*.

160 Dolan, Trepper, and Yalowitz, "Sex, Love, and Videotape: SFBT with Couples"; Weiner-Davis, *The Sex-Starved Marriage*.

161 Virginia Johnson and William Masters created this technique.

162 See, for example, Schnarch, *Intimacy & Desire*.

163 Human Rights Campaign (HRC), "National Coming Out Day"; HRC Foundation and PFLAG National, "Coming Out as a Supporter."

164 Poston and Baumle, "Patterns of Asexuality in the United States"; U.S. Census Bureau, "U.S. and World Population Clock."

165 See, for example, http://www.asexualawarenessweek.com.

166 Thanks to Karla Baur for this point.

167 "Leaving a Sexless Relationship (Tactfully)."

168 Chödrön, *When Things Fall Apart*.

169 Savage, "Savage Love: Wrong and Right."

170 Beattie, *Codependent No More*; "Codependency."

171 Poston and Baumle, "Patterns of Asexuality in the United States"; U.S. Census Bureau, "U.S. and World Population Clock."

172 Chödrön, *When Things Fall Apart.*

173 Smith, "Why Openness Is Awesome."

174 Brown, "Why Sham Marriages Between Gay Men and Women Are on the Rise."

175 Rodger, *Elliot Rodger's Retribution.*

176 Newman, "Fallout From Ashley Madison Breach Includes Extortion and Possible Suicides"; Segall, "Pastor Outed on Ashley Madison Commits Suicide."

177 Savage, "Ashley Madison Hack."

178 Anthony, "Just How Big Are Porn Sites?"

179 McKechnie, "Majority of Minors Engage in Sexting, Unaware of Harsh Legal Consequences."